A
Crash
Course
on
THE
NEW
AGE
Movement

A Crash Course on THE NEW AGE Movement

Describing and Evaluating
a Growing Social Force

⋆Elliot Miller⋆
FOREWORD BY WALTER MARTIN

BAKER BOOK HOUSE
Grand Rapids, Michigan 49516

The chapters in this book are updated and expanded versions of a series of articles which appeared in the *Christian Research Journal* (formerly *Forward*) during 1985–88.

ISBN: 0-8010-6248-9 (paper)

First printing, May 1989
Second printing, July 1989
Third printing, October 1989
Fourth printing, March 1990

ISBN: 0-8010-6251-9 (cloth)
First printing, May 1989
Second printing, July 1989

Printed in the United States of America

To **Corinne,**
without whose encouragement and support
this six-year-project could not have been completed.

Contents

Foreword

Lt is always a pleasure to be asked to write the introduction to a book that cannot help but be a landmark in the field of cultic and occultic research. This is such a book and I am well acquainted with its author's expertise as a researcher and writer in the field of New Age teachings.

Elliot Miller has made a real contribution to a proper understanding of the so-called New Age movement, which as he adequately demonstrates is a revival of ancient occultism and Hindu philosophy.

Throughout this volume he demonstrates a thorough grasp of both Christian and New Age theology. Chapters 3 and 4, outline and critique of New Age ideology, is a succinct analysis not found anywhere else in print.

The book covers subjects such as New Age evangelism and activism, the accelerated New Age phenomena of channeling, which he proves is pure spiritism, and his three appendices that can only be appreciated when one realizes that he himself was a former "New Ager" who made the painful journey from the New Age to Christ (Appendix D).

One of the great values of the book is that it answers the most common questions asked about the New Age conspiracy and fairly and cogently analyzes the impact of Eastern mysticism on objectivity.

No other book in print refutes so thoroughly the New Age conspiracy theory of writers such as Constance Cumbey and demonstrates both Christian compassion and apologetics when confronting New Age occultists.

The author's observations of breaking through the "relativity barrier," as he calls it, and effectively penetrating the semantic jungle of New Age vocabulary will continue to be a valuable tool for anyone seriously considering New Age thought.

There are other good books dealing with the New Age movement and the author has given us a detailed bibliography. But this volume is the only in-depth assessment from the mind of a former New Ager that answers so many relevant questions and refutes so consistently the tragic errors and flaws in the New Age movement.

I know of no one more qualified to write such a work and of no work that approaches the scope and depth of this growing field of concern.

Christians owe a debt to Elliot Miller for a painstaking scholarly and readable study that will exert influence for years to come on the minds of those who recognize the research and conclusions of a Christian scholar.

Walter Martin
Director of Christian Research Institute
Irvine, California
1988

Acknowledgments

It is appropriate that Dr. Walter Martin be first among those mentioned here. It was Dr. Martin who provided me (as he did with so many others) the original inspiration to enter this unconventional field of research. It was he who modeled for me the importance of careful scholarship, fairness, and biblically based analysis. And it was he who gave me the actual opportunity to do this kind of work on a full-time basis at the Christian Research Institute.

Of those who directly contributed to this work, none deserves mention more than my associate editor at the *Christian Research Journal*, Robert M. Bowman, Jr. Rob edited all of the articles from which this book's chapters are derived, suggesting several significant changes that were happily implemented.

As I wrestled with the difficult philosophical and scientific issues analyzed in chapter 4, I received much-appreciated help from Bob Passantino, William D. (Bill) Watkins, Dr. James Sire, and Dr. Henry Morris.

Not having a word processor until the final stages of the project, I am indebted to four extremely cooperative and long-suffering typists: Debbie Hall, Tanya Andersen, Linda Schultz, and especially Penny Luigs Spivey.

Finally, my wife, Corinne, deserves special mention. Because of her belief in this project she willingly (if not happily) accepted the fate of a "book widow" during the countless evenings and weekends that I was buried in research and writing. Also she often provided very useful "feedback" during difficult points in the writing process. Without her help I might still be lost in one of those literary labyrinths that writers have a way of wandering into.

What Is the New Age
Movement?

What is the New Age movement? Evidence of a forthcoming advance in evolution? Harbinger of the Antichrist? A passing fad? A conspiracy myth created by paranoid fundamentalists? Or is it so amorphous and multifarious that it is impossible to adequately characterize? The question posed by this chapter's title has been a live one in recent years, particularly for evangelical Christians. Answers have varied widely, including but not limited to those listed above. Discussions of the topic have frequently generated a great deal more heat than light.

This chapter is intended to shed some good light on the subject. In the process it will also ascertain whether New Age spirituality can in any sense be harmonized with that of historic Christianity.

The New Age movement (NAM) is not impossible to describe—just difficult. It is a complex sociological phenomenon not unlike the proverbial elephant discovered independently by three blind men: one came upon his leg and described him as a tree; another got hold of his trunk and likened him to a hose; a third stumbled upon his tail and insisted he was like a rope. That which may be true about parts of the NAM are not necessarily true of the whole.

13

Defining the New Age Movement

The New Age movement is best understood as a *network*—or, to be more exact, a *metanetwork* (network of networks). What is a network? According to New Agers Jessica Lipnack and Jeffrey Stamps (who have provided a useful analysis in their book *Networking*), networks are typically informal, loosely knit organizations which are very different in both structure and operation from other types of organizations: "Networks are composed of self-reliant and autonomous participants—people and organizations who simultaneously function as independent 'wholes' and as interdependent 'parts.'"[1]

Networks are "spontaneously created by people to address problems and offer possibilities primarily *outside* of established institutions."[2] There are many different *levels* of networking, so that one network can exist within a larger network, which in turn can exist within a still larger one (that is, a metanetwork). The borderlines of networks are characteristically fuzzy, "frustrating outside observers determined to figure out where a network begins and ends."[3] Networks tend to be decentralized, often having no single leader or headquarters, with power and responsibility widely distributed.

Bearing in mind my suggestion that the NAM is a network, one more characteristic of networks needs to be noted:

> Like the fly whose "one" eye comprises thousands of individual eyes, networks "see" through many perspectives, although the unknowing observer may think they have only one point of view.
>
> At times, a network seems to "see" with one eye and "speak" with one voice, testifying to consensus around an idea or a strategy. Such moments of unanimity are important, because they often reveal the essential common values and bonds that explain the unity among the diversity of network viewpoints.
>
> At other times, a network may appear to be a babble of disconnected concerns and interests, or an arena of internecine warfare. [Anthropologist Virginia] Hine calls this trait "the 'fission-fusion' characteristic that confuses observers and leads the bureaucratically minded to see networks as 'lacking' in organization." Networks not only tend to put up with disagreement, in many ways they depend upon it. The forthright independence of the members keeps the network as a whole from being dominated by

any single node. Hine writes that while it is a shared vision that keeps a network together, "it is the conflicting concepts of goals-means that prevent any one segment from taking permanent control over all the others." . . .

. . . The many perspectives of a network derive from the autonomy of its members. All have their own turf and agendas, yet they cooperate in the network because they also have some common values and visions.[4]

The New Age movement then is an extremely large, *loosely* structured network of organizations and individuals bound together by common values (based in mysticism and monism—the world view that "all is one") and a common vision (a coming "new age" of peace and mass enlightenment, the "Age of Aquarius").

New Agers may differ over such questions as when the New Age begins, whether it will be preceded by a worldwide cataclysm, how it will be politically structured, whether there will be a Christ-figure governing it, or who the true avatars (god-men) or messengers from the spirit world are (if there are any). Nonetheless, they agree that they can hasten the new order that they *all* await by cooperating to influence developments in our culture's political, economic, social, and spiritual life.

Within the New Age metanetwork and movement are hundreds of smaller (but still sometimes very large) networks and movements encompassing a wide variety of interests and causes (all compatible with the ends of the larger network). The consciousness movement (that is, those who have advocated developing altered states of consciousness as a means of expanding human possibilities—*see* chapter 2), the holistic health movement, the human potential movement—all have contributed generously to the New Age movement. So have the followers of many Eastern gurus and Western occult and "metaphysical" teachers. However participation in such movements as holistic health or human potential does not always indicate conscious or actual participation in the NAM (remember that networks have fuzzy borderlines). Nor do all Eastern or metaphysical movements believe in a coming new age; neither do they all participate in the networking process. (Such groups, like the Hare Krishnas and Christian Science, should really not be considered a part of the NAM, in spite of the many beliefs they hold in common with it.)

Additionally such secular movements/networks as ecology, "appropriate technology," the "peace movement," and future studies overlap the New Age network to varying degrees, though they are *by no means* entirely encompassed within it (*see* chapter 6).

The NAM is not a cult by any accepted sociological definition of the term. Although there are several cults which could be classified within it (for examples, Transcendental Meditation and the followers of deported Indian guru Bhagwan Shree Rajneesh), most are on the movement's periphery. Some, like the Movement of Spiritual Inner Awareness (MSIA) and the Sufi Order in the West, are more in its mainstream, but only because they are *less* exclusive than most cults. Cult membership is by far the exception and not the rule for New Agers.

New Agers tend to be eclectic: they draw what they think is the best from many sources. Long-term, exclusive devotion to a single teacher, teaching, or technique is not the norm. They move from one approach to "wholeness" to another in their spiritual quests (*firewalking* as a means to "personal transformation" has recently been a sensation!). *New Age Journal* observes that

> the many issues of the new consciousness are like peanuts: You can't eat just one. The stockbroker, for example, who began dabbling in alternative body therapies ten years ago has quite probably gone on to the likes of meditation or the ecology movement or Zen studies by now, and no doubt he notices the aperture in his personal cosmic egg getting wider all the time.[5]

Basic Beliefs

This eclectic tendency underscores the fact that New Agers consider spirituality much more a matter of experience than belief. Any teaching or technique that facilitates experience is welcome, but there is most often no loyalty to a rigid, elaborate system of belief.

Are there *any* beliefs that are universal—or almost universal—among New Agers? Some of them would answer *no*. (In fact, beliefs are often portrayed as direct impediments to enlightenment.) However, it should be obvious that certain assumptions cannot be separated from New Age thinking, or there could be no such thing as New Age thinking.[6]

As noted earlier, *all* New Agers believe that "all is one"— everything that exists consists of one and the same essence or reality. A second assumption is that this Ultimate Reality is neither dead matter nor unconscious energy. It is Being, Awareness, and Bliss (which is to say, a Hindu conception of God as an impersonal, infinite consciousness and force).

The first two assumptions imply two more: all that is, is God (which is *pantheism*); and man, a part of "all that is," is likewise divine. But how do New Agers answer the inescapable fact that most people do not at all *feel* one with God?

In agreement with all pantheists, New Agers explain that man is separated from God *only* in his own consciousness. He is the victim of a *false* sense of separate identity which blinds him to his essential unity with God, and this is the cause of all his problems. How then can man be saved (or *made whole*, as New Agers would prefer to put it)? It becomes a matter of *spiritual technology*.

New Agers believe that specific techniques for *altering* the consciousness (for example, meditation, chanting, ecstatic dancing, sensory deprivation) can enable the seeker to *consciously* (mystically) experience his (or her) supposed oneness with God. Thus, salvation for the New Ager is equated with *gnosis* (experiential knowledge). It is *self-realization* or the realization that one's *true* Self is God. Such mystical experiences are viewed as doorways to "personal transformation"—a lifelong growth process marked by increasing wholeness and personal power.

Experience and intuition are thus the final authorities for New Agers. Such subjectivism makes sense, *if* one believes he's in a universe where nothing ultimately exists but one solitary Self or subject. How can there be an objective authority? The very concept of objectivity loses ultimate validity and meaning in such a world view. Thus objectivity is not appreciated by New Agers as it has traditionally been in the West, though they like to consider themselves objective.

In addition to the above universal beliefs, most New Agers adhere to the ancient Hindu doctrines of reincarnation and karma. By the law of karma it is understood that whatever a person does—good or bad—will return to him experientially in an exact proportion of good or bad. Since most people are unable to experience all of the "bad karma" that they have accumulated in one lifetime, they are compelled to return in new incarnations until all of their bad karma has been balanced by good karma. Thus for those who accept such a scenario, *salvation is clearly a matter of works.*

Also central to New Age belief are a spiritualized doctrine of *evolution,* the conviction that personal transformation leads to planetary transformation, and the concept of the New Age itself (usually defined astrologically). Further discussion of these beliefs will be reserved until later in this and following chapters.

It should be pointed out that underlying the New Age belief system is an acceptance of most of the so-called truths purveyed by the secular establishment. While retaining strong elements of humanism, naturalism, and existentialism, New Agers have simply gone on to spiritualize the universe by making consciousness its essence, rather than matter. New Age activist Mark Satin writes that "consciousness is 'ultimately' determining. That is my perspective. It is not 'right' or 'wrong'—there is no 'ultimate' answer."[7] Denying that there is any ultimate objective truth we need to worry about (for example, a personal God with a definite will for mankind), New Agers see belief systems as worlds that we create to meet our cultural needs. When these "myths" are no longer serving the culture (which is how they tend to see the orthodox Judeo-Christian faith today), they should be discarded for the common good. (We will take a close look at this aspect of New Age thinking in chapters 3 and 4.)

Though New Agers have definite beliefs, this underlying utilitarian attitude explains their seemingly careless approach to issues of faith which, to the Christian, have ultimate consequences.

A Growing Force

Until the latter 1980s the majority of Americans were unfamiliar with the New Age movement. No doubt they had encountered certain elements of the New Age, like yoga, reincarnation, and astrology. And they might well have known someone who had been through an est "training" or practiced TM. But they lacked a clear perspective of the movement as a whole. This was largely because the media, on which they relied to stay informed, was itself oblivious to the movement's size and significance.

Commenting on this in 1982, popular New Age teacher David Spangler wrote in the Foreword to the book *New Times Network* that our newspapers, news magazines and television programs . . . suffer from a kind of evolutionary myopia, unable to see a larger context of growth and change in the world around them. If one looks beyond the range of the media, and examines some of the activities represented in this book, a different perspective emerges.[8]

It was not until late in 1986 and throughout 1987 that the New Age movement finally caught the media's attention. Credit for this goes to actress Shirley MacLaine's bold use of the media for New Age proselytization (see chapter 8); to the "Harmonic Convergence," a supposed "cosmic event" which in August 1987 brought roughly twenty thousand New Agers to "sacred sites" all over the globe; and to the massive popular interest in such New Age fads as "channeling" (see chapters 8 and 9) and the occult use of crystals (see Appendix A). Such a large and varied assortment of "true believers" (including many celebrities—see Appendix A) in the psychic and the occult provides just the kind of journalistic color the national media is always looking for. And so, one article or program on the movement after another began to appear, including a cover story in Time magazine (Dec. 7, 1987). Suddenly, the general public was well acquainted with the label "New Age."

Up to the time of this writing, however, the media's focus has remained almost entirely on the movement's more sensational and eccentric aspects, and thus they have treated it all as fad or fashion. As a serious cultural development, the New Age movement has yet to be discovered by the media at large.

The wishful thinking of its critics notwithstanding, this movement is not a passing fad. The forces responsible for it have been building steadily for several decades. It reflects rather a cultural revolt against secularism. It is a mass reaction against the spiritual void that the reign of secularism has left us with.

To be sure, since the 1970s this same dissatisfaction with materialistic values has produced a swelling of ranks within American evangelicalism. But many modern seekers, for a variety of reasons (including poor examples of Christianity), prefer more unconventional forms of spiritual expression. Thus by the late 1970s a Gallup survey could project that 10 percent of Americans had participated in some form of New Age mysticism.[9] Drawing upon this ground swell, the NAM has become a significant American spiritual and social force. Lipnack and Stamps have called it

"Another America"—a growing subculture existing alongside of the secular and religious establishments, competing with them for cultural dominance.

The NAM is decidedly a minority within our society, but a *mobilizing, active* minority. Its fortunes will ebb and flow with the political, economic, and spiritual climates. (For example, the economic recovery under Ronald Reagan was a setback for the movement, because it reenforced a trend toward conservatism; but the sexual scandals involving Jim Bakker and Jimmy Swaggart have helped the New Age cause, because they have reenforced—if not provoked—a widespread disillusionment with orthodox faith.) It currently has very little political power,[10] but an ever-expanding social influence (see chapters 5 and 6). It views its ideas and programs as the wave of the future (not without *some* good cause), and considers that it need only achieve a "critical mass" (not a majority) of public support to overturn the cultural strongholds of secular humanism and traditional religion.

As we proceed in this examination of the NAM, we will have frequent occasion to refer to its spokespeople (for a sampling of these, *see* the addendum at the close of this chapter). It should be remembered that since the NAM is a loosely knit network, and not a tightly run organization; participants are free to dismiss statements made by other New Agers as not representing their own views. Just as orthodox Christians all share the same basic world view and values, but can apply these values in very different ways, so it is with New Agers. I have generally sought to select quotes that represent the views of the entire movement, but quoting a New Age leader is not the same as quoting a spokesperson for a denomination, sect, or cult.

Understanding New Agers

Misunderstanding often inhibits fruitful dialogue with New Agers. They have been the victims of some rather unfortunate stereotyping, both by secularists *and* Christians. Secularists have often seen them as little more than flighty visionaries or as socially indifferent narcissists. Some Christians have viewed them as demonized Luciferians, consciously conspiring to usher in the

Antichrist, and have thus regarded them with mixed fear and loathing. Though there may be a limited basis in fact for some of these views, as general descriptions they are grossly misleading.

New Agers are generally sincere. Many are also intelligent; if one grants their basic worldview premises (which they assume to be self-evident facts), their beliefs are not as irrational and inconsistent as some think. (It is therefore these premises that the Christian must address in dialogue with the New Ager—*see* Appendix C.) They tend to be candid; even about their "conspiracy." (Marilyn Ferguson's *The Aquarian Conspiracy*, described in the addendum, is a forthright declaration of the movement's intentions and activities. If in any way it is misleading, it is due to excessive optimism, not sinister subterfuge.) Many New Agers are genuinely humanitarian, putting some Christians to shame by their willingness to serve humanity.

It is not that there is nothing sinister or dangerous about the New Age movement—but evangelicals should resist the temptation to try to locate the evil in simplistic black-or-white categories, for in so doing they will fail to see New Agers for who they really are. This will only reenforce the New Agers' *own* misconceptions about evangelicals, *and* their gospel.

Let us proceed, then, to seek a better understanding of New Agers, considering both those characteristics that relate them to other movements, and those features that set them apart and make them unique.

Life and World Affirming

In some respects, New Age religion can rightly be classified as a Western expression of classic monistic Hinduism (called *Vedanta*).[11] Their most basic beliefs (about God, the world, man, and salvation) are the same, as are the mystical experiences that are at the heart of both. Much of the New Age spiritual technology that produces these experiences has come straight from India, brought here and taught since the 1960s by Hindu swamis and gurus. Their followers make up a sizable—though by no means dominant—contingent of the NAM itself.

In spite of these commonalities, the New Age movement (*including* its Oriental components) is very different from traditional

Eastern mysticism. The key to this difference lies in the fact that New Agers are life and world affirming.

In traditional Hinduism the earthly is set in direct conflict with the spiritual, so that those who are serious about seeking God and salvation are expected to renounce the world of temporal pleasures and responsibilities. The world is *maya* (illusion), and is considered a formidable obstacle to eternal bliss. In the enlightened state, all is seen as God. Events in the world (being illusory) have no ultimate importance. Historic Hinduism is therefore world denying.

In keeping with their Western heritage, New Agers have rejected this aspect of Eastern mysticism. They affirm the value of temporal realities: people, nature, culture, education, politics, even science and technology. In fact, contemporary New Age thought represents an effort to graft the fruits of higher learning onto the various branches of mystical tradition.

Most New Agers are not romantically seeking to turn back the clock to a simpler time. They embrace the future, with all of its increasing complexity and automation, as long as things are developed along the lines of global peace, unification, and ecological balance. They stress a balanced exploration of both "inner space" (through meditation) and "outer space" (that is, the world external to the self).

One reason New Agers have rejected the traditional Hindu view of the world is that many of them have a social conscience. They desire to change the world—not drop out of it. Another reason is that almost all of them desire *personal* (earthly) as well as *spiritual* fulfillment.

The question might well be posed, "But isn't world denial a natural consequence of a monistic world view?" Historically, there seems to be a strong tendency in this direction, but New Agers are struggling to work out a metaphysical basis for their positive view of the world—a way to make social action and personal fulfillment compatible with mysticism.

In this regard some New Agers have proposed a "transmaterial" world view, which is (they claim) neither nonmaterialist (as with Hinduism), nor materialist (as with secular humanism). It agrees with the Hindus that on a certain level of consciousness (the "spiritual state"), all is seen as one, and there are no distinctions between, for example, subject and object, or good and evil. It would also agree with the materialist that on another level his perspective is valid. But New Agers argue for a third level, which incorporates both. Mark Satin comments, "In this state, objects, events, and self are neither separate, as in the material state, nor identical, as in the spiritual. Objects, events, and self are seen as separate *and* as flowing into a larger unity. As David Spangler puts it, difference is seen 'as really an enriching manifestation of this unity rather than a fragmentation of it.'"[12] In this perspective, the diversified created order can be viewed positively, rather than in the negative light in which Hinduism has long perceived it. The world, therefore, has value and purpose.

In this third state of consciousness, called the "religious state," the barrier that *maya* has long presented to ethics and social action (as in India) is seemingly "transcended":

> The religious state of consciousness is as valid as the others and as necessary to us, for without it we could have no morals, no guidelines for living. In the material state, morality is meaningless. An action works or it doesn't work, and that's that. In the spiritual state, morality is impossible; if you wish for something for your self, even guidelines or principles, you've already separated your self out from the One (and besides, everything is as it should be). But in the religious state, a moral principle is inherent in the universe, since *whatever is done to one part affects the whole*. As [Lawrence] LeShan puts it, "if one part moves another toward greater harmony with the whole, all of the whole—including the part that took the action—benefits"; and the reverse is also true. Therefore, "anything that moves a part toward its fullest development and fullest integration with the whole is good," anything that does the reverse is evil.[13]

But the question is, can such a convenient, arbitrary designation of "states" really sustain ethics?[14]

Hippies Come of Age?

The New Age movement bears a loose relationship, not only with Hinduism and the guru movements that have come from India, but also with the Western counterculture of the 1960s. It's true that many of the hippies of yesteryear are not a part of today's NAM (a healthy minority, in fact, are now Christians—*see* Appendix D), and most contemporary New Agers were probably never a part of the sixties counterculture. Nevertheless the 1960s counterculture is a *major* historical tributary among the several that have converged to become today's rushing river of New Age activity.

Theodore Roszak, who gave us *The Making of a Counter Culture* in 1969, observes, "People who grew up in the sixties have become part of the adult middle-class world . . . doing all the things people do—raising families, paying bills."[15] But because of their broad range of education and spiritual experience, Roszak points out, their values are different.

Though the hippie movement was pronounced dead sometime in the early 1970s, much of its spirit continues, having evolved into new cultural forms. Many New Agers carry on such sixties distinctives as (1) an antimaterialism which emphasizes a lifestyle of "simple living and high thinking" (though this in particular is far from true with all); (2) attempts to build alternative, utopian communities; (3) an exaltation of nature; (4) rejection of traditional morality; and (5) fascination with the occult. No New Ager would dispute the old hippie "gospel" that the answer to mankind's problems lies in the cultivation of "higher levels of consciousness."

Although the New Age movement has historical continuity with the hippie movement, in many ways they differ. (1) The NAM is not primarily a youth movement, but spans all ages. (2) New Agers are usually not distinguishable from the rest of society by outward appearance. (3) Hard-rock music is not a rallying point. Instead, they have developed their own "New Age" music (*see* Appendix A), described by *Newsweek* as

> a loosely defined school that encompasses . . . lyrical jazz folk . . . airy harp fantasies . . . spacey synthesizer noodlings. . . . What ties these musicians together is a vaguely mystical world view and a striving toward a relaxing musical mood.[16]

(4) Though revolutionary in its long-term objectives, the NAM is not anti-establishment in the overtly rebellious sense of the 1960s. (5) Whereas the sixties counterculture tended to be either radically left (socialistic) or anarchistic in political philosophy, New Agers have developed an entirely new approach, termed "radical center" (to be described in chapter 6). (6) New Agers have not generally continued the hippies' emphasis on free sex, though, as noted

above, their morals could hardly be called "traditional." (7) While psychotropic (mind-altering) drugs were the doorway to the spiritual realm for most hippies, the mysticism of the New Age movement is largely drug-free.

We see then that many New Agers could be described as "hippies come of age," but it would be a great oversimplification to suggest that the New Age movement is little more than a new name for the hippie movement. It represents a much broader cultural trend.

Health and Growth-oriented

The 1970s was a decade characterized by introspection—a search for what psychologist Abraham Maslow called "self-actualization." Thousands of young people, burnt out on the drugs and militant politics of the sixties, sought answers in cults or in a variety of Eastern and occult disciplines. But the same longings for qualitative change were being felt by the older and more established sectors of society. People of all ages desired to achieve meaning and direction in life, greater success and fulfillment, and increased physical and psychological well-being. These interests gave rise in the 1970s to the human potential and holistic health movements, which remain significant to the present.

Though they are not explicitly religious, both movements have built numerous bridges to the worlds of mysticism and the occult. So many ideas, practices, and techniques—as well as people—have crossed these bridges (both ways), that the various movements inevitably cohered, and assumed a common identity, which is the New Age movement of today. The overall body of New Age thought has been shaped by (and reflects), all of these influences.

New Agers as a rule then are very health- and growth-oriented. Much of the movement's activities centers around these themes.

It needs to be noted that there is nothing wrong (and everything right) with desires to grow and be whole. The quests for spiritual reality, authentic identity, satisfying relationships, and greater health are all, in and of themselves, desirable cultural trends. When carried out along biblical lines, they should be applauded. For the Christian the problem with the New Age approach to personal transformation is the metaphysical and spiritual context in which the concept is understood and pursued.

In the Bible, spiritual growth is equated with increasing dependence on Christ, and conformity to his will (for example, 2 Cor. 3:4–5; James 4:13–16; Eph. 4:15). In contrast, New Agers offer definitions like the following: "The personal and spiritual growth of a person can be described as the transformation from a dependent human being to one who knows and feels that he/she is in charge of his/her life and acts upon it."[17] These radically different conceptions of growth are perfectly consistent with the radically different universes that Christians and New Agers believe they inhabit.

Since for the Christian the distinction between Creator and creation is absolute and permanent, the limited creature must always depend on, and obey, the all-sufficient, sovereign Creator. Though personal growth may involve increasing independence on a *human* level, our relationship with *God* operates differently.

For the New Ager, though, the distinction between "creator" and creation is illusory, and so that which *is* all-sufficient and sovereign must be the self! In such a case, growth or transformation would logically involve recognizing this fact and acting on it, in ever-increasing self-sufficiency and control over one's own life.

When New Agers talk about "taking responsibility" and "being accountable," Christians can be disarmed, since these terms are part of their own vocabulary. Actually, the word *responsibility* can be used in very different contexts.

To the Christian, man is responsible and accountable to external authorities; beginning with God, and including those human authorities that he has instituted (for example, Rom. 13:1, 2). The New Ager, on the other hand, defines "taking responsibility" and "being accountable" ultimately in terms of the *self*. We have the power to create our own reality, but it will be created by external forces if we don't take responsibility for whatever happens to us. This is why human-potential-seminar graduates have been known to blame such adversities as cancer and rape *on the people who suffer from them.*

New Age belief in unlimited human potential—our power to "take responsibility" and shape our own future—is increasingly being applied not just to the individual but to society as a whole. New Ager and psychologist Barry McWaters writes of "the emerging potential of human beings to take responsibility, individually and collectively, for a positive future."[18]

Taking Responsibility for the Planet

New Agers are (understandably) very concerned about the many threats to global survival (such as the nuclear-arms race). They don't believe they have to watch helplessly as the fate of all humanity is shaped by the vested interests of short-sighted political and economic powers. Just as they've embarked on *personal transformation* by taking responsibility for their own lives, they believe that a critical mass of transformed individuals can take responsibility for society as a whole and bring about *social* or *planetary transformation*. Their highly optimistic view of human nature encourages them to believe that not only can the global crisis be survived, it can also be turned into an evolutionary opportunity to realize our *racial* potential in a relative utopia.

New Agers such as David Spangler recognize that this longing for a "new age" is not of itself new:

> The idea of the new age is rooted in one of the oldest human images, that of the holy (or holistic) human civilization. This image . . . is one of a human culture in full harmony and attunement within itself, with nature, and with God: a culture in which the divine perspective of love and wholeness can find full expression.
>
> The desire for such a civilization has empowered human striving and efforts throughout our history, particularly here in the West. It has been the impetus behind numerous millennial movements and eschatological expectations. It has been the imagination behind the idea of utopia.[19]

As "millennial" as the New Age movement may be from a sociological standpoint (and as indebted to Christianity as it may be for this emphasis), it does not believe in the biblical millennium (Rev. 20:1–6). Rather than base their hopes on biblical prophecy, New Agers appeal to astrology.

Belief that we are entering a more enlightened astrological age has been popular among occultists for nearly a century. The Introduction to *The Aquarian Gospel of Jesus the Christ*, a turn-of-the-century psychic "revelation," offers this classic definition:

> The Aquarian Age is pre-eminently a spiritual age, and the spiritual side of the great lessons that Jesus gave to the world may now

be comprehended by multitudes of people, for the many are now coming into an advanced stage of spiritual consciousness.[20]

For some New Agers the "Age of Aquarius" is little more than a convenient symbol for the anticipated new order, but for the majority, it is a deeply held religious belief.

New Age Religion: Anything But Christian!

Belief in an astrologically rather than a biblically defined new age is indicative of the fact that New Age religion is thoroughly occultic, and totally unchristian. Discernment of this truth is sometimes woefully lacking, even in traditionally Christian circles. As one of many possible examples, the Washington state-based Chinook Learning Community, a heavily New Age group similar to, and in close fellowship with, Scotland's Findhorn community (see addendum), receives an annual three thousand dollar grant from the North Puget Sound Presbytery of the United Presbyterian Church.

What makes "New Agism" unchristian? Intellectually, if the basic New Age beliefs outlined earlier are adhered to, the central components of the Christian faith cannot remain intact. If all is One (God), there can be no sin and death. The substitutionary death of Christ for our sins, which is the very heart of the gospel, becomes meaningless—even illusory.

It cannot even be said that Christ took our "bad karma" on himself. Karma is seen as an impersonal law in the universe, not the personal judge of the universe. It therefore is exacting, making no merciful provision for the sinner's atonement. (The difference between the two concepts of justice—a universal, unfailing law that works like gravity, and a sovereign, transcendent God—is accentuated in biblical passages like Ezek. 18:21–22 and Ps. 32:1–2.)

The New Ager will agree that Jesus Christ is God; his world view will allow that. But his world view will also compel him to say that Jesus is no more God than anyone else. The difference between Jesus and the rest of humanity must therefore be that he more fully realized and demonstrated the divine (Christ) potential we all have. His value to us becomes primarily one of example. New

Agers say that Jesus wanted us to become his equals, not to worship him.

New Age thinker Ken Wilber even suggests that the Christian clergy deviously changed Christianity from a mystical religion into a personality cult:

> A religion that is merely at the mythic level—such as fundamentalist Protestantism or exoteric (nonmystical) Catholicism—then a living mystic is a real problem for you, because the mystic claims that *everybody* can become one with God, and that means bypassing the middleman: the priest and his collection plates. . . . So the exoteric Christians did a clever thing: they allowed that Christ was one with God, but nobody else! Christ got "kicked upstairs," and from that time on, anybody who claimed to be one with God was pronounced heretical.[21]

But Christianity has *never been* anything other than a faith focused in the person of Jesus Christ as the unique God-man (2 Cor. 4:5; 11:2–3), and the highest spiritual attainment has never been mystical identification with God, but *fellowship* with the Son of God, and through him, with the Father (1 John 1:1–3; John 17:3; Phil. 3:8). *This* does not need any "middlemen" (1 Tim. 2:5), as Protestantism has always maintained.

By holding that "Christ" refers to a divine principle within *all* men, and that Jesus simply attained consciousness of it ("Christ consciousness") as we all can, New Agers seemingly resolve the dilemma that the obvious uniqueness of Jesus poses for their pantheistic world view. In other words, since his unmatched greatness would strongly support his claim to exclusive deity, the only way to escape this implication is to argue that he never made such a claim. By so doing, however, they brand themselves as "antichrist." For scholars agree that it was exactly *this error* (separating the man Jesus from the divine Christ), as promulgated by early Gnostics, that the apostle John was indicting when he coined that term (1 John 2:18–23).[22] In its historical context, "Christ" (Messiah) is *exclusively* the title of the prophesied human king of Israel (for example, Dan. 9:25–26).

Though some New Age groups identify themselves as "esoteric Christians," and most New Agers think highly of Jesus, their endorsements of him need to be evaluated in the light of 2 Corinthians 11:3–4, 13–15. It is there we learn that there can be a *counterfeit* Jesus, preached by counterfeit apostles who serve a counterfeit "angel of light" (Satan).

The New Age Jesus became "the Christ" only after purifying himself of "bad karma" through many incarnations, and even now (as many New Agers believe) he is only one of several "masters" who serve humanity from a higher (but not the highest) plane.

As relatively exalted as this Jesus may be in the *New Ager's* mind, he is a ghastly substitute for the Jesus of the Bible, the Creator and sustainer of the universe (Col. 1:16–17). Reverence for the New Age "Jesus" will not impress the historical, biblical Jesus, who is "ready to judge the living and the dead" (1 Peter 4:5).

A Return to Paganism

Not all New Agers profess affinity with Christianity, however. Many are becoming more open about the essentially *pagan* nature of New Age spirituality. In fact, there is a growing attraction in New Age circles to an "earth mother" deity, as opposed to a heavenly Father. Mark Satin comments on this trend:

> Significantly, among those of us at self-development stages six and seven, religious worship has already begun to rely less on the tradition of the sky god and more on the tradition of the earth goddess. As sociologist Robert Bellah sees it, "The sky religions emphasize the paternal, hierarchical, legalistic and ascetic, whereas the earth tradition emphasizes the maternal, communal, expressive and joyful aspects of existence.[23]

Among the books which Satin recommends is *God Is Red,* by Vine Deloria, Jr. (Delta, 1973). The message Satin gleaned from the book is that "we have more to learn from North American Indian spirituality than we do from Christianity."[24]

How could Westerners with a nearly seventeen-hundred-year Christian heritage drift so far from their biblical moorings? An insight can be gained from yet another affirmation by Satin: "A spiritual path is valid *for us* if it is appropriate to *our* needs as *we ourselves* define them"[25] (emphasis in original). What is revealing about this evaluation is that it is made without reference to the judgments or wishes of any power external to the self.

Due to the ever-increasing influence of secular ideas in our culture, for baby boomers like Satin the sovereign God of the Bible has been dethroned from the universe. In his absence, spiritual needs must be satisfied in seemingly novel ways. And though the autonomous seeker seems free to choose from a multitude of possibilities, the options open to the human condition turn out to be more limited. Ultimately, the forms of religion now being experimented with are little different than those employed by our prechristian forefathers.

In a tragic sense, the biblical proverb (2 Peter 2:22) is exemplified, "The dog [a word Jesus used for the Gentiles, Matt. 15:26] returns to his own vomit" (that is, the idolatry of his distant past). And modern man is doing so on a bridge built by his own intellect! (This fact is evident in the simultaneously sophisticated, imaginative, and yet tortured philosophizing that New Agers employ to justify this revival of the "earth tradition." *See* chapter 3.) The implications that this rising interest in paganism holds for Western civilization are disconcerting, to say the least.

Occultism: The Heart of New Age Religion

A study of religion in world history demonstrates the near universality of psychic phenomena and the mystical experience, as well as such practices as divination, magic, and spiritism. Only the biblical tradition really stands apart (for example, Deut. 18:9–14), offering a different kind of spirituality: the sovereign and gracious workings of the Holy Spirit among the covenant people of the true God.

Thanks to the profound historical influence of biblical faith in the West, pagan spirituality was forced to the cultural periphery and given the stigmatizing appellation "the occult." Now, in the form of the New Age movement,[26] paganism is attempting to regain *all* of its lost ground. By New Age design (*see* chapter 5), Western culture is being permeated with a variety of techniques for altering the consciousness and tapping "universal energy" (for example, yoga, "creative visualization," and "therapeutic touch" for healing). Because of the scientific or pseudoscientific language that is offered to explain these techniques, their occult connections often go unrecognized. In fact, the New Age's multiple doorways to spiritual power and experience *all* open up to the *same* world that has been populated for millennia by witches, shamans, and mediums.

What is the New Age movement? In this chapter I have attempted to answer that question from a number of angles, pointing to a variety of temporal factors, and emphasizing the sincerity and humanitarianism of many of its participants. But from a biblical perspective (which is to say, from the perspective closest to eternity that we are capable of), the New Age movement is *most* significantly a sophisticated, contemporary representation of the same old spiritual kingdom that has always stood in stark opposition to the kingdom of Jesus Christ (for example, Acts 13:8–12).

This fact is wearisomely demonstrated by the spiritual "entities" who through human "channels" supply much of the movement's teaching. They unfailingly make a point of attacking the unique deity of Christ, the atoning power of his death, and so on (*see* chapter 9).

New Agers desperately need this biblical perspective, lest they devote their lives to saving the world, only to find at the end they were serving the author of its destruction (John 8:44; 10:10). Once they come to know the *biblical* Jesus, they will find a resource for personal transformation that they have never dreamt of (2 Cor. 3:18), and a vision for human service grounded in the unshakable kingdom of God (Heb. 12:28). In *his* service, their idealistic energy will not be wasted (1 Cor. 11:34).

Addendum to Chapter 1: Who's Who Among New Agers

If a sign of a movement's vibrancy is an abundance of leading organizations and spokespeople, then the New Age movement is unmistakably throbbing with life. Due to space limitations, only a sampling can be offered here of even the most important names.

Groups

Findhorn: An almost legendary New Age community located in the north of Scotland which offers an ongoing educational program in the principles of New Age spirituality and world service; *Esalen:* The original "growth center," offers a plethora of workshops for mind, body, and spirit at its Big Sur, California, location; *the Unity-in-Diversity Council:* a New Age "metanetwork" of well over one hundred networks and groups rallying for global co-operation and interdependence; the *Association for Humanistic Psychology*; the *Association for Transpersonal Psychology*; *The Forum* (formerly est); *The Farm:* A countercultural community in Summertown, Tennessee, that does humanitarian work in America and abroad through its PLENTY Project; *Planetary Citizens:* A community and activist group committed to engendering "planetary consciousness" among New Age groups and in the general public.

Spokespeople

Significant thinkers: futurist Alvin Toffler; the late economist E. F. Schumacher; cultural historian Theodore Roszak; social historian William Irwin Thompson; biologist Jonas Salk; former *Saturday Review* editor Norman Cousins; psychologist Jean Houston; consciousness researcher Ken Wilber; physicist Fritjof Capra; the late anthropologist Margaret Mead; the late futurist Buckminster Fuller.

Political figures and activists: retired U.N. Assistant Secretary General Robert Muller; Planetary Citizens president and cofounder Donald Keys; futurists Barbara Marx Hubbard and Hazel Henderson; organizer and *New Age Politics* author Mark Satin.

Spiritual leaders: Author and former Findhorn leader David Spangler; medicine man Sun Bear; erstwhile Harvard psychology professor, now popular speaker Richard Alpert (a.k.a. Baba Ram Dass); "channel" Jach Pursel ("Lazaris"); Sufi Order in the West leader Pir Vilayat Inayat Khan.

Other influential spokespeople: Death-and-dying researcher and hospice pioneer Elizabeth Kübler-Ross; actress Shirley MacLaine; motivational speaker Rev. Terry-Cole Whittaker; est founder Werner Erhard.

Last but not least is lay consciousness researcher Marilyn Ferguson. Her popular book *The Aquarian Conspiracy* (1980) paints a broad picture of New Age activities and inroads into our culture, and suggests that this signals a transformation so radical that it may amount to an entirely new phase in evolution. By providing the movement with an optimistic view of itself, the book's publication did more to substantiate a sense of identity and vision for the NAM than has any other single event.

A "New Age" of Science
The Impact of Mysticism on Objectivity

Dianne Kennedy Pike, wife of the late Episcopal Bishop James Pike, expressly represented the sentiments of the New Age movement when she conveyed the following to author Brad Steiger:

> My personal conviction is that the Age of Aquarius has to do with our developing a large overview of how things are related. It's my hope and expectation that this . . . will be integrating the various levels of our consciousness—physical, emotional, mental, and spiritual—in one world view and one vocabulary and one way of talking so that we won't have the split that we've had for so many years, where we think that science and religion are talking about separate things. . . . We need a language in which we can talk about the spiritual forces and energies the way we are learning to talk about *other natural energy* in the universe. . . .
>
> I think we are now in a stage wherein mass consciousness can evolve to the spiritual level, and . . . it is at that level where there can be a reunification of religion and science. . . . I believe that a merging of the languages of science and religion will be one of the keys to the universality characteristic of the Aquarian Age (emphasis added).[1]

Indeed, in some scientific circles the traditional distinctions between science and religion do seem to be breaking down. Robert

35

Kirsch of the *Los Angeles Times* notes that there is currently "a drive to enlarge the scope of science, a tendency to examine questions which previously would be asked or emphasized only by those outside the boundaries of science."[2]

In this chapter we will take a close look at this phenomenon. We will consider the central place of mystical experience in the New Age movement, and how New Agers are appropriating science in order to authenticate this experience, for themselves and for society at large. Finally, we will consider possible effects of New Age entanglements with science on that enterprise.

Experience—The All-Important Factor

The rise of "New Age science" can only be adequately understood by reference to mystical experience. In the previous chapter we looked at how meditation, "creative visualization," chanting, and several other techniques for altering the consciousness play a pivotal role in the New Age movement. Such "psychotechnologies" are capable of interrupting or even bringing to a halt one's normal patterns of conceptual thought *without* extinguishing or diminishing consciousness itself. For the responsive subject, "ASCs" (altered states of consciousness) can produce a profound mystical sense of "transcendence" of individuality and identification with everything. Such experiences of undifferentiated consciousness suggest to the seeker that ultimate reality itself is undifferentiated; everything is one, and the nature of the One must be consciousness (since at the peak of the mystical state consciousness is virtually all that is experienced).

R. M. Bucke, a turn-of-the-century psychiatrist who popularized the term "cosmic consciousness" to describe these states, put it this way:

> This consciousness shows the cosmos to consist not of dead matter governed by unconscious, rigid, and unintending law; it shows it on the contrary as entirely immaterial, entirely spiritual and entirely alive; it shows that death is an absurdity, that everyone and everything has eternal life; it shows that the universe is God and that God is the universe, and that no evil does or ever did enter into it.[3]

The person who actively pursues or passively submits himself
or herself to ASCs is setting himself up for nothing short of a religious conversion: he will likely come out of his experiences persuaded that metaphysical reality is something similar to what
Bucke described. It can therefore be observed that ASCs are either a
passageway to Reality, or a passageway to delusion, but they are
hardly a neutral phenomenon to which one can repeatedly subject
himself while retaining a detached, "scientific" frame of mind.
Their impact on the psyche is too powerful, producing a subjective
entanglement in the dynamics inherent to the experience.

By their very nature, mystical states impart a sense of *absolute*
certainty. In the words of Alfred Lord Tennyson concerning experiences he had since boyhood: "This is not a confused state but the
clearest, the surest of the surest, utterly beyond words. . . ."[4] After
such experiences, New Agers tend to think that they *understand*
reality, while other, less enlightened souls can only *believe* it to be
a certain way.

Although New Agers do not generally repudiate normal reasoning processes, they do believe that they have experienced something that transcends them. Thus it is very difficult for rational
arguments (such as concerning the dangers of subjectivism) to penetrate their mindset: they simply assume that the one challenging
the experience has not had it—or he or she also would "know."

ASCs can have an especially profound impact on secular humanists who either never were exposed to, or have long since given up
on, traditional Christian spirituality. Cultural historian and "new
consciousness" advocate Theodore Roszak observes that "the spiritual void in our lives . . . is the secret of our discontent."[5] After
languishing in the arid wastelands of godless naturalism, and then
encountering the spiritual realm directly through ASCs, the
former skeptic's entire world is shaken. (For a personal account
of such experiences, *see* Appendix D.) Things he or she once considered impossible become a matter of personal experience. Ecstatic feelings, psychic power, even contacts from spirit entities, all
create hope for a more purposeful, satisfying life. A new world view
must be found to replace the shattered old one.

Awed by the discovery of an entirely new and (to him) uncharted
world of mystical experience, he will be prone to uncritically accept the explanations and interpretations of the experience that are

offered by New Age authority figures (especially if they have scientific or academic credentials). He will then be pliable in the hands of those who desire to conform his thinking to the distinctives of Aquarian Age ideology. The assurance derived from the experience will easily translate to an ideology that vindicates the experience, even if the same arguments would fail to impress the uninitiated. (This mystically generated credulity should be borne in mind when we examine New Age mythology in the following chapter.)

Desperately wanting to retain their new spiritual basis for life, such humanists will seek out ways to reconcile the apparent discrepancies between their old "scientific" (naturalistic) world view and their new mystical one. One of the strong appeals of the New Age movement is its attempt to bridge this gap—it seemingly allows one to accept modern evolutionary science while still offering the comforts of religion (for example, a purpose to life, the prospect of a blessed afterlife, a basis for ethics, and hope for humanity's future).

It would seem that this deep-seated psychological factor has strongly contributed to such New Age intellectual efforts as Fritjof Capra's *The Tao of Physics* (1975) and Ken Wilber's *Up from Eden* (1983), and their rapid and widespread acceptance. New Agers from a wide variety of disciplines and backgrounds would very much like to "matchmake" a union of science and (Eastern/occultic) religion. Not only would such a marriage vindicate the mystical world view in their own minds, it would offer powerful propagandistic leverage in a culture where science speaks almost *ex cathedra*. According to Marilyn Ferguson,

> Abraham Maslow [the "father of the human potential movement"] observed, although our visionary artists and mystics may be correct in their insights they can never make the whole of mankind sure. "Science," he wrote, "is the only way we have of shoving truth down the reluctant throat."[6]

New Agers are nowhere near achieving this objective, but their progress has nonetheless been noteworthy (*see* chapter addendum). It is conceivable that they could eventually succeed. What then would be the implications for science?

Subjective Science

Objectivity has commonly been considered essential to the scientific method.[7] In chapter 1 we observed that the monistic world view offers intellectual validation to a subjective approach to life, while devaluing objectivity. Mystical experiences also tend to both produce and progressively intensify a subjective orientation. When this psychospiritual transformation takes place in a scientist, it can profoundly affect his work. Dr. Edgar Mitchell is just one of many possible cases in point.

Mitchell, who holds a doctor of science degree, was the sixth man to walk on the moon. He was the lunar module pilot on Apollo 14.

On his return from the moon, while contemplating the earth, the astronaut (who had previously been interested in parapsychology) had a mystical experience. He told the magazine *Omni* that it was an "explosion of awareness, an aha! A wow."[8] *Omni* adds that

> what it meant to Mitchell was that God was real—although Mitchell's is not a biblical God—and something more. He came to realize that the universe is made up of matter and spirit but that they are not separate. The bridge is consciousness. God is something like a universal consciousness, manifest in each individual, and the route to divine reality and to a more satisfying human material reality is through the human consciousness.[9]

After this powerful experience, consciousness became Mitchell's dominant interest:

> To pursue these ideas, Mitchell changed his life. In October 1972, two years after Apollo 14, he resigned from NASA and the Navy and founded the Institute of Noetic (from the Greek *nous*, meaning mind) Sciences to study human consciousness.[10]

Mitchell became convinced that scientific methodology could be employed to explain telepathy, psychic healing, and other paranormal events. (This is the basic assumption underlying the discipline of parapsychology.) He wrote in the book *Mind at Large* that "there are no unnatural or supernatural phenomena, only very large gaps in our knowledge of what is natural. . . . We should strive to fill these gaps of ignorance."[11]

It is not that Mitchell believes that such phenomena have a *purely physical* explanation. Indeed, most scientists who subscribe to philosophical materialism do not recognize the reality of truly psychic phenomena, because their world view has difficulty finding a place for it.[12]

Mitchell's position can only be understood in the light of his acceptance of pantheism, where nature and God are considered one. Such a view not only makes nature divine, it makes God "natural." The category of the supernatural is ruled out, along with the miraculous. Once this view is adopted, the traditional distinction between science and religion quite easily becomes blurred. Everything, even God, can be explained in terms of laws or principles, and can be approached "scientifically." This is why in Eastern and occult literature it is common to read about the "science of yoga" (or god realization), the "science of soul travel," the "science of karma and reincarnation," and so forth. Even the miracles of Jesus are viewed in a so-called scientific light. He understood and manipulated nature's more subtle laws.

Typical of mystical teachers, Bhagwan Shree Rajneesh told his followers:

> The old religions are based on belief systems. My religion is absolutely scientific. . . . Of course, it is a different science than the science that is being taught in the universities. That is objective science. This is subjective science. . . .[13]

Since New Agers believe that the physical world is really made of consciousness, and that the mind of the individual scientist is part of this universal consciousness, the distinction between subject and object, between "subjective science" and objective science becomes difficult to define or maintain. Consciousness becomes the final explanation of *all* phenomena, psychic and physical. In such a context the marriage of science and mystical religion would seem inescapable.

In fact, Mitchell's Institute of Noetic Sciences (IONS) openly characterizes the "science of subjective experience" that they are recommending to the larger scientific community as "the esoteric core of all the world's religions, East and West, ancient and modern, becoming exoteric, 'going public.'"[14]

Many New Age thinkers, including IONS president Willis Harman, are calling for nothing less than a change in the scientific enterprise itself, including its purpose, methods, and scope.[15] Harman calls this proposed synthesis of modern science and ancient mysticism "multiple vision science" and says it

> would foster open, participative inquiry; it would diminish the dichotomy between observer and observed, investigator and subject. Investigations of subjective experience would be based on collaborative trust and "exploring together," rather than on the sort of manipulative deception that has characterized much past research in the social sciences."[16]

Such talk is reminiscent of a controversy that flourished in psychology a quarter century ago. This concerned (at that time) Harvard professors Timothy Leary and Richard Alpert. (Leary later became the infamous "guru" of the hippie movement. Alpert is now a popular New Age speaker and author also known as Baba Ram Dass.)

Leary and Alpert were not only conducting but *participating* in experiments with chemically induced ASCs. Leary insisted that "the subject-object method of research is inadequate for studies of human consciousness."[17] His point was that ASCs are so indescribable that they have to be *experienced* to be understood. Thus, competent research on the subject could not be conducted from a nonparticipatory standpoint.

To Leary and Alpert's colleagues, however, the once-respected researchers' participation in the experiments was transforming them from scientists into mystics (an allegation which the years that followed certainly substantiated). Reporter Dan Wakefield observed at the time:

> The question of who are "qualified researchers" has become increasingly controversial, and charges have been leveled at Leary and Alpert that their own use of the drugs has destroyed their objectivity as scientists. Dr. David C. McClelland, chairman of the Center for Research in Personality and the man who brought Leary and Alpert to Harvard, has said that the more they took the drug "the less they were interested in science." The *Archives of General Psychiatry* editorial warning against the dangers of the drugs noted that some researchers "who became enamored with their mystical hallucinatory state, eventually in their 'mystique' became dis-

qualified as competent investigators." On the other hand, mushroom expert Gordon Wasson has pointed out that such charges against investigators who have taken the drug lead to the dilemma that "we are all divided into two classes: those who have taken the mushroom and are disqualified by our subjective experience and those who have not taken the mushroom and are disqualified by their total ignorance of the subject."[18]

While many New Age scientists would disavow Timothy Leary and the use of psychotropic drugs, it is nonetheless widely acknowledged that such drugs can produce states of consciousness and personality changes essentially the same as those experienced through meditation, sensory deprivation, and other psychotechnologies. Therefore those who like Mitchell and Harman advocate integrating such experiences with science lay themselves open to some of the same objections that were rightly raised against Leary and Alpert.

Modern Physics and Ancient Mysticism

The impact of mysticism on science is not limited to such controversial fields as consciousness research and parapsychology. In 1979 Newsweek reported that "a new school of theoretical physicists, many of them based at the University of California's Lawrence Berkeley Laboratory, is using mystical modes of thought in an effort to create a unified philosophy of how the universe works."[19]

One U.C. Berkeley physicist, the celebrated New Age author Fritjof Capra, writes:

As Eastern thought has begun to interest a significant number of people, and meditation is no longer viewed with ridicule or suspicion, mysticism is being taken seriously even within the scientific community. An increasing number of scientists are aware that mystical thought provides a consistent and relevant philosophical background to the theories of contemporary science, a conception of the world in which the scientific discoveries of men and women can be in perfect harmony with their spiritual aims and religious beliefs."[20]

Specifically, scientists like Capra have been popularizing the idea that such twentieth-century developments in physics as quantum and relativity theories offer scientific backing to the beliefs of ancient mystical traditions. Many further argue that monistic and mystical perspectives are necessary to *understand* these recent discoveries, and to make further progress in the new frontiers of science.

The present work is not the place to attempt a detailed description of the new physics, nor to show the many ways in which New Agers like Capra use (and abuse) it for their own ends. The following examples of how New Agers make unwarranted "quantum leaps" from the hard facts of physics to their own metaphysical conclusions will have to suffice. To them, the interdependence of physical reality proves the oneness of *all* reality (including God and human souls); the fact that mass and *physical* energy are different aspects of the same thing proves that *psychic* energy is the universal, fundamental reality; the fact that objectivity is restricted at the quantum level demonstrates that "there is no absolute objective reality. . . . Objectivity is only a man-made concept . . ."[21]; the fact that our understanding of subatomic particles is significantly colored by our own minds suggests ". . . that consciousness may be an essential aspect of the universe, and that we may be blocked from further understanding of natural phenomena if we insist on excluding it."[22]

The End of Science

It is clear from our previous consideration of so-called subjective science that if the New Age interpretations noted above were to become widely accepted in physics, we would witness the marriage of a "hard" science to Eastern/occult mysticism. This could signal the end of classical objective science. Some New Age writers openly hope for this.

Marilyn Ferguson discusses the view of Gary Zukav, author of *The Dancing Wu-Li Masters* (a book similar to Capra's *The Tao of Physics*):

> In one sense, Zukav said, we may be approaching "the end of science." Even as we continue to seek understanding, we are learning

to accept the limits of our reductionist methods. Only direct [that is, mystical] experience can give a sense of this nonlocal universe, this realm of connectedness [that is, the realm of modern quantum and relativity physics]. Enlarged awareness—as in meditation—may carry us past limits of our logic to more complete knowledge. The end of conventional science may mean "the coming of Western civilization, in its own time and in its own way, into the higher dimensions of human experience.[23]

To be fair to Zukav I should point out that if his world view were correct, every statement just cited would be defensible. If consciousness were "an essential aspect of the universe," then it would be entirely conceivable that in failing to recognize this, conventional science would eventually come to the end of itself. It would also be reasonable to suppose that the various psychotechnologies (representing a new "subjective science") could pick up where traditional science left off, helping us attain knowledge experientially that had proved inaccessible to our "reductionist methods."

But what if mystical "enlightenment" is really delusion? If supposed insights gained from such an enlightenment were incorporated into scientific theories, science would run aground!

The world of the occult is brimming over with the fruits of "subjective science." There are accounts of contacts with every conceivable kind of unearthly being (*see* chapter 8); of journeys out-of-the-body and out-of-this world; of historical events inaccessible to normal investigation, but made available by obliging angels, hypnotically induced recollection of "past lives," or psychic inquiry into the "Akashic records" (the supposed "memory bank" of the Universal Mind).

Information gained from such unearthly sources is taken seriously in the New Age movement, and usually not considered any less reliable for not being objectively verifiable. Such an approach to truth spawns seemingly unending fantasies, most of which contradict each other at important points. If this approach was adopted by science, the outcome would be no different.

No Criteria?

The absurdity of such New Age revelations, and the conviction with which they are usually proclaimed, underscore the fact that spiritual or psychic experiences can be profoundly misleading. Christian author and lecturer Pat Means points out that

> the non-mystic might well interject the argument that no experience can prove anything to anybody except that one has, in fact, *had* an experience . . . does the fact that someone feels "enlightened" during meditation prove that he has had an experience with the Divine? No—it merely proves that someone feels "enlightened" during meditation.
>
> Even pro-mystic psychologist Carl Jung admits . . . "We can of course never decide definitely whether a person is *really* 'enlightened' . . . or whether he imagines it. We have no criteria for this."[24]

Jung exhibited commendable objectivity concerning the limits of spiritual experience. But what of his belief that "we have no criteria" for distinguishing authentic from imagined enlightenment? It would be folly for the serious seeker of truth to *assume* this to be the case. For if at some point in history the Ultimate Reality has objectively made itself known, then the seeker might avail himself of what Plato called "a safer and less hazardous passage . . . in a more secure conveyance, to wit, some word from God."[25]

A survey of world history reveals that amid the commonalities that can be observed in all religions, the God revealed in the Bible, the God of Israel and the Christian church, is unique.[26] Moses appealed to this indisputable fact when exhorting the children of Israel to keep Yahweh's commandments:

> Has anything been done like this great thing, or has anything been heard like it? . . . . has a god tried to go to take for himself a nation from within another nation by trials, by signs and wonders and by war and by a mighty hand and by an outstretched arm and by great terrors, as the LORD your God did for you in Egypt before your eyes? To you it was shown that you might know that the LORD, He is God; there is no other besides Him (Deut. 4:32b, 34–35).

A scientific approach to the histories of Israel and the Christian church will turn up data (like the Exodus from Egypt) that can only be adequately explained by reference to miracles. Nineteenth-century-higher-critical efforts to discredit Israel's own account of her history have themselves been progressively discredited by

twentieth-century archaeology.[27] Efforts to explain away Christian
claims have similarly been futile. The only satisfactory explanation for the rise of the Christian church is the bodily resurrection
of Jesus Christ from the dead.[28]

Only an antisupernatural bias would compel someone to seek
alternative explanations for these events. Such an approach is in-
defensible since it assumes miracles to be impossible *before* check-
ing the record of history to see if any have occurred. The available
empirical evidence supports the claim that a unique divine revelation is available to us in the Bible.

God *has* spoken, therefore, and given us answers to basic questions concerning himself, man, and the spiritual and physical
worlds. From this disclosure we learn that while God is intimately
involved with the world, he is essentially distinct from it (Pss. 90:2;
102:25–27; 113:4–6). We also find that God has created spheres and
personalities (angels) that are fundamentally not of this world
(2 Cor. 12:2–4; Matt. 18:10). In light of these facts we must conclude that the supernatural is a legitimate category.

Throughout the Bible we find that the supernatural realms are
capable of interaction with our natural world. However, because of
willful rebellion against God, men and some of the angels are morally fallen. Therefore, as a protection to man, the communion that
they are capable of is forbidden (for example, *see* 1 Cor. 10:20).
Thus the entire range of occult practices are prohibited (Deut.
18:9–14), as well as passive, trancelike states of consciousness,
which increase our susceptibility to demonic influence (we find
this chiefly in biblical condemnations of mediumistic trances, but
the same spiritual dangers can be shown to accompany other ASCs
as well).

Man's need for communion with the spiritual realm is not denied, but it must be met in the manner that God prescribes:

> And when they say to you, "Consult the mediums and the spirit-
> ists who whisper and mutter," should not a people consult their
> God? . . . To the law and to the testimony! If they do not speak
> according to this word, it is because they have no dawn (Isa. 8:19–
> 20).

Scripture ("the law and the testimony"), then, is the historically
reliable, objective criterion whereby the nature and value of spiritual experience must be determined.

The Limits of Science

It would seem that the primary failing of contemporary thought is its neglect of the logical and empirical evidence for biblical claims. This neglect, in turn, seems to result from a deep-seated antisupernatural bias. For modern man, *everything* must be explainable in natural terms.

Why, Christians ask, should it be a settled issue that all phenomena have natural explanations? What evidence is there that the universe is self-generating? What is there *within* the universe that is capable of *explaining* the universe? Why should science be equated with the philosophy of naturalism?

The scientific method deals with *empirical* data: it does not concern itself with whether metaphysical reality (that which is beyond observable processes) is natural or supernatural. Therefore, naturalism is a philosophical presupposition no more demonstrable by the scientific method than theism (belief in a transcendent God). And, the Christian would ask, is it more reasonable that a universe which exhibits temporal and dependent qualities throughout is *self*-producing, or that it is the product of a power that is *not* temporal and dependent, existing *outside* the system?[29]

Once the possibility of a supernatural creator is granted, there is no logically compelling reason to hold—as did the deists of two centuries ago—that supernatural forces could not continue to bring influence to bear on the natural world.[30]

Biblical theism establishes both a basis for, and limitations to, the scientific endeavor. It provides a basis because (unlike monism) it states that the world is objectively real, and was founded on rational principles capable of being discerned by rational minds (Pss. 104:24; 139:14). It sets limits, however, because (unlike naturalism) it teaches that the universe is not a closed system. Certain kinds of phenomena (both divine and devilish), not originating in the system, cannot be wholly understood in terms of natural processes.

Biblical prohibitions of occult involvement apply to researching scientists as much as anyone else, but useful scientific inquiry will not be stifled by this. Rather, biblical guidelines, if followed, would provide for the continued fruitfulness of science. The reasons for this will be evident as we proceed.

Almost anyone who has been deeply involved with the occult

will testify from experience that regardless of how much fakery may also exist, paranormal phenomena *do* occur (*see*, for example, Appendix D). The survival and growth of parapsychology—in spite of one hundred years of ridicule from outside the field, and experimental disappointment within—would be difficult to explain if there was *nothing* truly paranormal happening, goading researchers on to further experimentation.

When psychics are brought into the laboratory, however, the phenomena do not demonstrate the repeatability necessary for scientific verification, although they will at times occur. Furthermore, the energy employed in psychic healing, psychokinesis (the movement of objects by psychic power), and other demonstrations of "psi" (psychic ability) evades precise physical measurement.[31] As John Weldon has demonstrated in *Occult Shock and Psychic Forces*, there is little or no evidence in science *or* Scripture to support the hypothesis of "latent psi" within man.

New Ager Mary Coddington observes that

> for centuries men of genius have tried to harness this strange enigmatic force and enlist it to the aid of science. Thus far it has remained slightly out of grasp, eluding its would-be captors with an almost capricious tenacity and always escaping definition.[32]

These results defy the expectations of naturalism but conform to biblical theism's supernatural/natural distinction, which depicts the energy source behind occultism as both nonphysical and personal and therefore unmeasurable (in any direct sense) and unpredictable.

This inability to explain psychic phenomena in physical terms results in many conversions to the New Age world view. Unwilling to part with their antisupernatural bias, even after encountering the paranormal, the researchers resort to pantheism. As we saw earlier, this allows for a "natural" (though nonphysical) explanation. In this way they feel they can retain a "scientific" frame of mind.

The Christian sees, however, that there is nothing scientific about theories based on nondetectable, nonphysical energy systems. Nor is it unscientific to believe that science should be limited to the physical (that is, nonspiritual) world.

Just as the usefulness of the scientific method is exhausted at the point of explaining psychic phenomena, so with the subjective side of ASCs. The clear limitations on doing "competent research" of mystical states (such as was evident with Leary and Alpert) point to the fact that the participant has in some respects a spiritual (supernatural) experience. This requires biblical revelation to be adequately explained. The naturalistic observer will be unable to relate to experiences that are not strictly natural. The scientist who *participates* in order to understand may well encounter the spiritual realm, undergo the mystical conversion process, and lose his objectivity. Therefore, the "dilemma" that mushroom expert Gordon Wasson referred to is scientifically insurmountable.

I do not mean to suggest that acceptance of mysticism and monism necessarily equals a loss of scientific competency (in fact, Einstein was apparently a pantheist, and some of the leading for-mulators of quantum theory were attracted to Eastern thought). However where New Age thinking has penetrated science a dis-turbing loss of scientific objectivity is already evident. Were New Age influences to move from the fringes to the mainstream, there would be serious consequences.

It may seem ludicrous even to suggest that such a secular strong-hold could be overrun by mysticism. Certainly, it is hard to imag-ine. But the present dominance of skeptical naturalism in scientific circles is no safeguard against this eventuality. As long as scientists assume that there are *no limits* to scientific inquiry and explanation, they lay themselves open to the beguiling influences of supernatural darkness. Only theism, which provided fertile soil for the birth of modern science, can ensure its perpetuation. Through theism science can come to grips with its own bound-aries, and in so doing it will also regain an authentic sense of itself.

Addendum to Chapter 2: Some Ground Gained for the New Age

Mystical beliefs and supernatural phenomena are *slowly* but steadily weaving their way into the fabric of scientific thought and research. Efforts to link the "new physics" with Eastern mysticism (like Fritjof Capra's *The Tao of Physics*) have attracted considerable attention from the physics community. While a good deal of this attention has been critical, there is also much evidence of favorable interest and even wholesale acceptance.

The three most penetrating occult inroads into science, however, were pinpointed by Marilyn Ferguson in her 1973 book *The Brain Revolution:* "There is an enormous groundswell of scientific interest in practices considered quackery a brief decade ago, in altered states of consciousness, unorthodox healing, and parapsychology."[1]

In the field of consciousness research, conventional psychologists bring altered states of consciousness and psychic phenomena into the laboratory,[2] and often emerge with New Age world views. Many of the leading names in the field are New Agers or New Age sympathizers (for instance, biofeedback pioneers Elmer and Alyce Green, Robert Masters, Jean Houston, Lawrence LeShan, Stanislav Grof, Robert Ornstein, Stanley Krippner, and Charles Tart).

The same process of conversion in the laboratory often happens in parapsychology (for examples, and an excellent overall treatment of the subject, *see* John Weldon and Clifford Wilson's *Psychic Forces and Occult Shock* [formerly *Occult Shock and Psychic Forces*], Master Books).

Although parapsychology is still considered pseudoscience by much of the scientific establishment, it is gradually gaining ground. In 1969 it was granted affiliate status in the American Academy for the Advancement of Science, and in 1979 New Ager Jeffrey Mishlove received the first Ph.D. in parapsychology (granted by the University of California at Berkeley).

Stephen Schwartz, founder and head of Mobius, a firm exploring the practical uses of psychic abilities, comments:

> Physicists, among others, have taken a close look at paranormal abilities during the last decade. In 1979, nine respected physicists wrote "The Iceland Papers," detailing physical experiments on psychics. In the book, Brian D. Josephson, Nobel laureate of Physics at Cambridge University, wrote: "In recent years a number of reputable scientists have entered the field (of paranormal research) with expert knowledge of how to perform good experiments . . . still it appears that the phenomena occur."[3]

In medicine New Age advances have been most telling. Popular acceptance of "holistic health" and disillusionment with orthodox medicine are forcing desperate health professionals to experiment with dubious, sometimes blatantly occultic therapies. In the words of Robert Becker, professor of orthopedic surgery at State University of New York's Upstate Medical Center in Syracuse: "If the laying on of hands will do a better job for patients in this country, then I'm all for it. Let's just put it on as solid a scientific foundation as possible."[4]

Becker's comments reveal the seductive nature of the occult. It is hard to repudiate a practice that seemingly gets results, even if they cannot be explained scientifically. However, the kingdom of the occult never dispenses favors without requiring much more in exchange. When the psychic realm is given a flimsy "scientific foundation" upon which to extend its influence, both science *and* society will pay dearly.

The "New Myth"
An Outline of New Age Ideology

"The very chaos of contemporary existence provides the material for transformation. We will search [out] new myths, and world visions."—The Association for Humanistic Psychology.[1]

"I believe the most fundamental thing we can do today is to believe in evolution."—Robert Muller, Retired United Nations Assistant Secretary-General.[2]

Social optimism does not come easy in these latter years of the twentieth century. One hundred years ago many sincere Westerners anticipated that by our present time something close to an ideal society would have been achieved. Today in the light of the proliferation of nuclear-arms, escalating terrorism, and other global threats, people's hopes are more likely to be that civilization as we know it will still *exist* a century from now.

Ideologies that inspired political and social activism in the not-too-distant past have lost much of their visionary appeal. Sociologist Robert Lilienfeld speaks of a

> bankruptcy and decline of images and philosophies of society that until now have served as unifying ideas . . . European history of the past 100 years could be described in terms of a civil war among the exponents of major conceptions of society. With the bankruptcy of notions of the social contract and the military defeat of both Na-

zism and Fascism, the collapse of liberalism from within, and the evident loss of faith among socialists themselves in both the theory and practice of socialism in all its variants, we may be said to live in an "interregnum" [i.e., an interval in time between potent ideologies]. In this sense there is some small core of truth in the otherwise questionable notion of the "end of ideology."[3]

Lilienfeld is correct in noting that, in spite of the current lack of unifying ideas, ideology as a social phenomenon is still very much alive.

According to *The New Encyclopaedia Britannica* (fifteenth edition, "Macropedia") in the strict sense of the word, an ideology may be identified by five characteristics: "(1) it contains an explanatory theory of a more or less comprehensive kind about human experience and the external world; (2) it sets out a program, in generalized and abstract terms, of social and political organization; (3) it conceives the realization of this program as entailing a struggle; (4) it seeks not merely to persuade but to recruit loyal adherents, demanding what is sometimes called commitment; (5) it addresses a wide public, but may tend to confer some special role of leadership on intellectuals."

A New Ideology

Throughout this century a new ideology has been quietly emerging among an intellectual elite in certain scientific/technological, academic, liberal, and international political circles. It is based upon what some would consider the leading edge of scientific and sociopolitical theory. Starting with humanistic and evolutionary assumptions, it is global (rather than national) in its perspective, and is concerned above all with threats to world survival. Its distinctive emphasis is on finding *holistic* solutions to planetary problems, and this concern usually culminates in a vision of a united world community.

Depending on which aspect of the larger intellectual movement is being considered, different names are used to identify its adherents. In scientific and technological circles they are known as the "systems movement."[4] In the political arena they have no one label, but many identify themselves as "planetarians."[5] In psychology, they have assumed the epithet "The Third Force."

The new ideology is represented by such elite groups as the Club of Rome, the Institute for World Order, and the Society for General Systems Research and its sister organization, the International Federation for Systems Research. Its leading theorists include futurist Marshall McLuhan, philosopher Ervin Laszlo, and economist Kenneth Boulding. The late futurist and inventor R. Buckminster Fuller was also a prominent voice.

This intellectual elite should not be indiscriminately identified with the New Age movement. Some within it are not spiritually inclined, and most would shun the more outlandish New Age beliefs and practices (for instance, "channeling"—*see* chapters 8 and 9). However, quite a few in its ranks—including some leading names—are interested in mysticism. They believe it offers the spiritual dimension needed to complete their distinctive world view and ethics.

Certain of these ideologues have been actively involved with the "new consciousness" (or New Age) subculture (for example, cultural historian Theodore Roszak, futurist Willis Harman, psychologist Jean Houston, U.N. consultant Donald Keys, and the late anthropologist Gregory Bateson). Through their influence mystics and occultists who were not originally a part of this intellectual class have found within its writings the scientific and sociopolitical philosophies most compatible with their own beliefs and experience. Once having found each other, the ideologues and the "Aquarians" recognized their capacity to benefit each other, and to some extent have joined forces (the primary "glue" being those intellectual mystics who fully take part in both movements).

As a result of this convergence the new ideology is building momentum, not only among an influential but small class of intellectuals, but also a large, socially and politically active grass-roots movement.

The work of translating this highly technical, somewhat abstruse ideology into more popular New Age terms has been undertaken by a host of writers. None have been more successful, however, than Fritjof Capra in *The Turning Point—Science, Society, and the Rising Culture* (1982), and Marilyn Ferguson in *The Aquarian Conspiracy—Personal and Social Transformation in the 1980s* (1980).

The Turning Point, the more serious work, has served as sort of a manifesto of New Age ideology. A physicist at the University of

California at Berkeley, Capra has done an able job of synthesizing the views of the systems movement with the basic New Age belief system.

The Aquarian Conspiracy, while not strictly concerned with New Age ideology, has probably done more to promote it on a popular level than any single book. It provides an overview of a vast array of contemporary ideas and activities, and suggests that they may all be converging to produce a far-reaching social transformation (the "New Age"). Ferguson's book classically typifies the characteristic New Age optimism in the face of the present world crisis.

In the remainder of this chapter we will examine the basis for this New Age optimism as I outline the new ideology. Our focus will primarily be on its New Age form, as presented by Capra, Ferguson, and others. When relevant, however, the scientific and philosophical sources for New Age ideas will be considered.

The Paradigm Shift

New Agers are among the most vocal critics of worldwide political, economic, and military arrangements. Fritjof Capra notes in *The Turning Point* that

> more than fifteen million people—most of them children—die of starvation each year; another 500 million are seriously undernourished. Almost 40 percent of the world's population has no access to professional health services; yet developing countries spend more than three times as much on armaments as on health care. Thirty-five percent of humanity lacks safe drinking water, while half of its scientists and engineers are engaged in the technology of making weapons.[6]

Citing inflation, cancer, schizophrenia, and crime, Capra further points out that "it is a striking sign of our times that the people who are supposed to be experts in various fields can no longer deal with the urgent problems that have arisen in their areas of expertise."[7]

As far as New Agers like Capra are concerned, the inequities, the deficiencies, almost everything that is wrong with modern civilization can be blamed on a collective *intellectual* blindness: we are clinging to modes of thought that are themselves *out*moded. Marilyn Ferguson puts it this way: "We try to solve problems with our existing tools, in their old context, instead of seeing that the escalating crisis is a symptom of our essential wrongheadedness."[8]

It would follow that if enough people started thinking in a new, more appropriate context, a new age of peace and prosperity would be possible. New Agers say this change of thinking has already begun (mainly with them), and they call it "the paradigm shift."

A paradigm is a conceptual model that is used for interpreting phenomena. The concept of a "paradigm shift" was first introduced by science historian Thomas Kuhn in his 1962 book *The Structure of Scientific Revolutions*. As the title suggests, Kuhn's conception of paradigm shifts was limited to scientific theories, but New Agers apply it to world views of entire cultures. Bearing this in mind, let's allow Marilyn Ferguson to describe for us the dynamics of paradigm shifts:

> A paradigm shift is a distinctly new way of thinking about old problems. For example, for more than two centuries, leading thinkers assumed that Isaac Newton's paradigm, his description of predictable mechanical forces, would finally explain everything in terms of trajectories, gravity, force. It would close in on the final secrets of a "clockwork universe."
>
> But as scientists worked toward the elusive ultimate answers, bits of data here and there refused to fit into Newton's scheme. This is typical of any paradigm. Eventually, too many puzzling observations pile up outside the old framework of explanation and strain it. Usually at the point of crisis, someone has a great heretical idea. A powerful new insight explains the apparent contradictions. It introduces a new principle . . . a new perspective. By forcing a more comprehensive theory, the crisis is not *destructive* but *instructive*. . . .
>
> A new paradigm involves a principle that was present all along but unknown to us. It includes the old as a partial truth, one aspect of How Things Work, while allowing for things to work in other ways as well. By its larger perspective, it transforms traditional knowledge and the stubborn new observations, reconciling their apparent contradictions. . . .
>
> New paradigms are nearly always received with coolness, even mockery and hostility. Their discoverers are attacked for their heresy. . . .
>
> But the new paradigm gains ascendance. A new generation rec-

ognizes its power. When a critical number of thinkers has accepted the new idea, a collective paradigm shift has occurred. . . . After a time that paradigm, too, is troubled by contradictions; another breakthrough occurs, and the process repeats itself. Thus science is continually breaking and enlarging its ideas.[9]

By applying Kuhn's theory to the entire succession of world views embraced by human culture, New Agers are suggesting that our knowledge of *all* truth (not just scientific truth) accumulates and evolves in an entirely experimental manner. Consequently they hold that there should be nothing absolute or fixed about any particular belief system—including their own.[10]

In fact, as we noted in chapter 1, beliefs about reality are viewed as "myths" by New Age thinkers. They are to be evaluated more with respect to how well they serve the culture that holds them, than whether they are objectively true (since nothing can ultimately be "objectively true" in the subjective universe of monism). As mankind evolves, his myths must evolve with him.

At this point in his "evolution," man faces unprecedented complications and difficulties. New Ager and psychiatry professor Roger Walsh writes in *Staying Alive—The Psychology of Human Survival:*

> Our various economic, social, and cultural systems are becoming increasingly interdependent. The threat that some impoverished countries might be unable to repay the tens of billions of dollars of loans they have received sends shock waves through the international financial community. A recession in the United States leaves millions unemployed throughout the world. Ecological imbalances, atmospheric pollution, and radioactive contamination do not halt politely at international borders. With each new disruption it becomes more apparent that our biosphere—the totality of earth, water, air, plants, and animals—functions as an interconnected whole. A change in any part affects every part. Increasingly, we are forced to recognize that what we do unto others we are also doing unto ourselves. As Jerome Frank put it, "The psychological problem is how to make all people aware that whether they like it or not, the earth is becoming a single community."[11]

In our emerging planetary culture, New Agers say that a *new* myth is needed—one with a distinctly planetary, holistic character.

Systems: A Whole Is More Than
the Sum of Its Parts

To understand the nature of the new paradigm that New Agers are calling for, it will help to first understand what they consider the "old" paradigm to be.

Capra tells us that the old paradigm (among other points) looks at the world ". . . as a mechanical system composed of elementary material building blocks. . . ."[12] It largely originated with Rene Descartes, the seventeenth-century French philosopher and mathematician:

> Descartes' method is analytic. It consists in breaking up thoughts and problems into pieces and in arranging these in their logical order. This analytic method of reasoning is probably Descartes' greatest contribution to science. . . . On the other hand, over-emphasis on the Cartesian method has led to the fragmentation that is characteristic of both our general thinking and our academic disciplines, and to the widespread attitude of reductionism in science—the belief that all aspects of complex phenomena can be understood by reducing them to their constituent parts.[13]

New Agers affirm that due to the fragmenting effects of our over-emphasis on rationality, we have lost the intuitive awareness of our connection with the whole. This loss has serious consequences:

> To the extent we fail to recognize this interdependence and con-nectedness, to that extent we feel alienated, become ecologically insensitive, and are at risk for conflict with "others." Our current global crisis is making this fact desperately clear.[14]

We are told, however, that there is cause for hope. Science, the champion of the Cartesian paradigm which threatens to destroy us, is ironically now offering us a new paradigm which has the potential to heal us. Capra explains the new perspective:

> In contrast to the mechanistic Cartesian view of the world, the world view emerging from modern physics can be characterized by words like organic, holistic, and ecological. . . . The universe is no longer seen as a machine, made up of a multitude of objects, but has to be pictured as one indivisible, dynamic whole whose parts are essentially interrelated and can be understood only as patterns of a cosmic process.[15]

The thesis of Capra's *The Turning Point* is that there is a critical need for the holistic perspective of modern physics to be adopted by other disciplines like biology, psychology, and economics, as well as by the institutions and individuals that make up society as a whole.

Capra explains that this new vision of reality is known as the "systems view" and says that it

> looks at the world in terms of relationships and integration. Instead of concentrating on basic building blocks or basic substances, the systems approach emphasizes basic principles of organization. Examples of systems abound in nature. Every organism . . . is an integrated whole and thus a living system. . . . But systems are not confined to individual organisms and their parts. The same aspects of wholeness are exhibited by social systems— such as an anthill, a beehive, or a human family—and by ecosystems that consist of a variety of organisms and inanimate matter in mutual interaction. What is preserved in a wilderness area is not individual trees or organisms but the complex web of relationships between them.
>
> All these natural systems are wholes whose specific structures arise from the interactions and interdependence of their parts. . . . Systemic properties are destroyed when a system is dissected, either physically or theoretically, into isolated elements. Although we can discern individual parts in any system, the nature of the whole is always different from the mere sum of its parts. Another important aspect of systems is their intrinsically dynamic nature. Their forms are not rigid structures but are flexible yet stable manifestations of underlying processes. . . .
>
> Systems thinking is process thinking. . . .[16]

General Systems Theory

This view which Capra elucidates so well was first formulated in the 1930s by Austrian-born biologist Ludwig von Bertalanffy (d. 1972). By the 1950s his General Systems Theory (GST) had generated an interdisciplinary movement.

Although von Bertalanffy was not the first to advocate a holistic perspective (for example, *see* South African statesman-philosopher Jan Christian Smuts's 1925 treatise *Holism and Evolution*), he was the first to seek an all-encompassing scientific basis for it. His systematic development and application of holistic theory anticipated several modern movements. For example, holistic health, in theory if not always in practice, is perfectly consistent with the principles of GST.

While there are several movements that emphasize a holistic approach to a given subject (for example, health care, the environment, defense), the advocates of GST are unique in their *general* approach. GST proposes that there are several natural laws that determine the functioning of *all* systems (physical, organic, psychological, social, and even conceptual). Von Bertalanffy was convinced that an interdisciplinary study of systems would yield a mathematically precise, experimentally verifiable description of these laws. (Such an "interdisciplinary discipline" has yet to be established.) Then, he affirmed, the knowledge of organizing principles common to *all* phenomena would make possible the long dreamed of unification of the sciences (physical *and* social).[17]

Von Bertalanffy envisioned that, with science more unified and a systems view adopted, the presently overwhelming array of societal problems could be approached and resolved comprehensively. All factors would be viewed in the context of an interdependent whole. Capra explains why this holistic approach is especially relevant in today's increasingly interrelated world:

> Present-day economics, for example, remains fragmentary and reductionist, like most social sciences. It fails to recognize that the economy is merely one aspect of a whole ecological and social fabric. Economists tend to dissociate the economy from the fabric in which it is embedded, and to describe it in terms of simplistic and highly unrealistic theoretical models. Most of their basic concepts (e.g., efficiency, productivity, GNP) have been narrowly defined and are used without their wider social and ecological context. In particular, the social and environmental costs generated by all economic activity are generally neglected. Consequently, the current economic concepts and models are no longer adequate to map economic phenomena in a fundamentally interdependent world, and hence economists have generally been unable to grapple with the major economic problems of our times.
>
> Because of its narrow, reductionist framework, conventional economics is inherently antiecological. Whereas the surrounding ecosystems are organic wholes which are self-balancing and self-adjusting, our current economies and technologies recognize no self-limiting principle. Undifferentiated growth—economic, technological, and institutional growth—is still regarded by most econ-

omists as the sign of a "healthy" economy, although it is now causing ecological disasters, widespread corporate crime, social disintegration, and ever increasing likelihood of nuclear war.[18]

Thus, adopting the views of the systems movement, New Agers hold that a change from reductionistic to systemic thinking is a matter of primary importance (perhaps even life or death) for global civilization.

The Systems View and Mysticism

New Agers go further than the systems movement, though, by suggesting that this change of thinking requires acceptance of mystical modes of thought. This is the case first of all because New Agers tend to equate mysticism with intuition, and intuition undeniably plays an important role in systems thinking (for example, systems thinking requires synthesis as much as analysis: an intuitive ability to recognize wholes, or patterns of relationship). In the second place, since mystical states of consciousness tend to break down ego (that it, self-image) boundaries and create a sense of oneness with one's environment, New Agers assume that they offer an effective means for achieving the more holistic perspective that society needs.

For New Agers, then, mysticism is validated by the systems view, and the systems view is almost inconceivable without some measure of mysticism. Certainly, there are several areas of compatibility between the two.

One such area lies in their common tendency to view reality as more energy or process than substance or "thing." In GST this emphasis is focused in von Bertalanffy's conception of the organism as an *open system* (a central feature of his thought, which he proclaimed to be "an essentially new construct in biology"[19]). Citing the fact that all living systems continually exchange materials with their environment, von Bertalanffy argued that they are not just *in* a state of flux: they *are* flux. He wrote that "living systems are not *in being,* they are *happening.* They are expressions of a perpetual stream of matter and energy which passes through the organism and at the same time constitutes it."[20] He added that "what are called structures are slow processes of long duration."[21]

Systems thinkers point out that the process view of reality is also supported by quantum physics, where subatomic particles are often described more as events than things. Thus they claim both biology and physics lend profound corroboration to the systems approach, where all of reality is described more in terms of process (how does something operate?) than substance (what is it made of?).

The compatibility of such a perspective of the world with mysticism is evident when we recall (1) that mystics tend to see God more as a pervasive Energy (the "Force" of *Star Wars*) than an objective entity; and (2) that they generally identify the world with God. Thus, R. Buckminster Fuller perfectly expressed the process perspective:

> For God, to me, it seems
> is a verb
> not a noun,
> proper or improper. . . .[22]

Although, in the opinion of this writer (and I will elaborate on this in chapter 4), much of the holistic perspective need not be tied to a monistic world view, many of its advocates believe it has definite religious implications. Capra affirms that "the systems view of life is spiritual in its deepest essence and thus consistent with many ideas held in mystical traditions."[23]

New Agers even see "scientific" support in the systems view for their belief that consciousness is the essence of all reality. They arrive at this by defining "life" and "mind" strictly in terms of systemic (that is, self-organizing) properties, and then affirming that the same systemic properties are the fundamental force at work in the universe—the "universal mind."

Through such semantical legerdemain Capra (and von Bertalanffy before him) attempts to "transcend" the age-old dispute between mechanism and vitalism (that is, the belief that organisms are animated by a nonscientific force) and come out on the side of *both* materialistic biology *and* Eastern/occult mysticism:

The systems view agrees with the conventional scientific view that consciousness is a manifestation of complex material patterns. To be more precise, it is a manifestation of living systems of a certain complexity. On the other hand, the biological structures of these systems are expressions of underlying processes that represent the system's self-organization, and hence its mind. In this sense material structures are no longer considered the primary reality. Extending this way of thinking to the universe as a whole, it is not too far-fetched to assume that all its structures—from subatomic particles to galaxies and from bacteria to human beings—are manifestations of the universe's self-organizing dynamics, which we have identified with the cosmic mind. But this is almost the mystical view, the only difference being that mystics emphasize the direct experience of cosmic consciousness that goes beyond the scientific approach. Still, the two approaches seem to be quite compatible. The systems view of nature at last seems to provide a meaningful scientific framework for approaching the age-old questions of the nature of life, mind, consciousness, and matter.[24]

Emergent Evolution

Von Bertalanffy argued that this supposed self-organizing force behind the universe inherently tends toward *higher* organization. Invoking Aristotle's dictum that "the whole is more than the sum of its parts," he proposed that evolution is "emergent," operating in the following manner: the organizing force of the universe brings assorted objects into increasingly complex relationships. As this occurs properties emerge that are greater than the sum of these parts—a result of their interaction. These are entirely new and higher systems, such as life and mind. Evolution is therefore not random but purposive and creative. (In all of this, von Bertalanffy strongly resembles Jan Christian Smuts, though he plays the likeness down.[25])

The conception of "emergent evolution" belongs, not just to von Bertalanffy and Smuts, but to a larger philosophical movement dating from the latter period of the nineteenth century. This philosophical school, in fact, can legitimately claim to be the progenitor of the systems movement.

After the scientific establishment embraced Darwin's theory of evolution, sensitive minds quickly perceived its implications. If all of life arose strictly through chance mutation and natural selection, man was deprived of a spiritual base upon which to establish his ethics, hopes, and very identity. Without challenging evolution itself, several thinkers began looking for ways to overcome the futility it seemed to impose on man.

Earlier in the nineteenth century a context for such efforts had been created by the German philosopher G. W. F. Hegel. His view of history as God in process envisioned the world and mankind moving ever forward—by thesis, antithesis, and synthesis—to new degrees of freedom. It was not difficult to find a place for biological evolution in such a scenario. It was only necessary to add to evolution a creative principle beyond mutation and selection to guide things upward and (in some fashion) to legitimize spirituality.

Through the writings of such thinkers as Herbert Spencer, Henri Bergson, Lloyd Morgan, Samuel Alexander, Alfred North Whitehead, and, most importantly for the New Age movement, Pierre Teilhard de Chardin, a process philosophy[26] emerged which embraced evolution as the basis for, rather than the destroyer of, man's spiritual aspirations.

This well-established process view of God and history has been adopted quite naturally (because they identify the world with God) by New Age thinkers. Due to their highly eclectic propensities (as described in chapter 1), however, they have expanded the evolutionary drama of process thought into a full-blown mythology.

The Mega-Crisis:
Evolution in New Age Ideology

In chapter 1 it was noted that evolution is central to New Age belief. This fact can hardly be overemphasized. Evolution is inseparable from New Age conceptions of (to use Christian categories) God, creation, man, history, Christ (see particularly the teachings of David Spangler), salvation, "sanctification" or spiritual growth, and "eschatology" or beliefs concerning the kingdom of God and the culmination of all things.

For New Agers, evolution is God in process; hence, it is sometimes assigned a place in their world similar to that which the biblical God occupies for the Christian. For examples, note the quote from Robert Muller at the beginning of this chapter, or this comment made by New Age philosopher Ken Wilber after discussing the nuclear threat: "But *I really trust evolution*. I really don't think God would screw us around that bad. God might be slow, but God's not dumb" (emphasis mine).[27]

Without such faith in evolution, New Agers would be incapable of maintaining their distinctive optimism. As much as they may believe in the new paradigm's ability to rectify the world situation, what assurance is there that a significant portion of humanity would be willing to make the sacrifices demanded by such a change of thinking? History and today's newspaper offer little encouragement.

The new paradigm requires a new humanity. As Donald Keys put it:

> A new kind of world—the world into which we are already moving—requires a new kind of person, a person with a planetary perspective, with a different, more inclusive awareness, a person with a more humane and integral consciousness, capable of identifying with the entire human species and with all planetary life. This requires a leap to a quality of consciousness which most of us do not automatically possess. It implies a quantum shift to a state of being which is fundamentally different from the divided or fragmented consciousness which has gone before.[28]

New Agers have a historic sense in some respects comparable to that found in many Christian circles: this generation may stand at the threshold of history's consummation. British science writer and New Ager Peter Russell affirms that "the majority of human beings now alive may experience an evolutionary shift from ego-centered awareness to a unified field of shared awareness."[29]

Rapid social change resulting from the industrial and technological revolutions and the rising number of people who have experienced altered states of consciousness are interpreted as evidence that the pace of evolution has been dramatically stepped up. John White, who has written extensively on the interface between the New Age and science, expresses this conviction:

> Higher human development—evolution—has been accelerating in the last few centuries. The pace of change now is unprecedented in the life of our species and what is to come is, in fact, a new species. We are witnessing the final phase of Homo sapiens and the simultaneous emergence—still quite tentative because of the nuclear threat to all life—of what I have named Homo Noeticus, a more advanced form of humanity.
> . . . as we pass from the Age of Ego to the Age of God, civilization will be transformed from top to bottom. A society founded on love and wisdom will emerge.
> The change of consciousness underlying this passage involves transcendence of ego and recognition of the unity of life.[30]

The new humanity, therefore, will be characterized by the intuitive/mystical or holistic perspective already emerging in New Age circles; each individual aware of his (or her) oneness with God, the rest of humanity, and his environment. Consequently, the threats of war, ecological disaster, and socioeconomic collapse are expected to ultimately vanish.

At this point one might *still* wonder why New Agers are so hopeful. After all, it is one thing to *say* these global challenges will be answered by a "quantum leap" forward in evolution; it is another to *produce evidence* that evolution is in fact advancing. In spite of what may be said for technological advances, an objective look at the world situation would seem to indicate that in many respects things are only getting more fragmented and out-of-hand. In fact, as Keys notes, technology has only magnified and multiplied our problems:

> The unprecedented technological prowess developed by humanity during this twentieth century has brought us not only the crisis of the use of nuclear weapons but other major crises as well. The accelerating curves of overpopulation, wasteful use of resources, pollution, unemployment, disappearing agricultural land, the unmet basic human needs in two-thirds of the world and the threat of a runaway nuclear arms race appear to be converging rapidly into a global "mega-crisis". . . .[31]

In the words of Robert Burrows of the Spiritual Counterfeits Project, "Nothing undermines belief in evolutionary progress more than the gruesome realities of today's world."[32]

At this juncture, however, a seemingly unrelated trend in scientific thought rescues the New Age vision from ideological shipwreck. This is "punctuated equilibrium," a relatively new paradigm for understanding evolution, proposed in 1972 by paleobiologists Stephen Jay Gould of Harvard and Niles Eldredge of the American Museum of Natural History.

Punctuated equilibrium is quickly gaining ascendancy in scientific circles because the fossil record has not confirmed the expectations of the older and previously favored model of Neo-Darwinism. *Newsweek* reported in 1980 that

> the more scientists have searched for the transitional forms between species, the more they have been frustrated. . . .

Evidence from fossils now points overwhelmingly away from the classical Darwinism which most Americans learned in high school: that new species evolve out of existing ones by the gradual accumulation of small changes, each of which helps the organism survive and compete in the environment.[33]

Marilyn Ferguson describes the new model:

Punctuationalism or *punctuated equilibrium* suggests that the equilibrium of life is "punctuated" from time to time by severe stress. If a small segment of the ancestral population is isolated at the periphery of its accustomed range, it may give way to a new species. Also, *the population is stressed intensely because it is living at the edge of its tolerance.* "Favorable variations spread quickly," Gould said. . . .
Most species do not change direction during their tenure on earth. "They appear in the fossil record looking much the same as when they disappear," Gould said. A new species arises suddenly in the geological evidence. It does not evolve gradually by the steady change of its ancestors, but *all at once and fully formed."*[34]

According to Punctuationalism, then, a crisis in a species' environment can disturb its "stasis" or equilibrium and trigger rapid, radical evolutionary change.

Ferguson goes on to explain the relevance of punctuated equilibrium to New Age thinking:

(1) It requires a mechanism for biological change more powerful than chance mutation, and (2) it opens us up to the possibility of rapid evolution in our own time, when the equilibrium of the species is punctuated by stress. Stress in modern society is experienced at the frontiers of our psychological rather than our geographical limits. . . .
Given what we are learning about the nature of profound change, transformation of the human species seems less and less improbable.[35]

Punctuated equilibrium has provided New Agers with a positive context within which to interpret the negative realities of the world scene—a new world may be in the throes of birth.

Futurist and 1984 candidate for the vice presidency Barbara Marx Hubbard exudes confidence:

Crises always precede transformation. Before every great change in planetary evolution, problems emerge which appear insolvable—problems like limits to growth, stagnation, impending catastrophes, and disintegration. These crises appear to involve gigantic mistakes, but from a higher perspective the problems are "evolutionary drivers" which trigger innovation and transformation, as well as bringing out new potentials in us which introduce absolute newness into the world.

We are at the dawn of a period of "conscious evolution," when humanity first becomes aware of the process of Creation and begins to participate deliberately in the design of our world. . . .[36]

Conscious Evolution

The idea of "conscious evolution" is not peculiar to Hubbard, but is a central component of the emerging ideology. David Spangler, New Age teacher and spiritual leader, calls it "a new cultural myth."[37] Sri Aurobindo (d. 1950), an Indian philosopher-mystic who has inspired many New Age thinkers, said that "man occupies the crest of the evolutionary wave. With him occurs the passage from an unconscious to a conscious evolution."[38]

Barry McWaters, psychologist and founder of the Institute for the Study of Conscious Evolution, attempts a definition:

"Conscious evolution" is that latter phase in evolutionary process wherein the developing entity becomes conscious of itself, aware of the process in which it is involved and begins voluntarily to participate in the work of evolution. This can happen in a number of dimensions, in a number of ways, and in fact has been happening for a long while both in individuals and small groups. We are now approaching that moment in evolutionary history when Humanity as one self-conscious entity will assume this role.

In preparation for this unified function much work is required. And, in fact, many individuals and groups are working diligently. There is an *Aquarian Conspiracy.*[39]

McWaters's concluding statements make the ideological significance of conscious evolution evident. It provides a context and impetus for social and political action. Roger Walsh notes that conscious evolution:

can be seen as a call to each and every one of us, both individually and collectively, to become and contribute as much as we can. This perspective gives us both a vision of the future and a motive for working toward it.[40]

Specifically, what is the "vision of the future" that New Agers are "working toward"? Where do they believe evolution is taking us? The answer to these questions has both practical and mythical elements.

"Gaia": The World as Being

In practical terms, the New Age vision, as Donald Keys demonstrates, can be stated quite succinctly: "Humanity is on the verge of something entirely new, a further evolutionary step unlike any other: the emergence of the first global civilization."[41]

There is much that can be said about both the form (spiritual, social, and political) that New Agers see this world community taking, and what they are particularly doing to help bring it about. But these will be the subjects of chapters 5 and 6. Here we are concerned with the more abstract—the imagery that embodies the hopes of New Agers and inspires their commitment.

The U.N.'s Robert Muller invoked such imagery in an interview with Jessica Lipnack and Jeffrey Stamps, the authors of *Networking*:

> In essence, his message is this: Humanity is evolving toward a coherent global form best described by the metaphor of a human brain; each person, young or old, able-bodied or handicapped, is an important neuron in the emerging planetary brain that is constituted by the myriad "networkings" among people.[42]

To most New Agers, however, the emerging "global brain" is more than a metaphor. Marshall McLuhan asks, "Might not the current translation of our entire lives into the spiritual form of information make of the entire globe, and of the human family, a single consciousness?"[43]

The notion of humanity evolving into a single consciousness has great appeal to New Agers, who are always dreaming of attaining "higher levels of consciousness" and greater states of "oneness" with all of life. They discovered this conception in the writings of

Pierre Teilhard de Chardin (d. 1955). Ferguson informs us that Teilhard, a Jesuit paleontologist and philosopher, was "the individual most often named as a profound influence by the Aquarian Conspirators who responded to a survey. . . ."[44]

In Teilhard's process-oriented thought, consciousness is "defined experimentally as the specific effect of organised complexity."[45] Since, as he argues, an evolutionary pattern of *increasing* complexity can be observed in the physical world, it must also be true that "evolution is an ascent towards consciousness."[46]

Teilhard points to the successive emergence of the barysphere, lithosphere, hydrosphere, atmosphere, and "the living membrane composed of the fauna and flora of the globe, the biosphere. . . ."[47] He then affirms that with the emergence, in man, of conscious reflection a new "thinking layer" has been added, the "noosphere" (from the Greek *nous,* meaning "mind").[48]

Arguing that because it contains and engenders consciousness "space-time is necessarily of *a convergent nature,*"[49] Teilhard envisions a "mega-synthesis" of the noosphere:

> We are faced with a harmonised collectivity of consciousness equivalent to a sort of super-consciousness. The idea is that of the earth not only becoming covered by myriads of grains of thought, but becoming enclosed in a single thinking envelope so as to form, functionally, no more than a single vast grain of thought. . . .[50]

Donald Keys quotes Teilhard as predicting that this development will be accompanied by "the formation of an organico-social super-complex . . . the planetization of mankind."[51]

If a global brain is forming, does this mean that the globe *itself* has or will have a brain? In other words, is it now a conscious being, or will it eventually evolve into one? Many New Agers would affirm one or the other of these suggestions.

Teilhard himself wrote of "the still unnamed Thing which the gradual combination of individuals, peoples and races will bring into existence. . . ."[52] Today, this "Thing" has been given a name: "Gaia" (or alternately, "Terra"), after the Earth goddess of ancient Greek and Roman mythology. New Agers have been rapidly assimilating aspects of a number of pagan traditions that worship an "Earth Mother" into their own religious life.

It may seem astoundingly inconsistent for a movement that considers itself too sophisticated for literal belief in the Bible and its heavenly Father to wholeheartedly embrace the mythological concept of an Earth Mother. Be that as it may, in many respects it *is* consistent with their own underlying belief and value systems for them to do so. First of all, belief in a living, sacred planet is perceived as having immense ecological value; an answer to the exploitation and abuse of the Earth allegedly fostered by Cartesian mechanism and Judeo-Christian "dominion" theology (based on Gen. 1:23):

> The older indigenous societies never descended into a mechanomorphic view of existence. The "Indians" of north and south America, the Polynesians, Australian aborigines and other native peoples have gained a sense of the livingness of the Earth and its processes. They express a reverence for the Earth as a source of all material needs and perceive it as a conscious entity whose processes should be respected, be related to and be worked with harmoniously, not violated or exploited. . . . Humanity in extremis now appears to be more open to accepting in a functional way the essential reality and beauty of these awarenesses . . . . The young alumni of the "new consciousness" movement are developing their own experiential relationship to Terra's life processes.[53]

Second, belief that the integration of humanity with itself and all earth systems would cause something new and greater to emerge is perfectly consistent with the emergent evolution view that integrated parts create a whole greater than their sum. "Gaia" would simply be the next step up in a universe of ascending systems. As Capra sees it, "In the stratified order of nature, individual human minds are embedded in the larger minds of social and ecological systems, and these are integrated into the planetary mental system—the mind of Gaia—which in turn must participate in some kind of universal or cosmic mind."[54]

Finally, the new myth is consistent with New Age spiritual experience, which is the ultimate shaper of and authority for their beliefs. Keys notes that

> there is a direct connection between the subjective or inner experience of the individual person and the emergence of myth . . . myths such as Humanity-as-Being, Earth-as-Entity, or Human Community are experienced as self-evident and unquestionable facts in the inner life. A life of active spiritual pursuit provides an ultimate basis to realize the unifying oneness through which all life flows.[55]

(That these concepts are "experienced as self-evident and unquestionable facts" suggests that they are more than *just* myths to many New Agers.)

Because the new myth embodies the holistic paradigm, is exquisitely compatible with mysticism, implants an optimism that seemingly thrives in crisis, and inspires social activism, it is becoming an effective focus for New Age ideology. McWaters makes this clear in the following appeal:

> Clearly, a need from within calls for our attention at this moment in evolutionary time. The call is to serve the well-being of the living planet Earth, Gaia. . . . The call is to enter into a holistic consciousness from which all peoples, all forms of life, all manner of universal manifestation are seen as interdependent aspects of one truth.[56]

Whether the new myth offers a reliable basis for human hope—a true passage to planetary salvation—is another matter, to be taken up in chapter 4.

The "New Myth"
A Critique of New Age Ideology

All truth is God's truth." So the saying goes. And although recent applications of this dictum have generated some controversy,[1] it remains in principle a logical necessity. If a non-Christian scientist or philosopher discovers something that is *objectively* true, and the teachings of Scripture are also *objectively* true, then these truths must somehow exist harmoniously. And Christians can rightfully attempt to harmonize them *conceptually* as well.

The Christian is called to an uncompromising commitment to truth (2 Cor. 4:2; Eph. 6:14; Prov. 23:23; and so forth). Such a commitment cannot allow for a cursory and simplistic dismissal of entire systems of thought, even if those systems arise from unchristian sources. New ideologies are not born in a vacuum—they grow out of social and individual needs that are at times legitimate, and they likely contain *elements* of truth—truth which partly accounts for their powers of attraction.

The Christian response to New Age ideology, then, should be affirmative as well as critical. Positively, it must identify truth wherever it may be found, and demonstrate how such truth, far from proving a non-Christian world view, can be readily integrated into the Christian perspective. Negatively, it must point out that which is false, and expose the dangers which inevitably accompany falsehood.

The Paradigm Shift

With respect to revolutions in scientific thought, Thomas Kuhn's theory of paradigm shifts can claim both logical and historical support. But does our knowledge of *all* truth accumulate and evolve experimentally as many today think? Should *nothing* be final or fixed in our belief systems? Those who would answer *yes* presuppose that we presently possess *no* information that can be trusted as absolutely true—all current knowledge must be regarded as imperfect, though evolving toward perfection. But are there good logical and evidential grounds for such a conclusion?

The Christian can agree that imperfection and changeability are demonstrably the rule *within* creation, but this fact does not preclude the possibility that a perfect and unchanging being exists *outside* of creation, a being who is capable of introducing something final and fixed *into* creation. This is the biblical doctrine of *special revelation*. And it so happens that a weight of historical evidence can be summoned to prove that such revelation has in fact occurred (*see* chapter 2 and its endnotes for examples and references to scholarly works on the subject).

Reductionism vs. Holism

There is much in Fritjof Capra's critique of Cartesian reductionism and mechanism with which a Christian can agree. Although Rene Descartes was a professing Christian, his thought gave rise to a very unchristian rationalism and determinism which came to dominate the Western mind. As Capra pointed out, the progress of science is indebted to Cartesian analysis, but the emphasis on reductionism (in general culture as well as science) was carried to an extreme.

In Germany an effort to find Christian alternatives to this unbalanced situation was underway long before Capra and other afficianados of Eastern religions were voicing similar concerns. The Interdisciplinary Study Group of the Evangelical Church includes physical and social scientists, historians, and theologians.

In a paper entitled "The Spiritual Dimensions of the Scientific World," a former member of this group, Lutheran pastor Ulrich Duchrow, identifies several distinguishing features of the

Cartesian-Newtonian paradigm (which he labels "the spirit of classical physics and modern technics"). He further points out some unhappy consequences that follow when they are taken as "the whole of reality," which I will partially reproduce here.[2]

Objectivization has led to "the suppression of the subject and of those experiences and aspects of reality which cannot be objectivized." What *can* be made, *will* be made, with no regard for such subjective concerns as "sorrow and suffering, joy and happiness, love and hope and faith." *Manipulation* has involved the exploitation of nature and human beings which can result in "the ecological and social self-destruction of humankind." *Particularization* "splits the various aspects of human life into different realms," and "robs us of wholeness." *Determinism* and "the belief in unlimited growth which goes with it" leads us to conclude that "nothing can be done about all this because everything follows autonomous laws." Finally, a *linear view of time without direction* makes us believe that only that which can be scientifically reproduced is true. Therefore, we are oriented toward the structures of the past, no longer viewing the future as an open possibility for "hope, imagination, vision, and responsible action."

This brief consideration of the effects of excessive reductionism is sufficient to show that the cause of the church is not served by defending the "old paradigm" in all of its assumptions. Our modern technocracy has in many ways suffocated the spiritual and personal dimensions of man, and so there is a good measure of legitimacy to the current reaction against it. New Agers are correct in pointing out the deficiencies in our traditional reductionistic approaches to science, society, health, and life.

General Systems Theory

Is General Systems Theory (GST) the answer? Certainly, the holistic approach that it advocates would be useful. However, it does not appear likely that it will become established as a proven scientific theory. GST proponent Mark Davidson admits:

> All we have are premonitions, semi-philosophical intuitions, a few principles remote from mathematical rigor in description and prediction. Developing principles that apply to systems in general is a task far from being finished. We are aware of the problem even though remote from its final and elegant solution.[3]

If significant systems laws cannot be demonstrated for all phenomena, than neither can GST provide a basis for the unification of the sciences. Furthermore, several practical weaknesses have been pointed out within GST as a social theory.[4]

So while GST does not appear to be the planetary panacea it is sometimes described as being, the value of a systemic or holistic approach in many areas of life and science is undeniable. But is a change from reductionistic to holistic thinking *the* critical issue facing mankind today?

Misdiagnosing the Disease

In responding to Ulrich Duchrow's paper, Stephen C. Knapp of Partnership in Mission made the following poignant observation:

> Duchrow's transition from an all-pervasive "disease" to a single "cause" outside of ourselves, is necessary, perhaps, if one hopes to come up with some accessible and manageable "cure." Marx' concern to do something about these same effects led him to isolate their cause in capitalism (and the bourgeoisie) and to locate the cure in the proletariat's revolutionary action. But the risk in such a "narrowing" in order to make change "manageable" is that the cure will be "out of phase" with the disease. . . .[5]

What is the primary "cause" underlying the many symptoms of our global "disease"? Mark Davidson states that "the fault, as viewed from the perspective of Bertalanffian GST, is not in our stars and not entirely in ourselves—but substantially in our systems."[6]

Fritjof Capra offers a Taoist explanation for human self-centeredness—too much dependence on rationality: ". . . rational knowledge is likely to generate self-centered, or yang, activity, whereas intuitive wisdom is the basis of ecological, or yin, activity."[7]

To place the blame primarily on our systems rather than ourselves is to diagnose a symptom of the disease as its cause. To attribute human selfishness to an excessive rationality and lack of intuitive awareness is a confusion of categories: cognitive issues are being mislabeled as moral ones. Unselfishness is as plentiful among thinkers as mystics, and selfishness can be found in at least as many mystics as thinkers. In my extensive research of Hindu gurus I have encountered some of the most abominable examples of selfish, exploitative behavior I have ever come across.[8] Irrespective of their claims to be "enlightened," with their considerable experience in meditation and their highly acclaimed psychic powers there can be little doubt that their *intuitive capacities* are highly developed. Human selfishness, therefore, is a matter of the will, demanding a change of heart much more than the development of intuitive capacities.

We can conclude, then, that an overemphasis on the Cartesian-Newtonian paradigm has definitely contributed to the problems of modern times, and drastically needs to be corrected. However, a more *fundamental* cause of the megacrisis in our "post-Christian culture" is the widespread rejection of biblical truth and moral principles. To a great extent, Western nations have turned their backs on the revealed Word and will of the sovereign God and become a law unto themselves. In this sense at least they are humanistic, and such godless humanism can be traced back to that very seventeenth- and eighteenth-century embrace of rationalism which enthroned the old paradigm in the first place.

The answer, therefore, is not a new, *holistic* humanism. In any form, an ethic that makes man the measure of all things cannot possibly remedy the deeper dimensions of our crisis, for it is exactly this approach that is responsible for them. The breakdown of the family, its resulting injury to our young, and the spiraling statistics for such social ills as violent crime, drug and alcohol abuse, and sexually transmitted diseases are ultimately the results of *sin* (that is, the moral choices of individuals), not faulty systems.

Again, New Agers are right—we do need to reevaluate our cultural assumptions and structures in the light of a more holistic paradigm. But if such reevaluation is not informed by an uncompromising commitment to a biblical world view, the intended cure may only succeed at making the disease terminal.

Christianity vs. Holism?

We now turn to some deeper apologetic issues. New challenges are being brought to the Christian faith by New Agers, and also at times by the systems movement and process philosophers. Efforts are well underway to wed the holistic or systems view to mysticism, and such unchristian beliefs as "process" metaphysics and emergent evolution. The more acceptable such a synthesis becomes, the more outdated orthodox Christianity will appear, for our urgent need of a holistic perspective is becoming increasingly evident.

Systems and Mysticism

If a shift to a more holistic way of thinking is desirable, does this suggest, or even demand, a switch to mystical modes of thought? First of all, when New Agers equate mysticism with intuition they are confusing the distinct technical usages of the words *mystical, mysticism,* and *intuition*. Although mystical feelings of oneness with the universe do (infrequently) happen spontaneously, *mysticism* generally involves a determined effort to still the mind and empty it of conceptual thought. Such a practice is neither essential nor common to human experience.

Intuition, on the other hand, is one of the two basic means to human knowledge (along with reason), and is something that we *all* possess and exercise to varying degrees. Just like a detective, sculptor, or psychotherapist, a systems thinker could develop an intuitive ability to recognize patterns of relationship without becoming involved in any form of mysticism. In other words, while mysticism necessarily involves intuition, intuition does not at all necessarily involve mysticism.

Even if mysticism is not *necessary* for systems thinking, might it not be *desirable* as the perfect means for engendering a more holistic (and therefore responsible) social perspective? Historically, mysticism has rather been the perfect means for engendering social apathy. As was noted in chapter 1, New Agers are attempting to overcome this by developing a basis for ethics and an affirmative view of the world. Given their monistic, pantheistic world view, however, this will be extremely difficult to accomplish in the long run.[9]

The Christian world view, on the other hand, easily provides a basis for social concern and action (as the leading historical role of Christians in social reform and charitable work testifies). But can a holistic perspective be developed within a biblical context?

Biblical theology certainly does *not* allow for the New Age belief that everything (including God) exists within one interdependent whole. However, the holistic perspective that we have agreed would be beneficial for society pertains to *this* world—it need not include God to meet the needs we have considered. And the biblical picture of physical creation (*see,* for example, Gen. 1) is perfectly compatible with the now obvious fact that the universe is one enormously vast system. Furthermore, as many modern theologians have pointed out, the radical compartmentalization of Cartesian analysis is foreign to Jewish and early Christian theology (although this position has often been taken to an extreme—the Bible *does* recognize such differences as body-soul within creation). Therefore, the Christian is free to develop a "systems view" of the physical world compatible both with the facts of modern science and with the teachings of Scripture.

Systems and Process Metaphysics

Some will dispute this last claim. How can the Christian understanding of a substantial, objective world created by a substantial, objective God really be compatible with the view, emerging from modern physics, that fundamental reality is more an indivisible pattern of events (random "probability waves") than an assortment of isolated ordered objects? Doesn't this sound more like the views of some mystical traditions, where there is a "dance" but no "dancer"—where God and the world are more energy than substance, more "verb" than "noun"?

First of all, belief in a substantial, objective world does not need to equal a "naive realism" that imagines electrons revolving around their nucleus like planets around their sun.

Second, it is crucial to realize that the findings of physics are by definition *physical.* They offer no final answer to such *meta*physical questions as the existence and nature of God, or the existence and nature of the human soul.

Ian Barbour, an authority on the interface between science and philosophy/theology who is also a process thinker, wisely asks:

> For what reason do we reject the mechanistic world-view that once claimed support from classical physics: (a) was the mistake a *scientific* one, which we now reject because of new scientific discoveries, or (b) was it a *philosophical* and *epistemological* mistake involving an uncritical transition from physics to metaphysics? In

the second case we would conclude that a mechanistic world-view never did have legitimate justification, even when it claimed to be based on the best science of its day; and the lesson from the past would lead us to be wary today about extending modern physics into a new metaphysics.

Thus the primary significance of modern physics lies not in any disclosure of the fundamental nature of reality, but in the recognition of *the limitations of science. . . . The most we should expect from physics is a modest contribution to a view of nature at one limited level* (second emphasis mine).[10]

Our current knowledge of fundamental physical reality is still quite tentative, and scientists remain divided about the implications of their experimental findings. To say that process is more fundamental than substance in the universe may be as misleading as saying that time is more fundamental than space. They may be inextricably united in the larger scheme of creation.

It should be noted that in trying to use modern physics in support of Eastern/occult mysticism New Agers commit the very reductionist fallacy they condemn. Let us grant that microscopic entities *are* pure energy; does that mean that the material appearance of macroscopic entities is an illusion? If fundamental physical reality *is* "event," does that mean that the highest order of physical reality (man) cannot truly be substance? If in fact wholes cannot be understood by reducing them to their smallest parts, then why deny the reality of what so convincingly *appears* to be true on the level of human experience? Objects *are* substantial. People *are* "in being." Events *are* ordered.

Biblically we know that even if process *is* the fundamental created reality out of which God formed substance, substance remains the primary metaphysical reality, for God, the "I Am," is *not* process, nor in process (Mal. 3:6; compare with Exod. 3:14).[11]

Systems and Emergent Evolution

Is the universe a self-organizing system inherently driven toward higher organization? And can the emergence of widely diverse properties (including life and mind) be sufficiently explained by this tendency when coupled with the principle that a whole is more than the sum of its parts?

There is no biblical nor scientific reason to reject the proposition that a whole can be more than the sum of its parts. It can be clearly observed in nature that

> as more complex systems are built up, new properties appear that were not foreshadowed in the parts alone. Each of two separate hydrogen atoms will attract a third hydrogen atom; but when the two combine to form a molecule, the third atom will be repelled. New wholes do not of course contain any mysterious entities in addition to their parts, but they do have distinctive principles of organization as systems, and therefore exhibit properties and activities not found in their components.[12]

Such systems laws can easily be understood as part of God's original design.

It requires a giant leap of faith from such observable phenomena, however, to hold that such extraordinary, unique qualities as life and mind are simply more complex examples of the same cosmic pattern. There are no known experiments where such emergent processes can be replicated. Systems theorists offer us no explanation as to how inorganic parts brought into complex relationship could possibly produce *life*; or how organic parts brought into complex relationship could possibly produce *mind* (let alone the human psyche). They just assure us that they do.

An even greater downfall of emergent evolution is its claim that there is a *natural* organizing force behind the universe bringing assorted parts into *increasingly complex* relationships. This belief is flatly contradicted by the second law of thermodynamics, which states that all systems inherently tend toward entropy or *dis*organization.

It is not as though New Agers and systems thinkers are oblivious to the second law. But, they argue for another law (von Bertalanffy named it "syntropy") which counteracts entropy and accounts for the high level of organization and design that we see.

The reasoning employed here can be fairly represented as follows: (1) Entropy is a fact; (2) the existence of highly organized systems is a fact; (3) evolution is a fact; so (4) there must be an additional law to counteract entropy and account for evolution.

Here New Agers and systems thinkers are guilty of question begging. Why consider evolution a fact? Why postulate an unproven law (syntropy) to counteract a demonstrable law (entropy) in order to keep one model, when another model fits the facts of science as we find them? Creation is ultimately no more nor less "scientific" or "metaphysical" than evolution (see chapter 2's argument against equating naturalism with the scientific method). And it perfectly accounts for nature's order while in no way prohibiting its tendency toward disorder. (In fact, the biblical account would seem to *require* this as the consequence of sin—pronounced thousands of years before the second law was discovered. *See,* for example, Gen. 3:17–19; Rom. 8:19–22).

It can be concluded then that while historic Christianity may be incompatible with mysticism, process metaphysics, and emergent evolution, none of these elements are essential to a holistic perspective of life or a systemic approach to science. Therefore there is no justification for the New Age opinion that orthodox Christianity is ill suited for the needs of our time.

Evolution in New Age Ideology/Mythology

It is frequently assumed today that human evolution has been advancing with something like an exponential curve over the past few centuries. Those who reason thus unwittingly indulge in the fallacy of *equivocation.* In other words, they cite evidence for one meaning of the word *evolution* as support for a belief that pertains to a different sense of the word.

What we have witnessed over the past few hundred years is rapid *social* evolution: the development and (in *some* respects) progress of society due to advancing knowledge and technology. There is no essential connection between social evolution and *biological* evolution: the morphological and physiological change of a species over time. The fact that *society* has been rapidly changing does not prove that *man* has undergone any essential change. Even most evolutionary scientists would agree that over the past few centuries man has simply realized under favorable conditions a potential that he has had for thousands of years. Therefore rapid social evolution does not suggest, as John White thinks, that *Homo Noeticus* is waiting in the wings.

What about the increasing number of people experiencing altered states of consciousness? ASCs have always been just as possible as they are now, and at various times in various places mystical movements have thrived (for example: India in the eighth century B.C., and at several later points in its history; also fourteenth-century Germany). The fact that such states need to be induced, and come no more naturally now than they did millennia ago, should give pause to those who reason that their current prevalence signals a change in human nature itself.

Will punctuated equilibrium convert humanity's current megacrisis into an evolutionary leap forward? It should be noted first of all that even a serious Punctuationalist would derive little hope from the fantastic New Age application of this hypothesis. Second and more importantly, punctuated equilibrium is not at all established as a scientific theory. Creation science writer Henry Morris points out that "it has no known mechanism and has never been observed in operation."[13] Even many evolutionary scientists reject the model. *Newsweek* observed in 1980 that punctuated equilibrium

> is the theory of "hopeful monsters," a point of bitter contention among geneticists and biologists. To some geneticists, all monsters are hopeless. Such a major change in structure can only be the result of gross chromosome rearrangements. So many other delicate systems would be set awry as a result that the organism could not survive.[14]

We have seen that the "facts" summoned to support belief in "conscious evolution" and "Gaia" can just as easily be interpreted within a biblical framework. And while (macro) evolution has not been proven, biblical reliability has been.[15]

Nonetheless, might it not be desirable to keep the new myth alive for utilitarian purposes? In other words, wouldn't the earth and its ecosystems be better served by belief in a sacred planet than by biblical "dominion theology"?

A Biblical Basis for Ecology

It cannot be denied, nor should we wish to deny, that God told man in the beginning: "Be fruitful and multiply, and fill the earth, and subdue it; and rule over the fish of the sea and over the birds of the sky, and over every living thing that moves on the earth" (Gen. 1:28). But since when does the scriptural model of rulership allow for the ruler to exploit and abuse his subjects? On the contrary, it calls for care, protection, and wise, just administration (*see* Pss. 72; 82; Jer. 22:1–5; Ezek. 34:1–22).

When God entrusted the earth to man it did not cease to belong to him (Pss. 24:1; 50:12). Adam's responsibility in the Garden of Eden was to "cultivate and *keep* it" (Gen. 2:14). Man's role on the earth, then, must be understood in terms of *stewardship,* and stewards are responsible and accountable for that which has been entrusted to them (Luke 12:42–48; 1 Cor. 4:2). Since God established an order in his creation, and gave us the capacity to understand it, then to the best of our ability, we are responsible to maintain it.

Truth vs. Myth

The most serious error underlying New Age mythology is the unwarranted assumption (based in monistic subjectivism) that there are no truths "out there" that we need be concerned about. If, as Christians argue, the Bible is a trustworthy divine revelation, such thinking is grievously false, for God is an objective (not subjective) reality as far as humanity is concerned. Therefore, certain propositions are objectively true and others objectively false.

Because the Lord is a God of truth (John 17:17; Rom. 3:3, 4; Titus 1:2; 1 John 5:20), to disregard truth is both morally wrong and spiritually dangerous. Therefore, in spite of whatever ecological value the new myth might appear to have, we are obligated to reject it because it lacks a basis in objective reality.

The truth question makes our choice of a belief system a moral issue. This is evident in the scriptural warning that "the time will come when they will not endure sound doctrine; but . . . will *turn away their ears from the truth,* and will *turn aside to myths*" (2 Tim. 4:3–4). The sobering *objective* truth is that each one of us will one day face "the God who is there" (as Francis Schaeffer put it) in judgment, and he will hold us accountable for the truth he has made known to us. For many, this encounter will not be pleasant (Rom. 1:18, 25):

> For the wrath of God is revealed from heaven against all ungodliness and unrighteousness of men, who suppress the truth in unrighteousness. . . . For they exchanged the truth of God for a lie, and worshiped and served the creature rather than the Creator. . . .

In the light of such a solemn apostolic pronouncement, all who harbor even a residual fear of the biblical God must feel uneasy with Barry McWaters's call "to serve the well-being of the living planet, Earth, Gaia."

Undeniably, the earth has suffered much abuse under the pretext of biblical sanction. Human greed often twists Scripture to suit its own ends. The answer to this regrettable situation is not to abandon biblical truth for pagan mythology. We must recover a biblical appreciation for creation and man's role in it, without falling into the opposite and more damning error of worshiping the creature rather than the Creator.

Tracking the "Aquarian Conspiracy"
(Part One—New Age Evangelism)

Prominently displayed next to the EXIT doors at the local supermarket are free copies of a slick New Age "community resources" publication; everything from holistic dentistry to "gay spirituality" gatherings to past life therapy is advertised. The local junior college mails a catalogue of summer extracurricular offerings that include classes in yoga, tai chi, astrology, and psychic healing. In early 1987 the ABC television network airs a five-hour "miniseries" based on Shirley MacLaine's autobiography *Out on a Limb;* a classic piece of New Age evangelism. And the August 1987 "Harmonic Convergence" (a gathering of thousands of chanting and meditating New Agers to "sacred sites" around the globe to prevent global disaster and bring in the New Age) succeeds at becoming a major media event, with the result that the term "New Age movement" finally achieves familiarity with mainstream America.

Secular humanists tend to dismiss all expressions of occultism as fringe lunacy—not to be taken seriously. Evangelicals have often shared this view (perhaps because they've seen society's real spiritual threat as coming from the secular humanists themselves!). Nonetheless, occultism, as represented by the New Age movement, is rapidly becoming a force to be reckoned with in the Western world.

Western culture is being repeatedly barraged with New Age in-

fluences such as those described above. Much of this is best under-
stood as a massive social trend, spontaneous and unorchestrated.
However, to a significant degree it also represents an "Aquarian
Conspiracy": Marilyn Ferguson's term for a conscious effort by
New Age humanists to win cultural dominance over secularism
and traditional religion.

While the "conspiracy" is still far from its goal of supplanting
the establishment, its momentum continues to build at a steady
rate; even the relatively conservative Ronald Reagan years failed to
discourage or dissipate it. Over the past few years New Age writers
increasingly have shifted from calling their movement a subculture to referring to it as the "emerging mainstream."[1]

Hoping to hasten the Age of Aquarius, and to make sure there is
still life on this planet when it arrives, New Agers are actively
seeking to influence such social arenas as health care, psychology,
education, business, and politics.

This is not to suggest that everyone who in any way promotes
the New Age cause is a *conscious* participant in the Aquarian Conspiracy. For examples: many doctors who prescribe meditation for
their patients do so strictly because they believe in its therapeutic
value, not to win converts to the New Age movement; many parents who volunteer to teach in New Age education programs do so
because they want to help children cope with the pressures of
growing up in these troubled times, not to recruit young activists
for future Aquarian political objectives.

The fact that there are a variety of motives and perspectives
among those contributing to the New Age illustrates an important
point: it is wrong to view the rise of the movement as a carefully
engineered plot originating from a covert central network of in-
geniously devious conspirators (*See* Appendix B). However, as this
writer will demonstrate presently, it is equally wrong to assume
that there is *no* conscious collusion involved.

I have identified two distinct objectives to New Age social penetration. The first, "personal transformation," is evangelistic, and
the second, "planetary transformation," is sociopolitical. Both individuals and the very structure of society are targeted for change at
fundamental levels. In this chapter we will examine Aquarian
"evangelism." In Part Two (chapter 6) we will turn our attention to
New Age social and political activism.

Personal Transformation

New Age writers often point out that if "planetary transformation" (global political unification along New Age lines) is ever to occur, a "critical mass" of individuals must first experience "personal transformation"—the New Agers' psychic counterpart to Christian transformation through regeneration and sanctification. For this reason especially, New Agers are anxious to win people over to their mystical/occult perspective.

In the competition for souls, New Agers have a strategic (though, from the Christian perspective, unethical) advantage. Unlike the Christian gospel, which openly demands a faith commitment at the outset, conversion to New Age belief can be engineered subtly and deceptively. What in actuality may be Hinduism or occultism can be taught and administered in secular guise. Many seemingly innocent techniques for increasing health, enhancing creativity, and achieving deeper levels of relaxation, for example, are sometimes deliberately used by New Agers to effect this shift in perspective.[2]

First, an altered state of consciousness (ASC) is induced in the potential convert with the hope that it will trigger a mystical or psychic experience powerful enough to cause him (or her) to doubt his previous understanding of reality. If the subject's belief system has been shaken, he will be far more disposed to embrace a new world view than he would have been before submitting to this "nonreligious" exercise. Then he is exposed to New Age beliefs that supply him with a seemingly profound explanation of his experience. Since the monistic world view ("all is One") is derived from and closely related to mystical experiences, it will seem to fit the new way of viewing reality perfectly. In fact, for this reason even if the monistic interpretation is *not* offered, after going through such an experience a reflective individual may come to monistic conclusions on his own (the dynamics of this process and why it should not be trusted were elaborated in chapter 2). Marilyn Ferguson explains:

> . . . Exercises and experiments are designed for direct experience from a new perspective.
>
> For only that which is deeply felt can change us.

Rational arguments alone cannot penetrate the layers of fear and conditioning that comprise our crippling belief systems. The Aquarian Conspiracy creates opportunities wherever possible for people to experience shifts of consciousness.[3]

Holistic Health

Examples of this abound in the burgeoning holistic health movement. Ferguson observes:

. . . The proliferating holistic health centers and networks have drawn many into the consciousness [that is, New Age] movement. A nurse said, "If healing becomes a reality with you, it's a lifestyle. Altered states of consciousness accompany it, increased telepathy. It's an adventure."[4]

In spite of its many obvious accomplishments and benefits, there are widely recognized inadequacies in the overall approach of traditional medicine. Consequently, a virtual revolution has been transpiring in health care:

No one had realized how vulnerable the old medical model was. Within a few short years, without a shot's being fired, the concept of holistic health has been legitimized by federal and state programs, endorsed by politicians, urged and underwritten by insurance companies, co-opted in terminology (if not always in practice) by many physicians, and adopted by medical students. Consumers demand "holistic health," a whole new assortment of entrepreneurs promise it, and medical groups look for speakers to explain it.[5]

New models of wellness as well as healing are being popularized, some of them valid and helpful. For example, the Association for Holistic Health describes the holistic approach as being "person oriented rather than disease oriented," having as its objective "full vibrant health (positive wellness), not symptom amelioration," and focusing on "primary prevention rather than crisis intervention."[6] However, holistic thought and practice are so often interlaced with occultism that, in its search for alternative approaches to healing, an entire generation is in danger of being baptized in psychic power.

That this is so can be discerned from the pages of the *International Journal of Holistic Health and Medicine:*

> The Eastern philosophy/spiritualism movement has also contributed to holistic health by its appreciation of a unifying invisible dynamic force within and around the human body that is called "Chi" by the Chinese, "Ki" by the Japanese, "prana" by the yogis and numerous other names by various cultures throughout the world. Unlike the word "spirit" in the West, the words for this energetic force in the East generally have a very practical meaning and have direct and specific influences upon health.[7]

As we saw in chapter 2, this "invisible dynamic force" is scientifically undemonstrable, but nonetheless can be real. Historically, under various names such as those the author lists, the same force has always appeared in the context of spiritistic paganism. Thus the Christian has every reason to consider it supernatural, demonic, and dangerous.

Psychic Healing

Psychic healing, which—in spite of whatever immediate benefits it may deliver—opens people up to occultic deception and (ultimately) oppression, is rapidly becoming accepted as a valid form of therapy in the medical world. Fifty-eight percent of medical-school faculty members wanted to see the subject of psychic phenomena included in psychiatric training, according to a survey published in the October 1981 *American Journal of Psychiatry.*[8]

A good (though far from the only) example of psychic healing's infusion into traditional medical practice is "Therapeutic Touch." It has received federal funding, and been taught to many thousands of health professionals by New York University Nursing School professor Dolores Krieger.[9] "Essentially meditative,"[10] Therapeutic Touch is nothing other than the ancient religious practice of the laying on of hands for healing—attempts to dress it up in scientific language notwithstanding. Nor should it be confused with the *biblical* practice of laying on hands, which invokes the name of Jesus and the power of the Holy Spirit. Instead, it is based upon the Hindu doctrine that "prana" or "universal life energy" flows through the body. In a trancelike state, "the Therapeutic Touch

practitioner becomes a channel of universal life energy for the patient and then *helps the patient assimilate this energy*" (emphasis
added).[11]

Meditation

Adapted Eastern meditative methods are being prescribed by
thousands of American doctors as therapy for high blood pressure,
tension headaches, chronic fatigue, insomnia, and so forth. Harvard
cardiologist Dr. Herbert Benson, whose popular "relaxation response" technique is based on TM, told *Esquire* magazine that
meditation has "become an integral part of medical practice."[12]

Benson's experiments lend support to this writer's contention
that Eastern meditation cannot be desacralized (that is, isolated
from its historical religious and mystical context). Although he has
more recently concluded that meditation is more therapeutically
effective when *kept* in a religious context, for some time Benson
had attempted to administer his own meditative method in a
strictly medical, nonesoteric setting. Instead of a mantra, (that is,
the name of a Hindu deity, as is used in TM), he instructed his
patients to repeat mentally the word *one* (a "pleasant" word—
presumably neutral). In spite of these desacralizing measures, however, the ASCs created by Benson's relaxation response resulted in
religious experiences and conversions for many. As Benson wrote
in *Psychiatry:* "During the experience of one of these states, individuals claim to have feelings of increased creativity, of *infinity,*
and of *immortality;* they have *an evangelistic sense of mission,*
and report that mental and physical suffering vanish" (emphases
added).[13] Thus, an unknown but probably large population of
Americans who were merely seeking physical or psychological relief have been overtaken and won over by the very kinds of experience that are foundational to Eastern/occult mysticism.

Humanistic and Transpersonal Education

Aquarian Conspirators have especially marked out students for
conversion to the New Age. Brooks Alexander, co-founder of the
Spiritual Counterfeits Project and a keen observer of New Age
trends, explains why:

In the ideological contest for cultural supremacy, public education is *the* prime target; it influences the most people in the most pervasive way at the most impressionable age. No other social institution has anything close to the same potential for mass indoctrination.[14]

It began in the mid-1960s with the inroads of "humanistic education" into the public schools. Its originators claimed they had "developed techniques to help people validate themselves, to communicate more effectively with others, to enhance their self-concepts, to ask directly for what they want, to clarify their values, to express their feelings, to celebrate their bodies, to use their will, and to take responsibility for their lives."[15]

Just as humanistic psychology led to transpersonal psychology, which sought to complete the former approach by making room for the spiritual dimension in man, so humanistic education was followed in the early 1970s by "transpersonal" or "holistic" education. Jack Canfield and Paula Klimek, pioneers in this field, wrote in 1978: "Now is the time to combine both of these focuses [that is, humanistic and transpersonal], for the New Age means integrating the soul and the personality."[16]

Marilyn Ferguson exulted in 1980 that "the deliberate use of consciousness-expanding techniques in education, only recently well under way, is now in mass schooling."[17]

Right Brain Learning:
Smuggling Religion into the Schools

The discovery that the right hemisphere of the brain governs intuitive, creative, nonverbal activities has been seized by New Agers and used as a justification for bringing "right brain learning techniques" into the classroom. These include meditation, yoga, guided imagery,[18] chanting, mandalas (visual symbols used as aids to meditation), and fantasy-role-playing games. Children are being led into mystical and psychic experiences (including encounters with spirit guides called "Wise Ones") on the premise that this will develop their intuitive abilities and thus provide a more balanced, holistic, or "whole-brained" education.

Ferguson is very candid when she writes:

Like holistic health, transpersonal education can happen anywhere. It doesn't need schools, but its adherents believe that the
schools need *it*. Because of its power for social healing and awakening [such as, transformed children can transform society], they
conspire to bring the philosophy into the classroom, in every grade,
in colleges and universities, for job training and adult education.[19]

While the New Age movement is not a conspiracy in the highly
organized sense that some evangelicals have portrayed it, Ferguson's use of the word *conspire* is certainly appropriate here. Mario
Fantini, former educational consultant for President Gerald Ford,
acknowledged that "the psychology of becoming has to be smug-
gled into the schools."[20]

Canfield and Klimek counsel their fellow educators:

Centering [that is, relaxation exercises] can also be extended into
work with meditation in the classroom. (Advice: if you're teaching in a public school, don't call it meditation, call it "centering."
Every school wants children to be relaxed, attentive, and creative,
and that's what they will get.)[21]

The deception inherent in this nonreligious front becomes dis-
turbingly evident when the same writers describe the nature and
purpose of New Age education:

The word *education* comes from the Latin word *educare*, "to lead
out from within." What teachers are now interested in leading out
from within is the expression of the self—the highest qualities of
the individual student's unique soul.

>   What nature has disposed and sealed
>   Is called the unborn Self.
>   The unburying of this Self
>   Is called the Process of Education.
>   Tsze sze[22]

In other words, God has been "disposed and sealed" in the illusory identity of the student. It is the teacher's responsibility to
"unbury" or awaken within each child this sleeping Self (variously
called "God within," "Inner" or "Higher Self," "Inner Wisdom," "Infinite Potential," and so forth). This goal is the *cornerstone* of all
transpersonal education. It is believed that each student *already*

has all knowledge and wisdom. He or she needs only to be taught (through meditation, guided imagery, and so forth) how to tap it.

In 1977–78 the late Beverly Galeyan received two federal grants to prepare teachers of all grade levels to use transpersonal "confluent education" techniques in the Los Angeles city schools. The Association for Humanistic Psychology (AHP), which also helped sponsor the program, noted in its August-September 1980 newsletter: "The core of the curriculum is the cadre of guided imagery-meditation types of events experienced by the teachers for their own growth, and subsequently by the students."[23] In an article which followed those comments, Galeyan wrote:

> Another aspect of meditation is the increased capacity to contact and learn from the source of wisdom, love and intelligence within us—often called the "higher self"; God, universal wisdom or spirit, conscience. This is done through the symbolic use of light such as the sun, the sky, mountain tops, wise persons, golden liquid energy, and the colors white, gold, purple, and violet. Teachers who are deeply spiritual and who feel comfortable working with their own spiritual development may choose to offer spiritually-oriented meditations to their students. This is done when there is an explicit sense of appropriateness established between the teacher and the students, parents, school personnel and community.[24]

Values Clarification

Occasionally, Christian parents are vigilant enough to explode this constitutionally *in*appropriate "sense of appropriateness." But when the transpersonal elements of a program are detected and challenged, the authors of the program may simply remove those elements while continuing the program with its humanistic underbelly unscathed. This results in a hollow Christian victory. For example, Project Self Esteem (PSE), which has been broadly implemented by south Orange County, California, public schools, originally included a mystical-sounding-guided-imagery exercise (Galeyan's "symbolic use of light such as the sun"), and had other religious overtones. In the spring of 1985 Christian parents in San Juan Capistrano organized to oppose the program, legally and before their local school board. The creators of PSE, Sandy McDaniel and Peggy Bielen, quickly rewrote the curriculum omitting all portions that had provoked controversy. Now for many PSE is no longer offensive, and it continues to be used by Capistrano elementary schools. However, "values clarification" remains a central component of the program.

Formulated in the mid-1960s by social scientists Louis E. Baths, Merrill Harman, Sidney B. Simon, and others, values clarification plays a pivotal role in both humanistic and transpersonal education. Holding that values emerge from within and therefore should not be imposed from without (a view compatible both with basic humanism and the "Inner Wisdom" concept), it attempts to help students discover and clarify their *own* values. It has been widely implemented in public schools under the pretext that it is an appropriate approach to values in a pluralistic society, since it does not seek to impose any particular value system on the children.

There is a tacit value assumption involved in values clarification, however: there are no absolute truths; values are to be *subjectively* determined. Richard A. Baer, Jr., wrote in the *Wall Street Journal:*

> On the deeper level the claim to neutrality is entirely misleading. At this more basic level, the originators of Values Clarification simply assume that their own subjective theory of values is correct. If parents object to their children using pot or engaging in pre-marital sex, the theory behind Values Clarification makes it appropriate for the child to respond, "But that's just YOUR value judgment. Don't force it on me."[25]

Because New Age spirituality flows out of the fountainheads of humanism and subjectivism, the use of values clarification in the schools is just as important to the Aquarian Conspiracy as the use of meditation or mystically oriented guided imagery. In fact, where values clarification becomes established, it will likely be only a matter of time before meditation and guided imagery also appear.

Human Potential and the Workplace

Like holistic health and transpersonal education, the human potential movement has been subtly prompting widespread acceptance of the New Age world view. The *Los Angeles Times* observes: "For better or worse, the human potential movement has grown up to become a staple of our culture."[26] In such diverse settings as churches, schools, military bases, and prisons, "growth" seminars and workshops (usually billed as "nonreligious" and compatible with Christian faith) deliberately attempt to subvert participants' belief systems in order to replace them with definitions of human potential derived from humanistic psychology and Eastern mysticism. Methods used by "trainings" like Werner Erhard's the Forum (formerly est) and John Hanley's Lifespring include controversial "thought reform" techniques[27] and various "psychotechnologies" (for example, meditation and guided imagery).

Promising greater motivation and "vision," increased productivity and creativity, and improved teamwork and interpersonal relationship skills, the human potential seminars have especially attracted the business world.

As the USA continues to lose ground to such industrial competitors as Japan, Germany, and Korea, American businesses are being forced to rethink their operations, and learn from the competition. In so doing they have observed, for instance, that one of the ingredients of Japanese success is shared vision, values, and traditions among the work force.

In America's exceptionally pluralistic, fragmented, and undisciplined culture, such homogeneity would usually have to be created *in* the workplace. This requires leading employees through a powerful group experience that can change their thinking and values along common lines beneficial to the corporation. Enter the human potential movement, which is quite accomplished at producing such group experiences. Thus, the nation's leading businesses have been inviting the likes of "Transformational Technologies" (another Werner Erhard brainchild), Lifespring, Summit Workshops, and the Movement of Spiritual Inner Awareness (MSIA) to come and change their "corporate cultures."

For example, the list of corporate giants who have subjected their employees to the mind-bending influences of Transformational Technologies (TT) seems endless: IBM, RCA, Scott Paper, Lockheed, Boeing Aerospace, Ford Motor Co., NASA, Allstate, Sears, the Federal Aviation Administration, General Dynamics, and so forth. TT's 60-odd affiliates generate an annual income of over $25 million.

As impressive as these names and figures are, the inroads of such admittedly controversial personalities as Werner Erhard and John Hanley into business represent only the tip of the iceberg. The trend is much broader than the activities of these well-known human potential "gurus." Through what has come to be known as "organization development," New Age humanistic psychology has penetrated into the very soul of corporate America.

"OD"—Mysticism in the Marketplace

In 1982, University of Southern California School of Management professor Warren Bennis estimated that perhaps as many as 20 percent of the Fortune 500 corporations regularly devoted a portion of their budgets to "organization development" ("OD"): growth seminars, the teaching of interpersonal skills to managers and stress reduction techniques to employees.[28] By all appearances, the ratio is now much higher than 20 percent.

Consider the following revelations, which appeared in a September 28, 1986 *New York Times* article:[29]

- The magazine California Business reported recently that its survey of 500 company owners and presidents found more than half said they had resorted to some form of "consciousness-raising" technique. Although such "human potential" programs are more common in California than elsewhere, industry experts say that recently they have been the fastest-growing type of executive development program.
- At Stanford University's well-regarded Graduate School of Business, the syllabus for a seminar on "Creativity in Business" includes meditation, chanting, "dream work," the use of tarot cards and discussion of the "New Age Capitalist."
- Representatives of some of the nation's largest corporations, including I.B.M., A.T.&T. and General Motors, met in New Mexico in July to discuss how metaphysics, the occult and Hindu mysticism might help executives compete in the world marketplace.

As the trend intensifies, it inevitably provokes controversy. For example, during 1986–87 Pacific Bell, California's largest utility company, required its 67,000 employees to participate in quarterly, two-day "Krone" training (a.k.a. "Leadership Development") sessions, which have a decidedly esoteric character. (This is largely due to the fact that OD pioneer Charles Krone, who developed the program, drew many of his ideas from the teachings of Russian mystic G. I. Gurdjieff.) In the wake of employee and consumer outcry over enforced Eastern mysticism, "mind control," and the $147 million cost that was to be passed on to rate payers, the program was discontinued. But the skyrocketing growth of the OD field suggests that for every company that abandons a program like Krone training, several more start new ones.

Organization development had its beginnings in the 1950s with American businesses sending key management personnel to sensitivity training groups ("t-groups"). Soon it became common practice for such trainings to be held in the workplace (employee attendance often mandatory) so that the entire company could benefit from them.

> The organizers of these sessions discovered that both groups and the communication patterns within them evolve in a broadly predictable way. Once they understood how the members of a group learned to trust one another, these trainers were able to apply the lessons throughout business, using such techniques as teamwork and management retreats. The methods these consultants and their academic colleagues worked out were joined with studies of how organizations function and became known as the field of organization development (OD).[30]

Much of the theory applied in OD could be applauded by Christians as much as anyone else. For example, OD calls for a more holistic approach to business, and increased responsibility and opportunity for workers. But as the human potential movement blossomed in the 1970s, there was much overlap between it and OD, and the OD field became saturated with the former movement's distinctive, often unchristian, beliefs and practices.

"OT"—Change Agents for the New Age

In the early 1980s OD consultants who were also Aquarian Conspirators became dissatisfied with the field's lack of "vision." In other words, in spite of its New Age connections, OD as a specialized profession was largely concerned with simply helping corporations turn a greater profit. Instead, as this "maverick 10 percent margin within OD" argued, consultants should encourage businesses to think more about their "responsibility," "mission," and "self-realization."[31]

Thus, a new field, "Organization Transformation" ("OT"), has recently emerged. While developing its own identity, it remains to a degree within the larger OD network as both its spiritual and activist wing.

As its name makes clear, OT is concerned with *transforming* organizations, not just *developing* them. OT's more visionary consultants are avowedly committed to fostering both personal transformation (the spiritual "awakening" of a corporation's employees) and planetary transformation (the utilization of the corporation's resources and influence for promoting New Age sociopolitical causes).

Typically, the efforts of New Agers to bring an already humanistically oriented field more fully into alignment with the Aquarian Conspiracy meet with little resistance. By 1983 the OD Network's annual National Conference featured plenary addresses and workshops with titles like "Organizing for Quantum Transformation" (New Age leader Barbara Marx Hubbard delivered this keynote address), "Applying Spiritual Principles to Organizations," "Change Agents for a New Age," "Chumming—Attracting Your Organization to Transformation," "Managers and Executives for a New Age," "Transformation: Theory and Practice from Ancient Sources," and "Legitimizing Intuition in a Scientific Setting: Transforming Organizations from Insight Out." For whatever reason, "The Shaman as OD Consultant" was canceled.

The Christian Response

New Age penetration of Western civilization through such avenues as health care, education, and the workplace (many other areas could have been discussed, including, the media, the arts, and even the church—*see* Appendix A) is particularly troubling in what it portends for the future. As this chapter has documented, occult beliefs and practices are progressively interweaving themselves throughout our cultural fabric. Thus the New Age world view could well become dominant without society as a whole even realizing what happened to it. New Agers Jessica Lipnack and Jeffrey Stamps affirm:

> Social change starts with brief flickers and flashes . . . but when the shift to a new world view comes, it does so swiftly and suddenly.

Since most people are blind to the precursors of fundamental change, the new wisdom will seem to burst forth suddenly, fully formed and ready to address the myriad crises of the present.[32]

If New Age influences continue to grow (as it appears they will) it will become increasingly difficult for Christians to participate in day-to-day cultural life. Those who do will seriously risk being infiltrated and overpowered by anti-Christian spiritual influences. Christians who refuse to participate in New Age spirituality could conceivably be forced, not just to the periphery of the culture (that has already begun to happen), but *outside of it*. If and when New Age values become dominant the status of "inflexibly dogmatic" Christians as a very resented minority will be questionable indeed.

In chapter 7 this theme (what the future may hold) will be developed further, and the question of whether we should even bother to resist the Aquarian Conspiracy will be addressed. For now we will assume that Christians *should* resist New Age inroads in such areas touched on in this chapter.[33]

To be effective, Christian resistance should be carried out in a rational rather than emotional manner. We should studiously avoid making declarations about the New Age movement's size, hidden intentions, and so forth, *if we cannot clearly substantiate them*. New Agers already think of us as fearful, backward reactionaries, and to a degree this cannot be helped: we must *react* to their cultural onslaught. But when they detect hysteria in us (as, unfortunately, they often have) it only reinforces their entire false-belief system. This defeats our mission of evangelism, which is even more important than resisting their social influence. A rational presentation of our position, on the other hand, has the potential of breaking their stereotypes and thus opening them to the gospel.

If we are protesting the presence of New Age philosophy or practice in public institutions, we should avoid resting our case on theological premises. The secular public is not apt to appreciate our uniquely Christian concerns that "New Age thinking is unbiblical," or "Meditation opens the mind to the devil." The issue to stress is that New Age programs have religious connotations. If the program contains yoga, meditation, or talk of the "Inner Self" and "Wise Ones," its religious nature can be easily demonstrated to any open-minded individual.

It should be noted that this point has been successfully estab lished in the courts, as in a 1977 ruling of the District Court for New Jersey (upheld by the Circuit Court in Philadelphia) that Transcendental Meditation is religious, and thus unacceptable for New Jersey high schools. To be religious, something need not exhibit such traditional formalities as a sanctuary, clergy, and worship services.

It is important to understand, however, that something can *also* be religious (or at least *metaphysical,* and thus in the same "personal faith" category as religion) without employing traditionally religious practices or terminology (for instance, prayer, meditation, or reference to "God" or "salvation").

It's true that this is not as easy to establish. The courts have given mixed signals, for example, as to whether *secular* humanism is a religion.

Nonetheless, the Supreme Court *has* affirmed that one of the primary characteristics of a religion is that it adheres to and promotes "underlying theories" concerning such "ultimate realities" as man's nature and place in the universe.[34] Virtually all transpersonal/humanistic programs operate from such metaphysical assumptions. Thus, it can (and should) be argued that even those that use only values clarification are religious in nature.

Any public agency that promotes or facilitates (let alone requires) New Age ideas or practices is on precarious legal ground, because the First Amendment prohibits government from establishing religion. It also protects the individual citizen's right to free exercise of religion, which could be violated by mandatory New Age programs.

Parents need to remain alert to what their children are being taught or subjected to in the public schools, regularly discussing their experience at school with them, attending school-board meetings, and reviewing the school's curriculum. The Protection of Pupil Rights Act (a.k.a. the Hatch Amendment), which has been in force since 1984, gives parents the right to inspect *all* instructional material that is "designed to explore or develop new or unproven teaching methods or techniques." If such parental concern invokes charges of censorship from disgruntled educators, Christian parents can point out that as long as *their* religious beliefs and practices are carefully screened out of public institutions, it's only fair that those of competing religions and world views be likewise monitored.

What about the Christian whose *private* employer is demanding that he or she participate in a human potential seminar? In a 1985 interview with this writer,[35] Tom Brandon of the Christian Legal Society advised first a creative appeal to the employer, suggesting (for example) an alternative seminar which would satisfy the employer's job-related concern without violating the Christian's faith.

If the employer refuses to compromise, legal recourse is open. Brandon affirmed: "The employer is prohibited from discriminating against your religious convictions, and if you said 'I'm sorry, I cannot attend that, it violates my religious principles,' then according to Title Seven they have to make reasonable accommodation for that."

Brandon's opinion has since been confirmed by the Equal Employment Opportunity Commission. In response to several complaints filed by Christian employees, the EEOC issued a policy statement in the spring of 1988 which pronounces:

> Where an employee notifies an employer that his/her religious beliefs conflict with a particular training technique or method used in a "new age" training program, an employer may accommodate the employee's belief by substituting an alternative technique or method not offensive to the employee's belief or by excusing the employee from that particular part of the training program.[36]

The statement stresses that an employer "may not judge the veracity or reasonableness of the religious beliefs of an employee,"[37] and specifies: "That the employer or the sponsor of a "new age" program believes there is no religious basis for, or content to, the training . . . is irrelevant to determining the need for accommodation."[38] The policy further states that any employer who penalizes an employee for not participating in such a program "discriminates on the basis of religion."[39]

Christians who find the guidelines of the EEOC being violated at their jobs should not allow employer intimidation to keep them from standing up for their rights. Massive New Age encroachment into the workplace will only be checked when business gets a strong message that such enforced indoctrination will not be tolerated.

As for holistic health, Christians within the health professions need to oppose the implementation of therapies that lack a firm scientific basis, particularly if they invoke dangerous psychic forces.

Beyond this, there is a clear need for public education. When holistic healers talk about healing body, mind, and spirit, many assume that "spirit" is meant in a Christian rather than a pantheistic sense. When Therapeutic Touch practitioners, for example, claim they are utilizing "universal life energy," many are blind to the fact that this is a nonphysical, *psychic* energy. When New Agers *do* speak of psychic energy, many fail to grasp the spiritual and psychological dangers involved.

Sadly there are very few educational resources available. The works of Kurt Koch and those of John Weldon are important, particularly Koch's *Christian Counseling and Occultism* (Kregel, 1972) and Weldon's *Psychic Healing* (Moody Press, 1982) and *New Age Medicine,* coauthored with Paul C. and Teri K. Reisser (InterVarsity, 1988). The "Holistic Health issue" of the *SCP Journal* (Aug. 1978) contains some helpful articles (write Spiritual Counterfeits Project, P.O. Box 4308, Berkeley, CA 94704). Also, Douglas Groothuis has an informative chapter on holistic health in *Unmasking the New Age* (InterVarsity, 1986), and chapter 2 of this book, "A 'New Age' of Science," might prove insightful for some.

Ultimately, direct resistance can only go so far toward curtailing New Age advances. After exploring the world of New Age politics and activism in chapter 6, and its possible eschatological (endtimes) significance in chapter 7, I will conclude chapter 7 by pointing to some of the broader issues that the Aquarian Conspiracy raises for the church.

Tracking the "Aquarian Conspiracy"
(Part Two—New Age Activism)

There *is* an "Aquarian Conspiracy"—a conscious effort by a broad-based movement to subvert our cultural establishments so that we might enter a "New Age" based on mysticism and occultism.

In the previous chapter we saw how this conspiracy is seeking to transform society at the individual level through subtle, sometimes deceptive forms of evangelism. In the present chapter we will look at what the movement is doing to transform the very structures of national and global society.

Politically, what are New Agers trying to accomplish? Are they making any progress? It is my objective here to provide accurate and sober answers to these questions, neither overstating nor understating the present and potential power of the Aquarian Conspiracy.

New Age Activism—The Rise of the "Green Movement"

It was in the latter half of the 1970s that a social and political consciousness became widespread in New Age circles. In 1978 Mark Satin's *New Age Politics* was published, and California's

107

New Age Caucus was formed to marshal "new consciousness" people into a political force. Its founders wrote at the time:

> Force in politics means people—lots of people, organized people. Ten years ago or so, only the most perceptive prophet could have foreseen New Age thought leaving the incense-filled, esoteric chambers of its origin to expand dramatically all over the American scene. Ten years ago a New Age political movement would have drawn amused chuckles from established politicians. Today, however, such a movement would draw the politicians' anxious attention and respect . . . . There is an expectant feeling in the air. New Age people are sensing that the time is super-ripe for a fresh, original, nonpartisan New Age movement.[1]

At the time of this writing yet *another* decade has passed. How justified was the optimism expressed by the New Age Caucus? Undoubtedly, most New Agers expected things to go more their way in the 1980s than they actually have. Under Ronald Reagan's popular administration American foreign and domestic policy was almost the antithesis of what Aquarians would like to see. With former California Governor Jerry Brown and former US Senator Gary Hart (D-CO) no longer in office, New Agers are hard pressed to find a political "hero" who truly models their values among the nation's leaders.

It would be a mistake to conclude that because the movement's influence on party politics is minimal, its overall social and political influence is also minimal. For New Agers the use of *networks*[2] has largely replaced political parties as a means of impacting public policy and the character of cultural life.

The Networking Phenomenon

"Networking" has mushroomed among New Agers since the mid-1970s as a way to mobilize their numbers and pool their resources. Whether protecting baby seals on Canadian shores, installing "global education" programs in Colorado schools, or delaying construction of a nuclear power plant in California, networks can achieve social clout on a grass-roots level without reliance on party politics.

Networks are created and maintained by such means as computer conferencing, telephone and postal services, and periodic festivals and conferences, and can be composed of either individuals or organizations. Highly utilitarian, they are formed on the basis of shared interests and concerns, and are quickly disbanded if their purpose has been served, or if a more effective means for accomplishing the same end is perceived.

It needs to be clarified at this point that probably a majority within the social change networks cannot properly be called New Agers. Aquarians tend to claim everyone working in causes with which they identify as their own, but a high percentage of those in ecology, appropriate technology, peace, and other movements do not embrace pantheism and occultism. And so as we consider "New Age activism" it should be borne in mind that many of the activists may not be New Agers, though their activism is likely contributing to New Age ends.

Extent of Organization

Networking is essential to the New Age movement. But it should not be inferred from this that the New Age metanetwork is one smoothly coordinated "organism" obeying the well-defined messages of some "central nervous system." Just as differing perspectives as well as egos often keep Christians from cooperating, so it is with New Agers.[3]

Networking is much more common among New Age groups with shared *interests* (for instance, health and personal growth) than among those with shared *causes* (such as disarmament and human rights), for the latter must first agree on ways and means to their mutually desired ends before they can join forces.

The optimistic proclamations of Marilyn Ferguson *(The Aquarian Conspiracy)* and others have misled many evangelicals into believing that the New Age movement is more united than it actually is.[4] Ironically, many New Agers view the "fundamentalists" as the same kind of threateningly organized force as the latter view them.[5]

This history of weak organization recognized, it must also be noted that in the mid-1980s the long sought after convergence of New Age activists became more of a reality. At the 1986 Annual Meeting of the Association for Humanistic Psychology (AHP) in San Diego, Donald Keys, perhaps the movement's most brilliant political organizer, observed:

One of the most important things which is happening is . . . networking . . . is actually becoming functional now. A lot of us are on Peacenet [an international computer-based communications and information sharing system for "peace" activists] with our PC computers. There is a gathering awareness that we don't all have to be doing the same thing but we need to be knowing what each other is doing. . . . I believe that awareness is finally hitting reality now, and is taking form.[6]

The Green Movement

With New Age activists becoming more organized, a discernible political movement is taking form. It is increasingly being called the "Green movement." This is to identify it with kindred movements across the globe, most of which bear the same ecologically suggestive name. In Europe there are even Green political parties— coalitions of holistic ideological (see chapter 3), ecological, peace, and Marxist factions.[7]

The Cascadia Green Alliance of Seattle, Washington, surveys the international Green movement:

The West German Green Party, founded in 1980 and based on the four pillars of ecology, non-violence, grassroots democracy, and social responsibility, gained seats in the West German Parliament in 1983 and continues to gain support in local and national elections. Green representatives can be found in the European Parliament, and in the Belgian, Finnish, Dutch, Italian, and British Parliaments, as well as in local and regional offices in other countries. Political parties and organizations based on these values have also taken root in New Zealand, Japan, Canada, and more recently in the emerging green political movement in the United States.[8]

The Alliance proceeds to describe the rise of the American Green movement:

The birth of the Green movement in Europe drew inspiration from the many citizens' movements in America including peace, ecology, women's, civil rights and community movements. Linkages among these groups in recent years have begun to provide a strong basis for a green political movement in the United States. In August, 1984, a diverse group of activists and thinkers met in St. Paul, Minnesota to take the first step towards building a new organization that could form a powerful voice for the health of grassroots organizing in America. The group represented farmers and community leaders, peace advocates and activists in churches and synagogues, as well as environmentalists and educators. What brought them together was a shared sense that a movement for the far-ranging moral, political, and spiritual renewal of America had become [a] necessity. They launched the Committees of Correspondence as an organizing network to lay the groundwork for building such a movement, not to be a third political party but to bring together people from the broad array of issue, constituency, institutional and community groups who share a common set of values.

New Age Politics

If New Age influences continue to grow in the political arena (which they show every sign of doing), it will be important for those of us committed to a different "set of values" to be able to recognize them. What are the distinguishing characteristics of Green or New Age politics (using the word *politics* here to mean opinions and principles pertaining to the structure and policies of government)?

In my outline of New Age ideology (chapter 3) I explained that New Age sociopolitical theory is characterized by a holistic orientation that culminates in a vision of a united global community. These holistic and global threads run throughout the fabric of New Age politics, shaping its distinctive form.

In keeping with these essential features, additional qualities can be identified. The new politics is sometimes characterized as "radical center," and the German Green Party's slogan is "neither left, nor right, but out front."

What does that mean? The *Los Angeles Times* offers a succinct description: "The new politics has little to do with old liberal and conservative dichotomies. Rather it emphasizes appropriate scale, decentralization, fiscal conservatism and a lot of experimentation."[9]

Most adherents of New Age politics come from the left side of the political spectrum, but they have grown disillusioned with traditional liberal politics, whether moderate or radical. They criticize the "top-down bureaucracy," dependence on government, uncontrolled industrialization, and materialistic values that they often see fostered by both liberal democratic and Marxist regimes.[10]

Their advocacy of decentralization and self-reliance (as demonstrated by their effective use of networks) sounds like traditional Republicanism. But their underlying values are far from traditional. For example, Mark Satin writes that "a New Age oriented national government might" guarantee abortions for all women, regardless of age or parental consent; repeal all "laws creating 'crimes' without victims"; give young people of whatever age all of the rights and responsibilities of adults, including the right to live away from home without parental permission, or choose legal guardians other than one's parents; and "add 'the right to choose to die' to the bill of rights."[11]

The Emerging New Age Agenda

These underlying values—representing a new, spiritualized humanism—have led New Agers to adopt certain causes as their own. As unrelated to each other as human rights, population control, ecology, and disarmament may seem on the surface, New Agers conceive of them as interdependent facets of one comprehensive cause.

Why and how this is so can be explained in terms of a chain reaction, according to the following schema: Basic New Age *presuppositions* and *spiritual experience* give rise to a particular set of *shared values,* which engender corresponding *social concerns.* Depending on temperament and interests, individual New Agers identify with one or two of many possible causes consistent with their values. This motivates them to commit to *social and political action* in their areas of concern, which eventually necessitates forming *alliances* for greater political clout with others in different but compatible fields. As a result these assorted causes coalesce into a single political *platform* and *agenda.* In turn this inspires the formulation of a common sociopolitical philosophy that seeks the integration of all of these social causes in an underlying world view and value system.

This last phase will be a process of discovery and not invention, since it was a common world view and value system which stirred New Agers' interest in these causes in the first place. Thus at this point the chain has completed a full circle as the final effect attaches to and reinforces the first cause. And as the underlying beliefs and values and the relationship of the various causes become consciously identified and articulated, the political theorists can now identify a *grand solution*. This solution will answer all of the concerns included within the agenda while remaining true to the common value system.

I suggest that the Green movement has emerged along the lines of the above scenario, and their "grand solution" (my term, not theirs) is the formation of an all-encompassing, worldwide political system consistent with New Age values.

It will help to examine some specific New Age values and the causes to which they inspire commitment, and also to consider whether or not Christian values can lend support to the same causes. This will be important, on the one hand, because it is not my intention to suggest that every cause New Agers support should be avoided or opposed by Christians. On the other hand, Christians need to discern how even the agreeable New Age causes can figure into their grand solution. But before we move on to such a study, a crucial difference between New Age and Christian[12] political outlooks must be identified.

Warring Anthropologies

California State Assemblyman John Vasconcellos (perhaps the most aggressive Aquarian Conspirator in American politics) predicted in 1986 that the following ten years would be marked by a political struggle between the "fundamentalist" and humanist views of human nature. Vasconcellos, whose "self-esteem bill" (which establishes a task force to investigate the relationship of self-esteem to social problems, and recommend specific programs) was signed into law in October of 1986, argues that belief in the "inherent goodness of man" allows people to be affirmative, courageous, trustworthy, open, and free, while belief in "original sin" produces "a politics of repression and intimidation and shame and control."[13]

Christians strongly disagree. To believe that human nature is inclined toward evil simply produces a more realistic view of man (in light of actual human behavior) without denying his inherent worth and *capacity* for both relative and (through Christ) absolute goodness. A "politics of repression," on the other hand, could easily result from a naive utopianism (such as, the "New Age"), based on an optimistic anthropology, which would fail to see the danger of investing too much power in one "spiritually evolved" individual or group.

Another consequence of such an optimistic view of man is a heavy reliance on education and "positive reinforcement" (such as, Vasconcellos's bill) for correcting social problems and crime without the corresponding regard for discipline and punitive measures that Christians believe human nature requires.

It should be clear then that wherever else New Age and Christian political thought may be compatible, they radically differ over man's moral condition. And the very nature of a political structure is determined by such an assumption. (For example, because of a realistic view of human nature, the US Constitution's checks and balances of power have helped preserve American freedom for over two hundred years.)

Values and Related Causes

1. Survival

Survival may be the most critical value underlying New Age politics. In this respect New Age and secular humanists are no different, and therefore on many points they are able to form a common political front.

Evolution is foundational to modern secular belief, and (as we saw in chapter 3) according to both neo-Darwinian and punctuationalist theories, the evolution of a species is driven by the struggle to survive. For those who reject the concept of divine revelation, survival can appear to be the only discernible "value" operative in nature—the "law of the jungle."

Most New Age thinkers come from a background in secular humanism. Their New Age conversions lead them to renounce the materialism in secular thought, but as I've noted before, they never question evolution. Thus, although their values change in some respects, survival retains its primary position in their presuppositions.

Much of New Age interest in such diverse issues as the nuclear arms race, environmental pollution, overpopulation and starvation, and resource depletion can be explained in terms of personal and racial survival. In each case the grand solution is what Donald Keys refers to as "planetization."

Keys argues that the only realistic way the threat of nuclear holocaust (as the most crucial example) can be eliminated is to develop effective international security processes. In this view, the present nation-state political arrangement is decidedly *in*effective. In the words of former *Saturday Review* editor Norman Cousins, a long-time collaborator with Keys:

> Despite all the apparent evidences of civilization, we are really bumping along at a very low level and relying on philosophies that point us away from survival. The primitive nature of human society is reflected most of all in the inadequacy of the nation as a form of human organization. The nation came into being for the purpose of protecting the lives, property, and values of its citizens, but no nation in the world is able today to perform that basic function. Instead the nation has become a point of incendiary confrontations in a world too small for major conflict.[14]

Cousins adds: "We have a lot of loose cannons rolling around on the deck, and sooner or later one is going to go off if we don't tie them up and block them off."[15]

While not arguing that nations should necessarily be done away with altogether, Keys maintains that a "planetary management system" is a practical inevitability:

> In our discussion of the future of the planet, and the "planetization" of mankind, and the necessarily approaching global order . . . I think we can see that in a global sense there certainly is going to be, must be a new age, since what has preceded will no longer work. In fact, [it] is counter-productive, and dysfunctional in the future.[16]

Not everyone who believes that a new political age is mandated by our "shrinking world" is looking for the "Age of Aquarius." For example, there have been secular humanists promoting the idea of a "world state" throughout the century,[17] and many continue to do so today.[18] However, in the minds of those who have been influenced by occult teachings, what the secular "one-worlders" are calling for quite naturally merges with New Age mythology.

Even New Agers have no unified vision of how the global political entity will be structured. They just agree there needs to be one. Those who are in the esoteric tradition of Theosophy (for example, the followers of Alice A. Bailey and Benjamin Creme) tend to look for a centralized government administered by a spiritual hierarchy under the leadership of a "world Christ."[19] But most New Age thinkers are leery of a monolithic world government.

Opinions vary widely among the latter on what they *would* like to see.[20] It is common, though, for them to call for small-scale, largely autonomous communities at the local level connected via representation to larger regional bodies, with the same representative arrangement continuing up through levels to something like an empowered United Nations at the top. This final body's interrelated departments would handle matters of global concern, such as providing security, protecting the environment, and overseeing the equitable distribution of planetary resources. One writer even acknowledges a "well-founded fear that such a structure [a world government] could become tyrannical," and calls for "only that minimal degree of global organization required to handle problems that are irreducibly global in character and scale."[21]

Such talk of a united world easily sounds like pure utopian fantasy when one considers the major ideological and theological differences, the economic interests, the egos, and all else that keeps the world divided. However, when racial survival is one's only clear moral imperative, planetization becomes an increasingly reasonable proposition—even an evolutionary necessity. In the face of so many critical world problems, how else can racial survival be insured?

To those who have adopted such a seemingly humanitarian view, efforts to resist planetization and cling to national autonomy appear prideful, selfish, and dangerously divisive of the human family—in a word, *unspiritual*. But, from the Christian perspective, there is much more involved in this issue than national pride or selfish political or economic interests.

It needs to first be clarified that survival *is* a major Christian concern. "Fundamentalists" are often caricatured by humanists as *not* being concerned—even cheering global holocaust on, since most associate Armageddon with the second coming, and do not consider racial extinction a real possibility (Matt. 24:22). Sad to say, a small percentage of Christians *do* endorse a reckless approach to global threats, but such an attitude is *un*christian; it runs counter to New Testament teaching. Jesus placed higher value on individual human life than any other religious teacher (*see* Matt. 10:29–31; John 3:16), and called upon his followers to be peacemakers (Matt. 5:9). As consoling and encouraging as the biblical guarantee of racial survival is, it does not rule out the dreadful possibility of global holocaust and near-universal loss of human life. Therefore, a consistent, responsible Christian politics would place the highest priority on finding just, workable solutions to global threats and international tensions.

The difference between Christians and humanists, though, is that for believers physical survival does not *dominate* over all other values. Life is more than mere existence; it involves the privilege and responsibility of worshiping and serving God (Deut. 8:3). Most Christians in democratic lands (not to mention numerous other citizens) cherish their freedom as much as life itself, and desire a similar freedom to be extended to all peoples. Therefore any negotiations for nuclear disarmament or attempts to resolve any other global problem must in some way guarantee that freedom. Otherwise, ensuring *physical* survival for billions could simultaneously deny them the opportunity to hear about and thus obtain *eternal* survival through Christ.

It is not that most New Agers and secular humanists do not also value their freedoms. To the Christian, however, in placing physical survival above all other values they do not cherish freedom enough. For example, the late historian Arnold Toynbee, who was a globalist, wrote:

> It is most unlikely, I fear, that [a world state] will be established by the will, or even with the acquiescence, of the majority of mankind. It seems to me likely to be imposed on the majority by a ruthless, efficient, and fanatical minority, inspired by some ideology or religion. I guess that mankind will acquiesce in a harsh Leninian kind of dictatorship as a lesser evil than self-extermination or than a continuing anarchy which could end only in self-extermination.
>
> If the reluctant majority does accept this dictatorship on this ground, *I think they will be making the right choice, because it would enable the human race to survive.*[22] (emphasis added)

2. Unity and Interdependence

As we've seen repeatedly throughout this book, the most distinctive New Age belief—derived from mystical experiences—is that "all is One." This they hold in common with traditional Eastern mysticism. But, as we've also seen in previous chapters, New Agers diverge from the East in their affirmation that the diversity that exists in creation is not mere illusion but has intrinsic worth—the Whole is enriched by the interdependence of its parts.

For New Agers, then, the very concepts of *unity and interdependence* are almost imbued with a sacred quality. Anything which promotes them is generally good, and anything which disrupts them is correspondingly bad. Unity and interdependence become ends in themselves.

Coming from this perspective, it is no wonder that New Agers are attracted to "holistic" causes like ecology. This also helps explain why they so longingly look for the emergence of a worldwide political system: it would be the perfect sociopolitical expression of the unity and interdependence of all things.

This second value derives additional strength from the first, in that New Agers closely link interdependence with survival: "The concept of the 'mutuality of survival' is viewed as a consequence of interdependence, the belief that regions of the global community must establish 'organically' functional relationships if the planet is to survive."[23]

Christians should have no problem accepting that everything within the universe is interdependent, and that this God-ordained order should be respected in all human activities. It is perfectly appropriate for believers to be active in, for example, ecological causes (*see* chapter 4).

Unity is also valued in Christian teaching, based in the perfect harmony that exists between the Persons of the Trinity (John 17:20–21). However, since all is not one in essence, unity for the Christian is strictly a matter of the will, and must be grounded in conformity to *God's* will.

There are many creatures (earthly and otherwise) who are *not* in conformity with God's will, and to unite with them would be to rebel against God. Thus, the value of unity is conditional, not to be bought at any price. The worldwide unity based in humanism (that is, human autonomy) that planetarians desire would be the antithesis of the Christian hope in the kingdom (rule) of *God*. Therefore Christians must stand in opposition to it.

3. Autonomy

Although New Agers do at times speak of a redefined "kingdom of God," it is clear that *human autonomy* is an important New Age value. Basic humanism teaches that man is a law unto himself, but New Agers carry this assumption quite a bit further. For them, one's Self is ultimately indistinguishable from God. There is therefore no final power external to the self whose laws must be obeyed. Each person creates his (or her) own reality, good or bad, by the way he handles the law of his *own* being. If he can learn to harness the resources of his Higher Self, his possibilities are limitless (for more on this belief, *see* chapter 9).

Quite consistently, this belief provides the basis for the New Age emphases on self-reliance and self-development. And as diametrically opposed as the belief itself is to Christian theology, in its application it can at times be surprisingly compatible. For Christianity also emphasizes human responsibility (albeit, first and foremost to an objective God, then to others and self). Thus a New Ager and a Christian may both support free enterprise, or less federal funding for welfare and more for self-development programs.

New Age support for a host of "rights" issues (such as, human rights, civil rights, women's rights, gay rights) can also be traced back to their belief in and value of autonomy, or the sovereignty of the self. In other words, if we are all equally divine, then we each have the right to pursue self-realization without outside interference, as long as we don't interfere with others in their pursuit. Consequently, most would hold that no laws should be passed touching abortion or homosexuality, for example, since people have "the right to do what they please with their own bodies." (Of course, this is a fallacy where abortion is concerned, since the woman is destroying a body separate from her own. Furthermore, autonomy of the individual can also conflict with their interdependence ethic—that *whatever* a part does affects the whole.)

Since Christians believe that all men and women have equal worth as creatures in God's own image (Gen. 1:27; compare with Acts 17:26), there are many "rights" issues which they can wholeheartedly support (for example, the right of a qualified black female to the same job and salary as an equally qualified white male). In the case of acts such as homosexuality and abortion, however, we are not discussing questions of "equal rights" but of "moral rights."

Unlike the New Ager who recognizes no moral absolutes, the Christian accepts that God has revealed specific standards of lawful behavior in his Word, and we have no "moral right" to transgress them. And so the New Age assertion of autonomy and rejection of many biblical values is a *major* point at which New Age and Christian politics are at odds.

There are many additional values which could be identified, including the value of *balance* (that is, balancing polarities like mind/body or masculinity/femininity), arising out of an acceptance of Chinese "yin-yang" dualism; the value of *nonviolence* derived from belief in and reverence for the divinity in all things (it must be noted here that the espousal of a value and its consistent application are two different entities); and the value of that which is *natural* (over that which is restructured or treated by man), which is due partly to the identification of God with nature. But for brevity's sake, I will elaborate here on only one more New Age value.

4. Humanness

In keeping with their humanistic presuppositions, many New Agers attach great worth to the distinctive attributes of *humanness*. Rejecting views of man which reduce him to the level of a complex machine or an incurable savage, they celebrate man's higher qualities: his capacities for spirituality, morality, rationality as well as deep feeling, creativity, and meaningful relationships.

Politically this humanism translates into a deep concern about the dehumanizing effects of our modern technocracy. New Agers often argue that materialistic values and the uncontrolled industrialization and urban growth they produce are robbing us of life's greater riches, while depleting our natural resources and wreaking ecological havoc. They call for a cultural turning away from consumer values to a lifestyle of "simple living and high thinking." (Of course, many other New Agers are materialistic themselves.)[24] Such a life would seek fulfillment in spiritual development, participation in a caring community, and enjoyment of nature's wonders, rather than the endless acquisition of material "toys" and status symbols.

New Agers also argue that growth should be limited to an "appropriate" or "human scale" that protects the personal dimensions of life and keeps society manageable. For example, in *Small Is Beautiful,* one of the bibles of New Age politics, the late economist E. F. Schumacher argued that cities should be limited to a population of half a million. Beyond that, nothing is added to their virtue while the quality of life declines.[25]

Certainly, Christians will differ with New Agers and/or among themselves about how the depersonalizing effects of modern technology and urbanization should be corrected. But it would nonetheless seem that there is much room for agreement among New Agers and Christians here.

While Judeo-Christianity makes God the measure of all things rather than man, in the sense of valuing humanness it *is* "humanistic." In fact, in this sense it is *more* humanistic than both New Age and secular humanism, since neither the impersonal New Age god nor the impersonal secular universe can lend ultimate validation and worth to human personality. But the Bible, on the other hand, confirms man's sense of his own dignity and uniqueness by showing that his distinctive personal qualities reflect the very likeness of God.

Christians must take issue with the humanist stress on humanness, though, in terms of how far they carry it. They go beyond appreciation and respect to adoration and worship: an idolatry of the image of God in man. Christians know that the image, as great as it is, pales before that infinite and perfect Being from whom it is derived. *His* reality is something truly worth celebrating!

In summary we have seen that because of radically different world views, there are several points of irreconcilable difference between New Age and Christian values and political thought (for example, the relationship of survival and unity to other values, Christian rejection of New Age utopianism, and New Age rejection of many Christian morals). There are also, however, several areas of possible agreement (such as ecology, self-reliance as opposed to government dependency, human rights, and human scale).

No Place for Christianity?

Because their agendas can at times overlap, it is conceivable that New Agers and Christians might cooperate on some issues. But when they do, discernment is crucial. For if in seeking support for his or her cause (for instance, hunger relief) the Christian joins forces with the New Agers' alliance, he or she could unwittingly contribute to the New Agers' grand solution. This would not be worth any immediate benefits gained.

Why? In spite of frequent references to how "freedom of religion" would be an essential feature of the New Age, it is clear from their writings that virtually *all* New Agers are looking for a *spiritually* based society. And just as New Age (occult) spirituality is repugnant to, and incompatible with, Christian faith (*see* chapter 1), so orthodox Christianity is repugnant to, and incompatible with, the kind of global society New Agers are working toward. In the New Age there would be no comfortable (more likely no *tolerable*) place for true Christianity.

Current New Age teachings on evolution make it perfectly conceivable that an Aquarian regime would eventually justify persecution of Christians. The evolutionary and "paradigm shift" models for interpreting intellectual history make it appear axiomatic that humanity will eventually embrace the New Age belief system. Therefore, a "pluralistic society" would no longer seem necessary. It's true that New Agers often speak of valuing "unity in diversity" (and much diversity is tolerated in their midst), but the *ground* for this unity is *pantheism*. Christian theism is therefore *too* "diverse."

Furthermore, the New Age understanding of "conscious evolution" (*see* chapter 3) makes it the moral duty of government and citizens alike to contribute to the New Age and the growth of "Gaia," the living planet. Such concepts leave no room for the separation of church and state, and would make resisting the New Age a serious offense. Christian dogmatism could easily be viewed (in fact, already is) as antievolutionary: a threat to the global unity necessary for racial survival. And when survival dominates over all other values, the elimination of any perceived threat to it could easily be justified.

All of this sounds threatening—but it is one thing for New Agers to envision and even work toward a world order based on their beliefs and values, and it is quite another to succeed at bringing such an order into being. National coups are difficult enough to stage, let alone a world takeover that brings even the USA and USSR under its sway. How serious is the New Age threat to Christian interests? What is the current status of "planetization" and what are its prospects for the future? These questions will be addressed throughout the remainder of this chapter.

New Age Activism—The Progress of Planetization

The cause of planetization continually attracts new adherents in international circles. It has a broad base of support within the UN secretariat, and among disadvantaged and small countries in both hemispheres, public and private international organizations, and special interest groups. It is actively promoted by an international network of influential academics, industrialists, scientists, etc., such as those in the Club of Rome and the Institute for World Order.[26]

At present, however, planetarians have nowhere near the power necessary to make the world unite. Planetization is the furthest thing from the minds of nearly all who are leading the world's major powers, including the United States and Russia (although it is difficult to discern exactly *what* is in the mind of Kremlin leader Mikhail Gorbachev). When asked if our leaders see the need for an "evolutionary approach" to the new political reality, Dr. Jonas Salk replied: "No. Those already advantaged are resistant to change. It's the disadvantaged who desire change."[27] And if the super powers are resistant, who is going to make them conform?

On the other hand, changes in policy can come with changes in power. Encouraged by his planetarian rhetoric and the reforms he has initiated, New Agers have strong hopes that Mikhail Gorbachev will move the USSR fully into the Aquarian Age. And, with new presidential elections every four years, change is a way of life in American politics. Who knows, for instance, what alterations in foreign policy might be instituted if Jerry Brown made a comeback and was elected president?

For planetization to be embraced by the USA, Great Britain, and other democracies, however, it will require popular support. As Donald Keys puts it, "Changes have to come from changed understandings among large publics."[28] It is toward such an end that the Aquarian Conspiracy directs a good deal of its energy.

Prompting the Planetary Perspective

Just as on a spiritual level New Agers are attempting to initiate "paradigm shifts" to a mystical consciousness, so on a socio-political level they are attempting to provoke paradigm shifts to a planetary consciousness. "Planetary conscious" people are those who think in terms of the world and all of humanity ("inclusively") instead of in terms of their own nation, race, or religion ("exclusively").

Keys's own organization, Planetary Citizens, is in the forefront of this effort. Originally headquartered at the United Nations (where it was founded in 1970) and recently relocated in California, Planetary Citizens' key thrust is public education. They sponsored the Planetary Initiative for the World We Choose, which organized neighborhood "Issues Exploration Groups" in many countries. Any variety of global, national, or local problems would be discussed at these gatherings, and planetization would always be presented as the grand solution. Then these neighborhood groups convened in Toronto as a "Planetary Congress" in 1983. Their mission was to formulate a "Declaration on the World We Choose," to be passed on to politicians as a citizens' "global mandate."

Keys explains:

> Our goal is largely to try to orchestrate . . . a general awakening, a crossing of the threshold to a global awareness . . . for as large a part of the population of the world as we can. . . . There has to be some critical mass of public awareness of planetary consciousness before politicians will move, before foreign offices will get into gear, before teaching changes in the schools.[29]

In keeping with the objective of influencing world leaders, Planetary Citizens has more recently been sponsoring an "Independent Commission on World Security Alternatives" that is enlisting various peace, disarmament, and systems experts to draw up a "workable, believable, and non-threatening global [security] system."[30] This will require the "empowering of international institutions" (that is, the U.N.) to "make it stick."[31]

As to changing teaching in the schools, this has already been accomplished to a remarkable degree. "Global education" has been broadly embraced by the American educational establishment.[32]

Its advocates claim it is merely an approach to preparing students for responsible participation in the global age in which we live, but its materials are often biased *for* globalism and humanism and *against* nationalism and Christianity.

These materials are provided to the schools by *scores* of humanistic organizations, New Age and secular. One of these, Global Education Associates (GEA) of East Orange, New Jersey, is a particularly significant New Age group. Its efforts go far beyond bringing the planetary perspective to young people. Founders Gerald and Patricia Mische formed GEA with the intention of catalyzing a broadly based, multi-issue movement for "world order alternatives." Toward this end GEA publishes numerous impressive research papers on global interdependence and world order issues, conducts intensive educational programs for the general public (thousands have been given), and provides speakers and consulting services for schools, religious organizations, and community and issue groups. GEA is represented in over sixty countries, and works extensively with religious groups and professionals, particularly Catholic.

"Planetizing" the Activist Groups

Some New Agers, like those in Planetary Citizens and GEA, are entirely devoted to planetization: all of their efforts are to win converts to the planetary perspective. But most New Age activists are involved with more narrow issues or causes, like women's rights, ecology, or peace. Of these many are conscious Aquarian Conspirators: they view whatever problem they face over against the global solution, and direct their efforts in support of planetization whenever possible.

There is no simple way to diagram the extent of New Age infiltration in the activist groups and various humanistic associations. A particular organization committed to a cause or position included in the New Age agenda may or may not be directed by New Agers. For examples, the Sierra Club and the Audubon Society are essentially secular groups concerned only about environmental issues. But another environmentalist group, the militant Greenpeace (whose ship the *Rainbow Warrior* was assaulted in 1986 by the French with the loss of one life and much controversy), is thoroughly New Age and affirms that "our ultimate goal . . . is to help bring about that basic change in thinking known as 'planetary consciousness.'"[33]

Even groups like the Sierra Club, Amnesty International, and Zero Population Growth, which are not self-consciously New Age as a whole, may have several New Agers within their ranks, working to win their associates over to the mystical and planetary perspectives. Keys writes: "We can help to 'planetize' existing organizations and groups by joining with them in their efforts to promote human rights, peace, 'soft energy paths'; while working with them we can contribute the world-inclusive perspective."[34]

Once New Agers are established in positions of influence, they can bring their organizations into greater alignment with the New Age perspective. Marilyn Ferguson accurately observes:

> They often succeed in changing the emphasis in the organization's official publication; they bring in more innovative speakers for programs, run for office, and otherwise break the hold of the thinking of the old guard. The collusion is so low-key that no one notices. . . .[35]

And as more and more (sometimes powerful) organizations and activist groups fall under its sway, the political and social force of the Aquarian Conspiracy correspondingly accumulates.

If New Age activism is a force to be reckoned with (and has been for some time), why don't we hear more about it in the secular media? One answer to this curiosity is that most of the movement's strength lies in its networks. The network is a form of organization so intangible and inconspicuous that so far it has escaped the notice it deserves as an emerging, powerful sociological phenomenon.

Donald Keys has this to say about the comparatively scanty attention the movement has received:

> We mentioned earlier how the dominant, "straight" society has apparently not recognized the strength and pervasiveness of the new consciousness culture. Perhaps this is just as well, as so far a polarization between the old culture and the new one has been avoided. If the New Age movement does become a target of alarmed forces and defenders of the status quo ante, however, it

will offer a widely dispersed and decentralized target, very hard to identify and impossible to dissuade or subvert from its life-serving values.[36]

Shortly after Keys wrote these words in 1982 some alarmed voices were indeed raised, in the evangelical community at least.[37] After April 1982, when Benjamin Creme's Tara Center ran newspaper ads in major cities announcing that "The Christ Is Now Here," the many parallels between certain New Age teachings and popular end-time scenarios became common knowledge among Christians. With the New Age movement it appeared to many that the exact form of that deception with which the "man of sin" (commonly known as the Antichrist) would overpower the world was taking shape before our eyes (2 Thess. 2:9–10). In the following chapter we shall consider exactly what kinds of significance Christians should attach to this burgeoning Aquarian Conspiracy.

Is the End upon Us?
The Meaning of the New Age Movement for Christianity

Large sectors of evangelicalism appear obsessed with eschatology (that is, the study of biblical prophecy relating to the end times). Entire ministries have been founded on nothing else but this subject. Many study the daily newspaper religiously for any sign of prophetic fulfillment. Scenarios are continually constructed and revised to show how current world events will shortly lead to Armageddon. Many are more concerned about what *Christ* will do in the future than what he would have *them* do now.

It was not surprising that when the prophecy enthusiasts finally discovered the New Age movement the same sensational approach was applied. In dealing with the subject many authors have had such an eschatological bias (seeking always to show how it fulfills prophecy) that they have handled the facts selectively, and consequently left many Christians with a distorted picture of the movement.[1] Also, because many believers see the movement in exclusively eschatological terms, several moral and social issues that it raises for the church are never even considered (These will be discussed later).

With such doctrinal "winds" blowing, it's no wonder that some Christians who do not share this eschatological obsession are ready to dispense with an "end time" analysis of current events altogether. Sensing that the church needs to be more socially responsible, a growing number are being attracted to the *postmillennial* teachings of the "Christian Reconstruction" movement. Its teachers (such as, R. J. Rushdoony, Gary North, and David Chilton) affirm that the church is destined to conquer the world for Christ—both spiritually and politically—before he returns. Thus social and political involvement is understood to be part of the Great Commission to "make disciples of all the nations."

I sympathize with these efforts to find a biblical basis for social and political involvement, but I do not believe they have succeeded. The basis they have found, postmillennialism and *theonomy* (the doctrine that the law of Moses is binding on all governments), is not in my view biblical. Certainly, this book is not the appropriate arena to argue in-depth for a particular view of the millennium. It should be clarified however that I agree with the majority of evangelicals today who hold that premillennialism is the most natural interpretation of Scripture and a more realistic view of history—given the rebellious inclinations that are everywhere evident in man. It is hardly conceivable to me that God's kingdom could be established worldwide without a divine intervention of second coming magnitude.

I also concur with the "futurist" position that the events described in Revelation from chapter 4 on are in the future—yet to be fulfilled. I look for a literal, personal Antichrist riding atop a worldwide political, economic, and religious system (Rev. 13, 17–19, and so forth).[2]

If one holds to premillennialism and futurism, it should be clear that to dispense entirely with a prophetic consciousness on the ground that so many take it to an extreme is to fall into the *opposite* extreme. Jesus said: "When these things begin to take place, straighten up and lift up your heads, because your redemption is drawing near" (Luke 21:28). Christianity *is* an eschatological faith.

So, does the New Age movement, along with other world events, signal that the end is upon us? I do not presume to have the final answer, nor do I think anyone else should (Acts 1:7; Luke 12:40).[3] Therefore, some reasons will be offered why the New Age movement *might* be the precursor to the Antichrist, and also some reasons why it *might not* be. I will then suggest a perspective that integrates both of these possibilities.

Why It *Might* Be

Obviously, even before the New Age movement came into focus there were several reasons for thinking that the end might be near. For me the strongest of these is the re-establishment of the nation of Israel in 1948, and their repossession of Jerusalem during the 1967 Six Days War. This seems profoundly significant in light of Jesus' words in Luke 21:24:

> And they [the Jews] will fall by the edge of the sword, and will be led captive into all the nations [fulfilled in A.D. 70 and the years following]; and Jerusalem will be trampled underfoot by the Gentiles [true until 1967] until the times of the Gentiles be fulfilled.

And, from events described in the verses following Luke 21:24, it would appear that after the "times of the Gentiles" the end is not far.

It's hard *not* to think eschatologically in the days in which we live. Past, present, and future considered, one could easily conclude that the human race is reaching its limits in the present system of things. By this I mean that in attempting to govern himself apart from God, man has dramatically lived out his potentialities for both genius and wickedness; now it appears as though he is backing himself into a corner where every possible outcome has apocalyptic associations. Global famine? Environmental disaster (for example, the depletion of our atmosphere's ozone layer)? Nuclear war? A world government to prevent the above?

There are undeniable pressures toward planetization. As the late anthropologist Margaret Mead observed: "Our technology has increased the size of interdependent units to include the entire planet."[4] Politically, economically, environmentally, culturally, it is now impossible to remain isolated.

There are many global problems that can only be resolved through international cooperation. And through such technological advances as jet travel, satellite communications, and the information explosion unleashed by the computer, the media, and so forth, for the first time in history a functional "global village" is really feasible.

Because of these new pressures and capacities, it is entirely conceivable that *ultimately* a world state will be established, in spite of all that now stands against it. Donald Keys may be right when he argues that planetization is an inevitable outcome of human development, given enough time:

> Humanity is coming to the end of a long road. The world *will* organize as a community or human life will perish. If some elements of humanity should escape destruction, then the drama of evolution towards world community will begin again, and in time these remnants of humanity will once more arrive at the same decision point which we are now facing.[5]

According to the biblical record, this world community would have been organized long ago at Babel, but God scattered the people by confusing their languages (Gen. 11:1–9). For ages the language barrier and all the other differences that came to exist between people stood as insurmountable obstacles to unification. But in our own day the effects of Babel seem to be ominously wearing off. Robert Muller, retired U.N. Assistant Secretary General, proclaimed:

> For the first time in history we have discovered that this is *one* planet on which we live. Now it remains for us to discover that we are also one human family and that we have to transcend all *national, linguistic,* cultural, racial, and *religious* differences which have made our history. We have a chance to write a completely new history.[6] (emphases added)

Both at Babel and today we find an effort to realize humanity's *collective* potential for greatness apart from the rule of the sovereign God.

This leads to another reason why the move toward planetization might eventually succeed—it may be energized by Satan as no previous human endeavor has been. It would appear from Scripture that Satan has a specific objective directing his multifarious activities: to unite the world in a religiopolitical system which worships him and follows him in repudiating Yahweh (*see* Rev. 13:4).

Apparently, he would have had this at Babel (Gen. 11:4 shows this inchoate "world state" was not based in true religion), but God prevented him. The reason is not difficult to discern: the Lord still had a redemptive work to do on the earth and required a nation (that is, Israel) separated from the rest of humanity through which to accomplish it.

Now, however, Christ's work of redemption has long since been completed, and if the "times of the Gentiles" are fulfilled then it would seem only one event must occur before Christ's reign can hold sway over all the earth: judgment must fall on this wicked world system for its history of revolt against God. And it is God's pattern to allow iniquity to ripen to its complete expression, so that when his all-consuming wrath is revealed it will be entirely deserved (Rev. 14:14–20; compare with Gen. 15:16).

Thus, Satan will briefly be allowed to have his day (Rev. 12:12), and those who have willingly rejected the gospel will be punished with a delusion that will cause them to worship the Antichrist— the act that will finally incite the outpouring of God's wrath (2 Thess. 2:8–12).

By its all-out effort to overcome the global crisis by affirming human autonomy and self-sufficiency (the desire of which caused man to fall in the first place: Gen. 3:4–6), rather than by repenting before God, the New Age movement fits into this eschatological scenario like a hand in a glove.

As I have noted previously, most New Agers are sincerely concerned about salvaging the world, and much that they are calling for is even compatible with Christian values. But the kind of enlightened global society they desire could never be realized apart from a radical transformation of human nature—as they themselves recognize. Christianity offers such a transformation in the "new birth," but New Agers advocate instead a *psychic* birth—a quickening of spiritual consciousness and power *apart from* Christ's atonement and the regenerating work of the Holy Spirit. This results in a sense of peace and wholeness which fails to touch the dynamic, sometimes inscrutable operation of the sin nature. Such "transformation" opens up possibilities for a more refined, even apocalyptic kind of evil to emerge.

Those of us who personally experienced this brand of transformation (*see* Appendix D) before truly being transformed through faith in Christ are especially able to appreciate that mystical states of consciousness have powerful eschatological potential.[7] There is no corrective dynamic such as Christians know through the Holy Spirit's conviction. The sense of "transcending" normal consciousness and connecting with "Universal Mind" can produce such self-assurance that the need to check one's beliefs for truthfulness or actions for morality can easily be forgotten. In fact, many conclude that they have gone beyond the "illusory duality" of good and evil.

Certainly, such altered states of consciousness do not long remain separate from the beliefs and practices of the occult. And as we consider the Western occult movements that have been gathering momentum since the early nineteenth century, we must ask ourselves if there might be a larger satanic design behind them than simply leading individual souls astray. While there is a temptation to dismiss these groups as "fringe," it must be pointed out that if (1) Satan's objective is to unite the world under a man wholly given over to him, and (2) the occult world is uniquely Satan's domain, then (3) it should not be surprising to find occult movements actively engaged in promoting such a world.

This is exactly what we find. The teachings of Alice A. Bailey, for instance, call for the same type of selfless devotion in preparing the world for the New Age "Christ" that the New Testament calls for in service to the true Christ. All personal attraction to "world glamor" (a favorite Bailey term for the distracting allurements of the illusory emotional or "astral" plane) is to be subjugated, so that the "divine Plan" may be furthered. While it is extremely doubtful that Satan reveals his true "plan" to any of his disciples, if there are enough correspondences at crucial points his purposes *will* be furthered by those who naively think they are serving the "Masters." And although some evangelicals have exaggerated this point, there *are* striking correspondences between premillennial, futurist interpretations of biblical prophecy and spiritistically inspired teachings about the New Age.[8]

Why It *Might Not* Be

After looking at several reasons why the New Age movement could lead the world to Armageddon, a natural question presents itself: Why should we bother to resist the social advances of a movement which may well be destined to succeed (until the return of Christ)? The answer lies in the fact that as grim as things may look, *nothing is conclusive at this point.*[9]

First of all, we have to take into consideration the difficulties involved in interpreting as-yet-unfulfilled biblical prophecy. I built my case for why the end *might* be near on the assumption that the popular premillennial eschatology is basically correct. But the church's cultural position has had much to do historically with whether popular eschatology has been premillennial, post-millennial, or amillennial. A mistake perpetually committed throughout church history has been to impose the contemporary situation upon biblical prophecy so that Scripture is forced into *its* mold.

This can be an understandable error. After centuries of inquisitions and repression of truly biblical movements, what good Protestant *wouldn't* have thought, as the Reformers did, that the pope was the Antichrist and the Catholic Church "Babylon the Great" (Rev. 17)? Who else was the "bad guy" at that time? Yet very few of us accept this interpretation (at least that the papal office is the Antichrist) today.

While it can be argued that prophetic passages which were previously misunderstood are now being clarified by events taking shape to fulfill them, some humility is still needed. It remains very easy to make the old mistakes, and many of us stand guilty. For instance, in *Peace, Prosperity, and the Coming Holocaust,* Dave Hunt argues that today's computer technology will allow for the fulfillment of Revelation 13:16–18.[10] He predicts that eventually the credit of everyone on earth will be registered with a central computer, and each person's credit number will be "indelibly impregnated" on his or her body, "exactly what the Bible predicted 1900 years ago." But this ignores the precise wording of the passage, which says that no one will be able to buy or sell without "the name of the beast or the number of *his* [that is, the Beast's] name" (v. 17). If everyone will have the *same* number, then it would not involve an *individual's* line of credit. While computer technology could indeed develop as Hunt predicts, the *biblical text* gives us no reason to think so.

Another mistake we are capable of making is to conclude that a man is the Antichrist or a movement Babylon just because what he or it advocates corresponds to what we *expect* from Antichrist or Babylon. In this case, our eschatology may be biblical but our judgment of timing and identification of events may be faulty.

Hitler appeared a convincing candidate for the Antichrist at the time, and when the League of Nations was formed in 1919 many Christians thought it must be Babylon. But it failed in its mission and was disbanded in 1946.

This shows that the mere fact that the New Age movement is proposing a world order fraught with ominous implications does not *prove* that the end is upon us. What we think is Babylon may be just a wave in an advancing tide: another phase moving in Babylon's direction, but not that entity itself. Therefore, it is equally possible (from our perspective) that the end will have come within ten years or not have arrived in one hundred.

"Salt" and "Light"

Paul tells us that the "mystery of lawlessness" was at work even in his own time (2 Thess. 2:7). Satan has always known what he wants to do, and no doubt continually attempts to bring it about. Whenever his influence is in the ascendant (for example, as with Hitler), the evil designs of the "spirit of antichrist" (1 John 4:3) become more visible. But Paul also speaks of God's restraining influence, which holds Satan back until the appointed time (2 Thess. 2:6–7).

While the *primary* mission of the church is clearly evangelism, I believe we are also called to be instruments of God in loosening Satan's murderous grasp on the world. In Matthew 5:13–16 Jesus tells us that we are the "salt of the earth" and the "light of the world." As *salt*, our spiritual influence should act as a preservative (which was a common use of salt in biblical times), retarding the world's "ripening" toward its inevitable putrefaction. As *light*, our *active* presence is intended to keep the world from being engulfed by the powers of darkness. We should therefore be seeking in every way to bring a Christian influence to bear on our culture. We have a moral obligation to our children to make our society as safe and wholesome a place as possible for them to grow up in.

Because of this responsibility, as long as we stand a "fighting chance" (that is, society has not *entirely* hardened its collective heart against us and the gospel) we should never retreat from the spiritual battle that is being waged over our culture. If we do and the end does *not* come, we will have handed the destiny of Western civilization over to godless forces by *default*.

It has often been advised that Christians should be spiritually prepared for the end to come today while committing themselves to productive earthly endeavors as though it will not be arriving for centuries. This seems to accord with Jesus' teaching on the subject (Matt. 24:42–51; Luke 19:11–27). By maintaining *both* a heavenly *and* an earthly perspective, we can remain alert to the possible prophetic significance of world events without abdicating our responsibility to bring a Christian influence upon them.

Lessons to Be Learned

In our resistance of New Age inroads, though, should we be in every way "defenders of the status quo ante," as Donald Keys put it (*see* pp. 126–27)? I am convinced we need to recognize that in some respects the rise of the New Age movement is a reproof to the church for our undiscerning identification with society's status quo, and our considerable neglect of social matters. There are lessons to be learned from the Aquarian Conspiracy.

A Prophetic Void

New Agers are now occupying a prophetic void which the church has failed to fill. Not only have we failed to take a clear stand against certain cultural sins and vices which New Agers decry (for example, materialism, racism, neglect of the poor and oppressed, environmental abuse), too often we have been caught up in them ourselves. We have allowed our Christianity to be defined by our culture rather than challenging our culture by our uncompromising Christianity. In this sense the situation is not *simply* a black-or-white battle of New Age subversion versus some vague equation of Christianity with the "American way."

Historian Arnold Toynbee pointed out how in the past the church's refusal to reform itself gave rise to major antichristian movements:

Communism has been called a Christian heresy, and the same description applies to Islam as well. Islam, like Communism, won its way as a programme of reform for dealing with abuses in the contemporary practice of Christianity. And the success of Islam in its early days shows how powerful the appeal of a reforming heresy can be when the orthodoxy that this heresy is attacking is reluctant to mend its ways.[11]

The same phenomenon may well be happening today.

A Service Void

New Agers are also occupying a "service void"—meeting needs in areas the church has neglected.

As we saw previously, Aquarians have been in the forefront of reforms in health care, education, and business personnel "development." They have also led the way in such social innovations as food co-ops (providing alternatives to overpriced, chemically overtreated foods), hospices for the dying (which allow for a more humane environment than traditional institutions), local bartering systems and "skills banks," and women's "health collectives" aimed at protecting women from medical abuses (for example, unnecessary hysterectomies and mastectomies). Thus people in need must often go to New Agers for help, and in the process are exposed to occult spiritual influences.

Certainly, Christians also are involved in meeting needs (such as, ministries to substance abusers, unwed mothers, and the homeless). Nonetheless, there is a distinctive orientation to our social and political involvement. It is more supportive than transformative of established institutions and social processes.

A Need to Innovate

Because our faith has been historically embraced by the cultural establishment we are readily disposed to expend our efforts upholding or defending the traditional. But we are less inclined to concern ourselves with finding biblically acceptable solutions to the most strongly felt needs created by our rapidly changing society.

New Agers, on the other hand, do not perceive themselves tied to the established system. They feel, in fact, that a new system is needed. So they are more disposed to be *innovators*, developing alternatives to inadequate or outmoded social structures.

This makes clear that if the *church* does not act to meet legitimate social needs, they will be met by those outside the church, who will then have a greater stake in the emerging culture. In the meantime, the church will be increasingly perceived as irrelevant—part of the obsolete system.

It is quite understandable that when Christians do become politically and socially involved (as we increasingly have since the mid-1970s), it is usually to address immediate Christian concerns (for example, abortion, pornography, the stranglehold of evolution in the public schools). And generally speaking such efforts to uphold our Christian heritage and values *are* vital to the health of our nation—I do not mean to diminish them. But "conservative" is not *always* synonymous with "biblical." If we take a *predominantly* reactionary stance, and leave it to others to be on the "cutting edge" of social and political reform, we can only lose ground in the long run.

If we truly wish to influence world events, we must give more than superficial thought to how problems like the arms race, hunger, human rights violations, the energy crisis, and pollution can be solved. The global "megacrisis" *is* real, and will not go away by our ignoring it. To avoid these issues because New Agers are involved in addressing them is to allow *them* to be the ones who shape the solutions. If equitable, workable alternatives to the humanist's planetary society are not offered, the world will have no other option as global pressures mount. Global cooperation is surely needed to resolve these problems, and this will likely call for some adjustments in present political structures. But centralization of planetary power in one political entity is not necessary, nor is a world based on humanistic and New Age values. Such "solutions" could easily create more problems than they would solve—even if they *didn't* lead to the Antichrist.

A Need to "Infiltrate"

One more thing we can learn from New Agers (without copying their deceptive tactics) is to "infiltrate" the institutions of our culture. A Christian perspective desperately needs to be reintegrated into such fields as education, science, politics, the media, and the arts. Christianity *is* entirely relevant for the times in which we live, but we are largely failing to *demonstrate* this fact.

What then have we learned in the past few chapters? Faced with the rise of the Aquarian Conspiracy, the church needs both to discern and resist its cultural penetration. But we also need to respond to this challenge prophetically and creatively. For, while the first two responses are crucial, without the latter two they will ultimately prove inadequate. The bottom line is that if we want Western society to move once again in a biblical direction, we have to be willing to get more (redemptively) *involved* in society.

We have the numbers to create a "critical mass" of our own. But will we catch the vision and expend the effort? Ultimately, the answer can only be supplied by each one of us individually.

Channeling: *Spiritistic Revelations for the New Age*
(Part One—Background)

Anew wave of spiritism is sweeping America—the biggest since the initial American outbreak of the phenomenon in the mid-nineteenth century. The word *spiritism* refers to the practice of attempting communication with departed human or extra-human intelligences (usually nonphysical) through the agency of a human medium, with the intent of receiving paranormal information and/or having direct experience of metaphysical realities.

The current receptivity of the American mind to contact with spirits is reflected in a mid-1980s opinion poll conducted by Andrew Greeley and the University of Chicago's National Opinion Research Council. It reports that 42 percent of American adults believe they have had some type of direct contact with a person who has died. A decade earlier only 27 percent made the same claim.

The contemporary eruption of spiritism is called the "channeling" movement. Channeling could be called "Spiritism New Age Style." In his recent book, *Channeling: Investigations on Receiving Information from Paranormal Sources* (the only significant analysis of the modern channeling phenomenon that has yet seen print), New Age educator and psychologist Jon Klimo concisely depicts the exploding interest in this occult practice:

141

Cases of channeling have become pervasive. An increasing number of people are now seeking and following the guidance provided through channeling. Accounts of the phenomenon are sweeping the media. Dozens of new books said to be channeled are cropping up in bookstores. Millions of readers have been introduced to the phenomenon through actress Shirley MacLaine's recent best-selling books featuring her own dramatic, positive experiences with channels. All of this activity and visibility points to the fact that something very interesting and unusual is going on, and on a wide scale.[1]

What Is Channeling?

We will look presently at the differences between channeling and previous varieties of spiritism in America. It is sufficient to note here that channeling in all respects fits the definition of spiritism given above.

Although some (not all) New Agers would debate this, most cases of channeling can be described in terms of voluntary possession. Klimo observes:

> . . . channeling may be characterized primarily in terms of an *identity* (the source), apparently foreign to that of the channel, exercising *control* over the perceptual, motor, cognitive, or self-reflective capacities of that person once he or she has relinquished or altered control or sense of self-identity.[2]

Channeling vs. Biblical Prophecy

In their definitions of channeling non-Christian observers typically assume that it is fundamentally the same as the biblical phenomena of prophecy and inspiration. Even many professing Christians fail to see that there is anything unchristian about channeling. Laura Cameron Fraser, the Pacific Northwest's first woman Episcopal priest, chose to resign as rector of Saint Michael and All Angels parish in Issaquah, Washington, rather than renounce her belief in a channeled entity named "Jonah."[3] In defense of her involvement with channeling, which included conducting an informal class on the subject in her home, Fraser said: "My first exposure to channeled works was the Bible itself. It's hard to see what else we might mean when we say 'inspired writings.'"[4]

The Bible, however, portrays the practice of spiritism as the direct antithesis of inspired prophecy and Scripture:

> "When you enter the land which the LORD your God gives you, you shall not learn to imitate the detestable things of those nations. There shall not be found among you . . . a medium, or a spiritist, or one who calls up the dead. For whoever does these things is detestable to the LORD; and because of these detestable things the LORD your God will drive them out before you. . . . The LORD will raise up for you a prophet like me from among you from your countrymen, you shall listen to him" (Deut. 18:9–12, 15).

> And when they say to you, "Consult the mediums and the spiritists who whisper and mutter," should not a people consult their God? Should they consult the dead on behalf of the living? To the law and to the testimony [that is, Scripture]! If they do not speak according to this word, it is because they have no dawn (Isa. 8:19–20).

From these passages it is evident that Scripture condemns spiritism, not because people are seeking supernatural information and guidance (for which we have a legitimate need), but because they are seeking it from the wrong source. "Channeling" is not God's designated and approved means for communication between his realm and earth.

To seek supernatural information beyond what God has revealed can be likened to the primal sin in the Garden of Eden, when Eve partook of the forbidden fruit from the tree of the knowledge of good and evil (Gen. 3:1–7). Such an action is deemed evil because it disregards God's express will, and also because it maligns his character—implicitly suggesting that he is withholding something beneficial from his creatures, rather than trusting that he has good reasons for only revealing certain things.

Although the Bible does affirm the existence of good spirits (unfallen angels and "the spirits of just men made perfect"), efforts to contact them are never encouraged but rather prohibited. Saul lost his kingdom when, desperate for advice, he asked a medium to bring up the departed prophet Samuel, rather than inquiring directly of the Lord (1 Chron. 10:13–14).

Scripture allows that real spirits, capable of divulging extraordinary information, can be involved in spiritism (Acts 16:16–19), but it depicts them as deceptive and malevolent—in a different category than the good spirits mentioned above. The information they give is such a supernaturally sophisticated mixture of truth and error that their followers are incapable of sorting it out, and thus become entrapped in a web of deceit, suffering moral deterioration from involvement with such evil beings.

Biblical prophecy and inspiration differ from channeling, then, in that when they occurred, only the infinite-personal God of Israel spoke through the human instrument.

Another difference is that the biblical prophets and writers did not work themselves into a trance to "channel" God's words, as channels typically do for their "entities." It was always God who took the initiative, bringing his word to man, even in the cases when a trance was involved (as when a prophet saw a vision).

In spite of popular misconceptions (that is, the erroneous "dictation theory"), the Christian concept of inspiration is especially different from channeling. It holds that in the writings of Scripture a unique miracle occurred as part of God's special revelation of his salvation plan. The writers wrote from their own minds and circumstances, but were so moved and superintended by God that what they wrote was exactly what he wanted written—both their words and his. This is as opposed to channeling, where the personality of the channel moves aside so that another personality can communicate.

From Mediums to Channels—140 Years of American Spiritism

Deuteronomy 18:9–14 shows not only that spiritism had nothing to do with biblical prophecy, but also that it had a lot to do with the paganism of the time. In fact, spiritism has played a part historically in virtually all forms of paganism. Those who have allowed spirits to use their bodies in this way have been called a variety of names, including "shaman," "witch doctor," "medicine man," "oracle," "fortune-teller," and "seer."[5] In our own culture the common term has been "medium," but in recent years it has been largely abandoned in favor of "channel" or "channeler," reflecting, in part, a desire to break free of the negative stereotypes that have come to be associated with mediums over the years.

Although *medium* and *channel* can be and are used interchangeably, to many they represent two different eras: the spiritualist movement of the latter nineteenth and early twentieth centuries and the current New Age movement. This distinction is evident in parapsychologist D. Scott Rogo's definition:

> Mediumship is the art of bringing through spirits of the dead specifically to communicate with their relatives. Channeling I define as bringing through some sort of intelligence, the nature undefined, whose purpose is to promote spiritual teachings and philosophical discussion.[6]

The Spiritualist Movement

The evolution from traditional mediumship to contemporary channeling has been gradual. The original spiritualism had its start in 1848 in the Hydesville, New York, household of farmer John Fox. Rappings in the wall, presumed to be from an itinerant peddler who had been murdered on the premises and buried under the house, attracted great crowds, eventually giving rise to a transatlantic obsession with contacting "the Other Side."

Seances became common, complete with rappings and table tippings. "Sensitives" (people believed to be naturally endowed with the "gift" of mediumship) would "go into trance" so that people in attendance could make contact with their departed loved ones. "Automatic writing" (in which the medium's hand writes material not originating from his or her conscious mind, as though a spirit is in control) also became popular. Organizations like the Society for Psychical Research in Britain were formed in the interest of verifying the phenomena.

The modern spiritualist churches continue the tradition of this original movement, often employing many of the outward trappings of Christianity (for example, church services with sermons, evangelical hymns, and so forth) while remaining pantheistic ("everything is a part of God") at their theological core, with a strong emphasis on universalism (that is, that there is no hell—everyone will be saved).

Theosophy and Its Offshoots

When Russian-born spiritualist medium Helena Petrovna Blavatsky founded Theosophy (with the help of Colonel Henry Steele Olcott) in 1875, the slow transition toward modern channeling began. Instead of transmitting messages from "Uncle Harry" or "George Washington," Madame Blavatsky began to receive and transcribe spiritual teachings from superhuman "masters" or "mahatmas" allegedly living in the Himalayas. With its evolutionary and hierarchical view of the universe, and its syncretistic blending of multifarious Eastern and Western religious sources, the resulting material (including her two chief works, *Isis Unveiled* and *The Secret Doctrine*) laid the foundation for the modern New Age belief system.

Interest in Theosophy waxed strong (particularly in higher social circles) right as excitement about spiritualism began to wane, and thus a host of imitators appeared on the scene. In 1889 Blavatsky lamented:

> Every bogus swindling society, for commercial purposes, now claims to be guided and directed by "Masters," often supposed to be far higher than ours! . . . Only fourteen years ago, before the Theosophical Society was founded, all the talk was of "Spirits." They were everywhere, in everyone's mouth; and no one by any chance even dreamt of talking about living "Adepts," "Mahatmas," or "Masters."[7]

Since Blavatsky the Masters, those "highly evolved" custodians of earth's spiritual progress, have found no shortage of willing mediums, "prophets," "amanuenses," and so forth, to give voice to their teachings about the coming New Age, and what their disciples must do to prepare for it. Alice Bailey, through whom the "Tibetan master Djwhal Khul (D.K.)" wrote twenty-five books between 1919 and 1949, is the most notable example of these. Each of these channels would become the founder of a movement, and within each group the founders of competing movements would typically be looked on with suspicion, if not disdain.

Spiritistic "Bibles"

Additionally, over the past century several channeled "bibles" claiming to offer revelation especially suited to modern times have appeared, the most significant of which are *The Urantia Book* and *A Course in Miracles*.

The Urantia Book was received via automatic writing by anonymous individuals in the 1930s. It is 2,100 pages long and details a vast aggregate of ascending universes and evolving beings, and purports to disclose previously unknown information about the histories of the earth ("Urantia") and Jesus.

Extremely popular in New Age circles since its publication in 1975, *A Course in Miracles* is a three-volume set consisting of a large *Text* (622 pages), a *Workbook for Students,* and a *Manual for Teachers.* It was reportedly dictated clairaudiently between 1965 and 1972 to the late Columbia University psychologist Helen Schucman, who was a self-professing atheist at the time she first heard the inner voice. The Course sums up its message as follows: "Nothing real can be threatened. Nothing unreal exists. Herein lies the peace of God."[8] Although it liberally employs Christian terminology, such terminology is thoroughly redefined, so that the *Course* is in fact no more Christian than any New Age spir-itistic tome.[9]

"Seth" and the Rise of Contemporary Channeling

While writing poetry one evening in September 1963, author Jane Roberts (then thirty-four) of Elmira, New York, had a sponta-neous visionary experience.

> Suddenly my consciousness left my body, and my mind was bar-raged by ideas that were astonishing and new to me at the time. . . .
>
> Because of that experience, I began doing research into psychic activity and planned a book on the project. In line with this, my husband, Rob, and I experimented with a Ouija board late in 1963. After the first few sessions, the pointer spelled out messages that claimed to come from a personality called Seth.
>
> Neither Rob or I had any psychic background, and when I began to anticipate the board's replies, I took it for granted that they were coming from my subconscious. Not long after, however, I felt im-pelled to say the words aloud, and within a month I was speaking for Seth while in a trance state.[10]

So began the teaching career of "Seth." With her husband, Rob, taking verbatim shorthand dictation, twice a week Roberts would go into a trance and allow Seth to expound on metaphysical and physical subjects such as "the nature of physical matter, time, and reality, the god concept, probable universes, health, and reincarna-tion. . . ."[11] Portions of the resulting voluminous "Seth material" were organized into several books, including *The Seth Material*

(1970) and *Seth Speaks* (1972). Roberts also channeled a few books from other entities, and wrote a few more herself before she died in 1983.

The Seth writings have attracted a readership numbering in the millions. This attraction can be explained by pointing to the exceptional qualities of both Roberts as a medium, and the material she channeled.

Unlike the stereotypical medium, Roberts was intellectually engaging, articulate, personally believable, seemingly modest and unambitious when it came to her own personal following, and comparatively objective and nondogmatic about her experiences with the beyond.

The Seth material itself stands out as perhaps the most intellectually sophisticated and therefore believable of all spiritistic revelations. It has helped many one-time skeptics to accept the plausibility of such phenomena.

This widespread interest in Seth gave rise to the current channeling movement. Although Roberts's Seth had said that he would never speak through anyone but Jane, as early as 1972 Los Angeles New Ager Tom Massari was claiming to be a channel for the entity. Since Roberts's death at least a dozen "Seths" have appeared, one of the most popular being channeled by Jean Loomis of Connecticut. Additionally, throughout the '70s and '80s, and particularly over the past few years, a host of new entities have cropped up, all repeating in their own individualized (and usually far less sophisticated) terms the basic message of the Seth material: "You create your own reality."

With Seth was opened a new chapter in the history of American spiritism. All but unheard of before, it would soon become common for a disembodied entity to be more well known than his channel. By means of Seth's popularity the idea of receiving spiritual instruction straight from the Other Side (rather than through some human guru) caught on. This meant that it was no longer necessarily important how spiritually qualified an individual was to teach, since in the case of channels it was believed that a different, far wiser personality was actually doing the teaching. And yet, the person who offered his or her body to the spirit world for such use was still capable of reaping the fame and fortune that often follow spiritual stardom. A new vista of opportunities was opening for the many—particularly since it was now fashionable to believe that channeling was not a "gift" reserved for a select few, but a natural human potentiality that could be awakened and cultivated by all.

This popular rejection of the old idea that only a select few (like Blavatsky and Bailey) are chosen as mediums marks a key difference between the contemporary channeling scene and the previous era of Theosophical-style mediumship. The current sentiment is well expressed by author Hal Zina Bennett:

> Being an ardent Protestant by nature, I believe that the temple doors should be thrown open to the masses, and that we should each move forward to claim our God-given ability to have access to the Divine. Although from a historical perspective there was a time when a spiritual elitism was necessary, the single most important message of today may be that it is a time for the full democratization of our spiritual capacities.[12]

Today's channeling is also distinguished by the fact that the entities have left the cover of the dimly lit parlor or study and are increasingly coming into the public spotlight—at New Age expositions and fairs, in front of large audiences in hotel ballrooms, and even before the entire nation on television and radio. Although teaching remains their primary function, they now also provide counseling services, answer questions on call-in radio programs, and engage in witty dialogue with television talk show hosts.

Who's Who (or What) in Channeling

As a result of heavy media exposure in recent times, the names of certain channels/entities are becoming somewhat recognizable to the American public. We will look now at the three most popular channels and their entities, and then consider a sampling of other lesser-known but still popular personalities.

J. Z. Knight/"Ramtha"

Undoubtedly the most famous (or infamous, as the case may be) entity is "Ramtha," channeled by J. Z. Knight, an attractive former cable TV subscription saleswoman who lives in Yelm, Washington.

Knight has a Baptist background and "once claimed she had read the Bible, front to back, at least six times."[13] At some point in her fundamentalist experience, Knight suffered a change of attitude:

"I saw a lot of people condemned because they wore lipstick or they danced, or things like that," she remembers, or because they were black, she adds. She loved God, she says, and the emphasis on fear dismayed her.

Her mother, once "really intense" in the Baptist church, dropped out.

"They would tell me that my mother was going to hell and burning because she didn't go to church . . . I'd grab my mother and I'd love her . . ."

Soon after attending a bristling Baptist revival that frightened her thoroughly, J. Z. had what she believes may have been her first psychic experience.

At an eighth-grade slumber party, she looked out the window to see a huge, pulsating, blood-red object—oddly reminiscent of the preacher's warning that when the devil came, the moon would turn to blood.

Intense though those experiences were, J. Z. doesn't remember any particularly notable occurrences until Ramtha came into her life, she says (ellipses in original).[14]

That moment arrived, as the story goes, on a Sunday afternoon in February 1977, when J. Z. and her second husband (she is now involved in her third divorce) were devoting a weekend to experimenting with the alleged power of pyramids to preserve foods.

By Sunday afternoon they had become giddy, laughing so hard that tears came to their eyes. Looking up from her laughter, J. Z. saw what appeared as though "someone had taken a handful of gold sparkles and sprinkled them from the ceiling."[15] Peering closer to make sure it wasn't merely the light reflecting through her tears, J. Z. saw the sparkles take the transparent form of a bald, warriorlike man nearly seven feet tall. "I am Ramtha, the Enlightened One. I am here to help you over the ditch," he said.

And thus began a period of nearly two years in which Ramtha appeared to J. Z., monitored her thoughts and talked with her constantly as he taught her. After innumerable "adventures" and experiences, even a period in which she feared he might be the devil, she came to know, trust and love him immensely.

With J. Z.'s approval Ramtha then began to speak through her as a trance channel. The early audiences were small intimate gatherings in private homes. As the word grew, so did the audiences and the distances from which people would come to hear Ramtha speak.[16]

Now Knight regularly travels across the country for weekend "dialogues," usually held in hotel ballrooms, where as many as 800 people at a time gather to spend an evening in the presence of Ramtha. Ramtha's followers are estimated at 35,000, and include or have included a number of prominent actors and actresses, including Shirley MacLaine, Linda Evans ("Dynasty"), Burt Reynolds, and Phillip Michael Thomas ("Miami Vice").

What is so special about Ramtha, that "he" can attract such an impressive following? The answer lies partly in the mystique of a 35,000-year-old "Lemurian" warrior-king who conquered fabled Atlantis and made his way into India, before becoming enlightened and ascending to the higher planes—to be later exalted as the Hindu god Rama. And as far-fetched as this story may sound, the change that transpires in the feminine and seemingly fragile Knight when Ramtha takes over her body is enough to win over even most who come to her dialogues as skeptics.

Her movements, expressions, and voice take on a decidedly masculine quality. An unearthly perspective and insight into the lives of complete strangers is demonstrated. A radically different personality consistently comes through, with its own distinctive message, humor, intensity (Ramtha can remain highly animated for hours on end with no sign of fatigue), and (particularly distinct) speech patterns:

> I am Ramtha the Enlightened One. Indeed! Servant unto that which is termed as it were indeed the supreme cause, servant unto that which is termed the divine source, lover of that which is termed as it were indeed the divine presence, indeed that which is termed life, indeed that which is termed God, so eloquently put as it were indeed into that which is termed a singular word in what is called your understanding. Indeed![17]

Difficult as Ramtha's delivery may be to follow, in the minds of some it adds support to the notion that the one who is speaking is from a far-distant time, unaccustomed to modern patterns of speech.

Ramtha's continuing popularity is far from universal, however—even in New Age circles. One reason is his predictions of natural catastrophe, which have prompted as many as fifteen hundred Ramthaites to migrate to the Pacific Northwest. Channeling advocate Craig Lee is correct when he writes that "many [New Age] people now speculate that whatever [positive] energy came through J. Z. Knight has either shifted, departed or been replaced by a less benign entity."[18]

Jach Pursel/"Lazaris"

While attitudes toward Knight/Ramtha are mixed in the New Age community, channel Jach Pursel's popularity has been steadily rising without the same kind of attendant controversy. His entity "Lazaris" is favorably featured in Shirley MacLaine's 1987 book, *It's All in the Playing.*

Pursel claims Lazaris first came on the scene in October 1974, when he was a regional insurance supervisor in Florida. At the time he was too busy "climbing the corporate ladder" to be interested in spiritual things, but his wife Peny (who has since remarried) was very involved in "metaphysics," and he would occasionally meditate with her—only to doze off each time. On one such occasion, after he had seemingly fallen asleep, Pursel began to speak with a different voice. Asking him questions, Peny became convinced that another being was speaking through him. The same phenomenon repeated itself on several occasions, but Pursel could never remember the episodes. He recalls his reaction after he finally heard a tape of one session: "As soon as I heard this voice, I shut off the machine. I walked for about an hour. I was scared. I did not understand. I cried for awhile. Then, somehow, it became all right."[19]

Pursel named the entity "Lazaris" (pronounced with the emphasis on the middle syllable). Channeling Lazaris eventually became full-time work. Pursel spends as many as forty nonsleeping hours a week in an unconscious state while Lazaris conducts public lectures, weekend workshops, and private consultations.

Pursel, when himself, is intelligent and seemingly sincere, but rather ordinary and unimpressive—not the type one would expect to be at the forefront of the channeling field.

Lazaris speaks with an accent that at times sounds British, at times Scandinavian. Unlike Ramtha, his speech patterns are relatively normal and coherent. His talks display the orderly development of a prepared lecture.

Lazaris's appeal lies partly in his relaxed, amiable manner (Pursel's corporation, Concept: Synergy, promotes Lazaris as the "Consummate Friend"), partly in the practical, "how to" orientation of his teachings—he offers specific steps and techniques for implementing his principles.

Lazaris's popularity can be better understood by pointing to the similarities between him and Seth. Like Seth, Lazaris claims to be a multidimensional, multipersonal being (the one difference being that while Seth said he was "no longer focused in physical reality," Lazaris affirms that he has *never* assumed a physical form). Also like Seth (though not to the same impressive degree), Lazaris's teachings exhibit a sophisticated grasp of both metaphysical and psychological concepts. If one granted the truth of pantheism (which, obviously, I do not), Lazaris would be a comparatively believable entity.

Another thing Lazaris has in common with Seth is imitators. To counter this Pursel stresses on his videotape *Awakening the Love* that those who are also claiming to channel Lazaris are either "wrong or they're lying."[20]

Kevin Ryerson

The third of the "big time" channels is thirty-seven-year-old Kevin Ryerson, based in San Francisco and Santa Barbara, California. Ryerson differs from both Knight and Pursel in that he is more well known than his entities, of which there are several and not just one. Like Pursel, Ryerson enjoys widespread respect in the New Age community. Highly articulate about his work, and "professional" in his attitude toward it, his integrity has not been seriously challenged.

Ryerson's involvement with the paranormal goes back to his childhood in Sandusky, Ohio: "When all other kids were putting together model airplanes, I was studying ESP and Zener cards," he remembers.[21]

At the age of twenty-two Ryerson joined a meditation group based on the teachings of Edgar Cayce. (Cayce [d. 1945], famed for his psychic diagnoses of medical problems, apparently channeled some unnamed entity, who many New Agers believe was his "Higher Self.") Ryerson was a struggling graphic artist at the time, and hoped to tap some hidden reservoir of creativity through meditation. After six months of these sessions he surprised the group during one meditation by breaking into a demonstration of spontaneous channeling. An entity named "John" identified himself, and gave a metaphysical discourse to the group.

Over the following six months Ryerson experimented with himself until he was able to enter an altered state of consciousness and channel at will. For about a year he channeled for friends "as a kind of hobby," noticing that his channeled discourses paralleled those of Jane Roberts and Edgar Cayce, but he still wasn't convinced of their authenticity. Then, as he recalls:

> One day a medical doctor came in and reviewed several case histories with Spirit [that is, the entities], and I was astounded to discover that a large bloc of information came through on physiology, anatomy, and knowledge of the case histories that I didn't possess on a conscious level. I concluded that channeling could be a very valuable source of information and began to explore other areas of information that could be accessed—ranging from reincarnation and the essential nature of human beings to geology, physics, and future technologies.[22]

This emphasis on channeling scientific as well as metaphysical information is indicative of Edgar Cayce's influence on Ryerson, and no doubt Ryerson sees himself as carrying on the Cayce tradition. He has worked extensively with Dr. William Kautz, a former staff scientist at SRI International who now heads up the Center for Applied Intuition in San Francisco. The center is attempting to bring scientific respectability to channeling by using teams of reputable channels ("expert intuitives") like Ryerson in an effort to generate solutions to unsolved scientific problems.

Ryerson's career has been distinguished more by his interest in demonstrating the verifiability and practical value of channeling than by teaching. His entities do teach, though, usually in the context of private consultations or "readings." One such was the reading he held with Shirley MacLaine, which was instrumental in her New Age conversion, and which MacLaine, Ryerson, and two of Ryerson's entities reenacted in the January 1987 ABC miniseries *Out on a Limb.*

Unlike Ramtha, Lazaris, and others, Ryerson's entities do not claim to be particularly exalted beings, just disembodied spirits in between incarnations, trying to make the earth a better place to live (after all, Ryerson says, they've got to return here). Five in all, they include "John," supposedly an Essene scholar from the time of Jesus; "Tom MacPherson," an Irish pickpocket who lived in Elizabethan times; and "Obadiah," a Haitian herbalist and storyteller who lived 150 years ago.

The personalities are colorful, and the characterizations done well, so that watching Ryerson in trance could be entertaining if one lacked the Christian discernment that something very demonic is going on. That discernment is only reinforced by the entities' teaching, which is consistently occultic and antibiblical.

Lesser-Known Channels and Entities

One of the fastest-rising stars in the channeling galaxy is "Mafu," channeled since June of 1986 by Los Angeles housewife Penny Torres Rubin, a former Catholic. (Like J. Z. Knight and a high percentage of the others, Rubin has divorced and remarried since becoming a channel.) Mafu claims to be a member of the "brotherhood of light" in the "seventh dimension," last incarnated as a leper in first-century Pompeii. Torres has an entourage of devoted followers, has received a good deal of media attention, and has had, she claims, audiences with several very important people. (She was even supposed to have met with Moamar Ghadafi in September 1987.)

One observation that is likely to haunt Torres is that Mafu is almost a "carbon copy" of Ramtha. The speech patterns, persona, and teachings are all almost identical.

Another popular entity is "Dr. Peebles," who claims he was a Scottish physician and metaphysician in the nineteenth century. His shrill but cheerful-sounding voice opens every discussion with "God bless you," and then proceeds to offer medical or spiritual advice.

Dr. Peebles speaks through two Los Angeles channels: William Rainan, a psychic and teacher of the art of mediumship, and Thomas Jacobson, one of Rainan's former pupils who appears to be more in demand than his teacher. Previously having hopped from job to job, Jacobson, the son of a Congregational minister, now has "his own radio program, crowded workshops, and considerable financial success."[23]

Verna Yater, founder of the Spiritual Sciences Institute based in Santa Barbara, was rated at the top of a group of psychics tested by the Edgar Cayce-founded Association for Research and Enlightenment. She channels "Indira Latari," supposedly a nineteenth-century Hindu woman. Dialogues with Indira are featured in *The Butterfly Rises*, a recent book by Santa Barbara writer, philanthropist, and social activist Kit Tremaine. Yater also channels "Chief White Eagle," a Cherokee medicine man. The "chief" produces "powerful healing sounds," and gave a couple of live demonstrations of these eerie tones over national radio December 1, 1987. This occurred when Yater and Thomas Jacobson (along with their entities) were celebrated guests on the "Michael Jackson Show."

Unlike any of the channels we have considered so far, Darryl Anka, a thirty-six-year-old special effects designer from Los Angeles, claims to channel a *physical* being—physical, but not earthly. Anka's entity is "Bashar, an extraterrestrial from the planet Essassani."

Essassani is believed to exist "approximately 500 light years away," but we can't see its star because it is "in a different vibrational plane from us. . . ."[24] The inhabitants of Essassani are humanoid, we are told, "with large upturned eyes. They average five feet in height and have whitish, grey skin color. The females have white hair usually, and the males have no hair."[25]

This typical "space brother" (as outer space entities are often called) scenario runs like this: Bashar originally made contact with Anka by allowing him and some friends to see his spaceship in broad daylight over Los Angeles. The sighting spurred Anka into occult involvement, and during a channeling class Bashar made further contact. They now regularly "link up" telepathically so that Bashar can help earthlings with their spiritual evolution (since how we progress here affects the entire universe).

The list of channels and entities goes on and on. Psychic and parapsychologist Alan Vaughan channels "Li Sung," a small-town philosopher from eighth-century northern China. Nutritionist and psychic healer Iris Belhayes channels "Enid," an "earthy" Irish woman from the nineteenth century. Psychic healer Azena Ramanda is among the many who claim to channel "Saint Germaine," an Ascended Master from the "Seventh Ray." Psychic

Virginia Essene is one of an unfathomable number who claim to channel "Jesus." Former country and western singer Jamie Sams channels "Leah from Venus." Former legal secretary Taryn Krive channels "Bell Bell," a "giggly six-year-old from the legendary lost civilization of Atlantis."[26] For those who would prefer a "female" spirit channeled through a male rather than the more common reverse, full-time medium David Swetland channels "Matea," a "35,000-year-old spirit who once stalked the Earth as a 6-foot 8-inch black female spice trader."[27]

It seems as though there are disembodied voices claiming to be virtually every kind of entity people are capable of believing in (and is there any limit to that?). In her book *John Lennon Conversations* (Coleman Publishing) Linda Deer Domnitz channels the late rock star. "Merlin the Magician" dispenses his sage advice through a number of channels, including LA's "Diana, channel of light." The former luminaries of Scotland's famed Findhorn community (including Dorothy Maclean, Eileen Caddy, David Spangler, and R. Crombie "Roc" Ogilvie) have channeled everything from nature spirits, to fairies, to elves, to the Greek god "Pan," to angels, to "God."

"Group entities" are sometimes channeled:

> A group entity or group mind is described as a coherent bundle of still-individual or once-individual beings. As the individuals spiritually evolved, they claim, they reached a point where further growth meant pooling themselves into a larger Self.[28]

And, not to be outdone:

> ... physician/researcher Andrija Puharich, Israeli psychic Uri Geller, Texas channel Ray Stanford, and numerous others have separately experienced channeling from "Spectra," which is said to be an "extraterrestrial higher intelligence *from the future*," possibly computerized.[29]

One of the latest New Age crazes in Southern California is channeling dolphins. Sea World, San Diego's renowned aquatic park, has almost become "holy ground" in some circles. It was "shortly after an emotional visit to the Sea World aquatic exhibit"[30] that Neville Rowe, a former electrical engineer from Australia, became the first to channel the lovable sea mammals.

Rowe, who dresses entirely in aqua "down to his socks," offers group experiences with the dolphins. An advertisement entices the curious:

> Most in the group have experience of the dolphins' environment. Some find themselves swimming with them, some feel the water around—all feel their great love.
>
>   The dolphins are highly evolved and loving creatures, eager to assist us understand our oneness with all life on this Earth. They are more than willing to share their joy with us—to teach us to play![31]

And that about sums it up. Despite the tremendous diversity of these entities, there is a striking unanimity to their message: "All is one. You are God. You create your own reality." The channeling universe is one teeming with every conceivable kind of intelligent life, and each has one overriding concern: to help humankind make it safely into the New Age. (Apparently man's failure to realize he is God places him near the bottom of a myriad of evolving beings, even needing help from dolphins!)

The Current Channeling Craze

In previous chapters I purposely (to be fair, and for apologetic purposes) focused on the best examples of New Age thought and idealism. Therefore, this chapter and the next are helpful for achieving a more balanced perspective of the NAM. For channeling is "pop" New Age. Most New Agers include channeled teachings among their spiritual fare, and a growing number are making them their steady diet. Channeled teachings are certainly consistent with those of the larger NAM, but for the most part they lack the sophistication to sidestep the logical conclusions of such teachings. Thus, the unself-conscious narcissism and incredible gullibility that they feed on are an embarrassment to the NAM's intellectual and apologist wings. For example, the July 1987 issue of *Cycles* ("The Scientific New Age Magazine") laments:

> It's just more fuel for the fire of those who would consume us: the masses who just want to dismiss all of us as kooks and crazies, the ones who want to discredit the valiant and momentous ex-

periments of this loosely federated New Age only because it is unfamiliar and threatening.

What a shame. What a terrible shame.[32]

Such an outcry is a voice in the wilderness though. The mass of
New Agers march on after every new voice that sounds from beyond, naively assuming that if it's able to produce some kind of
psychic result in their lives it must be what it claims to be. And no
better example of this uncritical mindset can be cited than Shirley
MacLaine, who in turn has led thousands more down the same
paths of spiritual and intellectual abandonment.

The Influence of Shirley MacLaine

Although she is not commonly thought of as a channel (she does
claim to channel her Higher Self), Shirley MacLaine has been channeling's greatest friend. She has reverently sat at the feet of all of
the major channels, and by her endorsements has catapulted the
careers of each in his or her turn. Her own teachings (as presented
in her seminars) are derived from these sources and thus are indistinguishable from them.

The influence of Shirley MacLaine has been staggering. Her spiritual books have sold over five million copies. The *Out on a Limb*
miniseries, though not a ratings success (in spite of Kevin Ryerson's channeled prediction that "it will get the highest share of
anything on TV this year"[33]), has sparked an unprecedented interest in metaphysical subjects, particularly channeling.[34] William
Kautz and Melanie Branon predict that the miniseries

> will probably go on record as having drawn more public attention
> to "raising consciousness" in the 1980s than TM did in the
> 1960s. . . .
>
> The discoveries she shared have served as a primer in meta-
> physics for millions.[35]

MacLaine takes her role as chief evangelist for the New Age seriously. She immediately followed up her TV special with nationwide two-day seminars called "Connecting with the Higher Self."
These led fourteen thousand of her admirers into a step-by-step
acceptance of the New Age and channeling (using didactic and
consciousness-altering methods).

Also in 1988 MacLaine broke ground on her planned three hundred-acre-spiritual center in Crestone, Colorado (near Pueblo), funded by the proceeds from her seminars. She says one of the purposes for conceiving the center was "so everyone will know there's a place they can go for a really trusted trance channeler."[36]

A Booming Business

If people would travel all the way to Colorado for a "trusted" channel, we might assume that not every channel practices his/her profession from the purest of motives. And this is not difficult to understand, considering that there is now big money in channeling.

Ironically, by exciting public interest in channeling, MacLaine herself has contributed to this state of affairs. The *Los Angeles Times Magazine* reports that

> Neville Rowe, a Los Angeles channeler who charges $100 an hour, is pleased with the surge in interest, but also a little frustrated: It seems that MacLaine has not only inspired more customers, she has also inspired more people to become channelers themselves, so the competition is increasingly fierce.[37]

According to the *Times*, whereas a decade ago there were two known professional channels in Los Angeles, there are now well over 1,000.[38] Channels are now compelled to employ Madison Avenue psychology in the selling of their spirits. One full-page advertisement for two male channels closes hard: "As you are reading this, you can feel the call of your Higher Self. Be honest enough to listen. Be strong enough to act. Call now for more information."[39]

The channeling business is booming, not only in Los Angeles, but in San Francisco, Seattle, and dozens of other cities as well. People now go to channels, says Craig Lee, "the way they went to psychoanalysts in the 50s, or encounter groups in the 60s, or est weekends in the 70s."[40]

What kinds of services do channels provide? An advertisement for Taryn Krive gives a good idea:

> Through Taryn, a number of Spirit Guides bring forth their teachings and messages. They will answer your questions regarding this life and other lives. They will help you identify your life lessons

and unblock your highest potential for living and loving. They will help you to fulfill your life plan and advance to your next level of development. . . .

- Learn to communicate with your Higher Self.
- Meet your Spirit Guides.
- Learn to recall past lives and release their influences from the present.
- Develop your channeling abilities (conscious channeling, automatic writing, trance channeling).[41]

As always in a free market, the cost for these services varies according to the demand for the provider. In 1987 for a group session J. Z. Knight charged $400 per person, Jach Pursel $275. Private consultations with Pursel, for which there was at that time a two-year waiting list, cost $93 per hour. Kevin Ryerson charged "$250 per session, [and] has had so many inquiries at his San Francisco office that he is referring business to other channelers."[42] But, those who could afford such exorbitant prices could always find some entities within their means, like "Merlin and the Spiritual Hierarchy," who conducted group sessions once a month at the Sherman Oaks (California) Women's Club for only $12 per person.

The Appeal of Channeling

Evangelicals naturally stand back in astonishment at the channeling craze. Why would anyone part with $400 (or even $12) to spend a few hours in the presence of a medium? Haven't these people heard of the devil?

Christians need to remember that, in spite of the historic strength of evangelicalism in America, we are living in a biblically illiterate "post-Christian" culture. Most New Agers did not come to their present beliefs directly from Christianity but via secularism. (Even those who considered themselves Christian likely had a very watered-down, secularized faith.) Thus they retain the secular skepticism toward the Bible, both in its claim to be a special revelation from God, and in its depiction of an objective, personal devil. In fact, the very suggestion that something may have its source in the devil is all but taboo today, indicating to the contemporary mind that one is closed-minded, reactionary, and hopelessly out-of-date. Another factor which needs to be considered is that people from secular backgrounds are often acutely aware of a spiritual void within, and are looking for answers. When all of these considerations are taken together, it is easier to understand the present excitement about channeling.

There are several reasons why channeling is popular today. In an age when people frequently struggle with feelings of low self-esteem, powerlessness, and guilt, channels tell them that as gods they are worthy of self-love and respect, they are powerful beings, and there is nothing for them to feel guilty about. To a culture spoiled by conveniences like microwave ovens and automatic garage door openers, the entities typically offer instant and easy enlightenment.[43]

At bottom, however, is the need for answers. People want answers to everything from the ultimate questions about life and death to the more mundane problems they face in their daily lives. Rather than settling for advice from a mere human, even an "enlightened" human, through channeling they believe they have found access to a source of wisdom that transcends the human viewpoint.

Obviously, those on the Other Side are knowledgeable about things beyond the ken of mortal man. When someone who has experienced death reports back that all is well, the New Age doctrine that there is no death suddenly seems verified.

Channeling's ultimate appeal is its claim to connect man with a realm of reality greater than his own. As parapsychologist and channel Alan Vaughan observes: "The thrill, the immediacy of that contact with another consciousness, may be the driving force behind the phenomenal growth of the practice of channeling."[44]

There is more than a bit of irony in all this, though. The New Age movement has historically been attractive to secularists partly because it denied the need for special revelation (that is, the Bible), basing its rejection on the humanistically appealing premise that all answers can be found within. By its current obsession with channeling, however, the NAM is admitting by its actions that looking within is not sufficient—external help and information are necessary after all.

In Part Two we will explore the dimensions of this irony as we take a detailed look at the channeling experience, and the "revelations" it has produced.

Channeling: *Spiritistic Revelations for the New Age* (Part Two—Analysis)

Actress Shirley MacLaine calls trance-channel Kevin Ryerson "one of the telephones in my life,"[1] through whom she believes she can communicate with beings in distant dimensions. When the enthusiasm of celebrities like MacLaine is combined with the sensational nature of the phenomenon itself, it's little wonder that channeling has become a focal point of national attention.

In Part One we also gave channeling a good bit of attention, but from a Christian perspective. We saw that channeling is a New Age form of spiritism, a practice common in pagan religions, but distinct from biblical prophecy and inspiration. We traced its gradual emergence out of nineteenth-century American spiritualism, and noted that the modern movement got its start through the work of medium Jane Roberts and her entity "Seth." Seth has been followed by hundreds or even thousands of new entities, the most prominent of which are "Ramtha," channeled by J. Z. Knight, and "Lazaris," channeled by Jach Pursel. Thanks partly to the influence of MacLaine, channeling has become a booming business, its appeal being explained by several factors, particularly its claim to connect people with a source of wisdom and guidance that transcends the human viewpoint.

Now, with such basic information as background, this chapter will focus on some rarely considered (at least in any depth) aspects of channeling: the experience itself, and the teachings which result from it.

The Channeling Experience

As the channeling experience becomes increasingly common-place, it will generate more and more interest from such fields as sociology, psychology, and parapsychology. Already, scientific studies have been attempted, like the doctoral research of "trans-formational psychologist" Margo Chandley (International College, Westwood, California). Often, the questions such research attempts to answer would be of interest to all observers, regardless of their biases.

Who Becomes a Channel, and How?

Chandley's study produced some interesting data:

Childhood traumatic experiences were shared by twelve of the thirteen channels she researched. The experiences ranged from epileptic seizures, a shock from a fall, sexual or emotional abuse, neglect or abandonment by parents or peers. She said the channels withdrew into an interior life.

Also they all had had abnormal or mystical experiences—always when they were alone—between the ages of 3 and 11, Chandley said. Most had been raised Catholic. "They were already open to the idea of hearing voices. Saints have lives in other dimensions."[2]

My own research has detected an additional pattern: in all or nearly all cases some form of trance-inducing or occult (and thus biblically forbidden; see Deut. 18:9–14, and so forth) activity was engaged in prior to the alleged contacts from their spirit guides.

In most of the well-known cases, the prospective channel hears a voice asking him (or her) if he would be willing to serve as a channel for information needed to help mankind out of its present crisis. (Interestingly, the contactee is often first troubled by the thought: "This is the devil." But the entity's charm and seeming benevolence eventually win him or her over.) But with channeling's rising popularity, a new scenario is becoming common: the initial efforts to establish contact are made on the human side, by New Agers who have taken courses and/or read books on how to become a channel.

One such book, *Opening to Channel*, describes the feelings associated with the channeling experience:

> Some people go through shudders or strong physical sensations as guides come in, but that is rare. These sensations can usually be eliminated as the person opens and learns to handle the larger energy flowing through his or her body. The most common sensations are heat and tingling.[3]

Types of Channeling

Although by definition all channeling involves communications to humans from a supposedly nonhuman source through a human medium, the manner in which these communications take place can vary widely.

In *clairaudient* channeling (example: Alice Bailey) the message is believed to be dictated telepathically to and repeated by the human "amanuensis" or "messenger," who remains fully conscious and in control of his/her faculties.

A more clear-cut form of possession is *automatisms* (example: *The Urantia Book*), in which the spirit is thought to bypass the medium's mind and communicate via direct control of his or her body. Automatic writing, the Ouija board, and use of pendulums are all in this category.

Light-trance channels are common in contemporary channeling (examples: Darryl Anka/"Bashar", Alan Vaughan/"Li Sung"). Because they do not enter a deep-trance state, they are at least partially conscious when channeling, and have some memory of the experience afterward. Jon Klimo calls it a "temporary cohabitation of the seat of consciousness."[4]

In contrast, *deep* or *full-trance* channels (examples: Kevin Ryerson, Jach Pursel/"Lazaris") compare their experiences during channeling to sleep, and have no recall on resuming normal consciousness. Their voices and personalities usually undergo more noticeable changes than light-trance channels, presumably because they have *fully* vacated the seat of consciousness.

Full-body or *incarnational* channeling (examples: J. Z. Knight/ "Ramtha," Penny Torres/"Mafu") is similar to deep-trance channeling, except that instead of unconsciousness, the channels report experiencing something like the New Age conception of the death state, in which the spirit leaves the body and moves toward a distant light. It is this belief, that the channels have fully vacated their bodies and the entities have moved in, that gives this form of channeling its name. Consistent with this, entities such as Ramtha, Mafu, and Azena Ramanda's "Saint Germaine" do not exhibit the physical restrictions common to deep-trance entities (for example, sensitivity to light), but freely move about and interact physically and visually with their audiences. One other common characteristic is a convoluted and broken speech pattern that is peppered with repetitive phrases like "that which is termed" and "indeed."

Because of its newness and rarity, it is easy to view full-body channeling as a conscious creation of Knight, which Torres, Ramanda, and others have copied. But from the Christian perspective, there is no reason to deny the *possibility* that it is rather an advanced form of possession, suited to an acceleration of satanic deception in our time.

Some New Agers deny that channeling *is* a form of possession, since the channels "willingly allow entities to communicate through their bodies."[5] Others would agree that the word *possession* applies to any situation, voluntary or involuntary, in which an individual's speech and behavior appear to be taken over by another. The only difference is that in voluntary possession the controlling entity chooses not to force himself upon his human instrument. The Christian explanation for this seeming benevolence is that in voluntary possession the entities have elected to use the channel as an instrument of mass deception, and an enthusiastic channel serves that end better than a debilitated victim of unwanted possession. Nonetheless, we shall soon see that such voluntary relationships at times become involuntary.

Since Christians usually believe in spirit possession as a possibility for today, it is natural for them to assume that those teaching unchristian doctrines who also *claim* to be possessed, are indeed what they claim. But, lest I be justly accused of oversimplifying matters, there are other possible explanations that deserve consideration.

What's Going on in There?

Regardless of his or her biases the careful observer will find the question of what is really happening when a channel channels a difficult one to answer. This is partly because channeling is an intensely subjective phenomenon, involving unobservable parts of the channel's being. It is also due to channeling's complex and heterogeneous nature: at times it can seem convincingly supernatural, while at other times exceedingly natural. And this applies not just from channel to channel, but within the overall material of almost every channel individually.

The ambiguity surrounding channeling has generated some skepticism even in New Age ranks. For example, Ken Wilber, a highly regarded New Age thinker, expressed doubts about *A Course in Miracles,* a highly regarded channeled work:

> ... there's much more of [channel] Helen [Shucman] in the *Course* than I first thought. She was brought up mystically inclined. At four she used to stand out on the balcony and say that God would give her a sign of miracles to let her know that he was there. Many ideas from the *Course* came from the new thought or metaphysical schools she had been influenced by. . . . I found also that if you look at Helen's own poetry, you're initially very hard pressed to find any difference between that and the *Course.*[6]

It is interesting to note that channeling forerunner Alice Bailey said that 85 percent of channeled material comes from the personal subconscious minds of the channels.[7] Many of today's channels would substantially agree. Channel Joey Crinita of Canada believes that channeling is often nothing more than a form of self-hypnosis in which the imagination creates its own characters.[8]

If it is not that uncommon for *New Agers* to invoke theories of "dissociation" (in which part of the mind splits off from the whole and acts as a separate personality) to explain some channeling, one can imagine how appealing this explanation is to psychologists. It allows one to acknowledge the sincerity of the channel (which is often quite convincing) without having to allow for an otherworldly source.

Conscious fraud should not be discounted, though, at least in some cases. Highly theatrical channels such as J. Z. Knight particularly invite suspicion. As quoted in *Newsweek,* a former Ramthaite once saw Knight impersonate Ramtha without going into trance: "We thought she did a better job of doing Ramtha than Ramtha. In fact, we couldn't tell the difference."[9]

Such inconsistencies buttress those who would write off all channeling as a "scam." However, to those who have no bias against the supernatural as such, it should be clear that some channeling phenomena are *not* fraudulent, and might be best explained supernaturally. For example, cases of involuntary possession resulting from channeling feature symptoms so unusual that German psychiatrist Hans Bender found it necessary to create a new classification: *mediumistic psychosis*. Klimo reports:

> Some of the cases he reported would seem to us to be genuine channeling. Some of the incidents involving malignant-type entities led to (unsuccessful) suicide and murder attempts.
>
> By using automatisms, Bender said, splits of mediumistic psychosis led to disruption of normal personality that was different from schizophrenia. It does "not shatter the psyche into pieces," he wrote, "rather it creates functional units which act more or less independently of each other. It is not a splitting off, but a functional liberation of partial systems. . . ."[10]

It may be difficult to explain in strictly psychological terms why mediumship should produce its own unique set of disorders, but it is not difficult to explain biblically: Scripture leads us to expect just such derangements from involvement with demons (*see* for example Mark 5:1–7).

We have, therefore, three tenable explanations for the channeling experience: psychological dissociation, conscious fraud, and actual spirit possession. Each has its merits, but none seems sufficient to explain all phenomena.

Here I will venture to discuss a personal experience bearing upon this problem of ambiguity—my May 4, 1987, encounter with Mafu on the "Stanley Tonight" television talk show (KTTY, San Diego). As the spokesperson for orthodox Christianity on the program, I prayed for the "discernment of spirits" (1 Cor. 12:10) to know who or what I was dealing with, and I trust that is what I received—in two stages.

On the one hand, I did not sense anything directly or essentially supernatural about the *person* (supposedly Mafu) who was sitting next to me. On the other hand, I did discern *in* that person a seemingly supernatural ability to twist truth and manipulate the audience. What was particularly revealing was that the most powerful demonstration of this "gift" occurred early in the interview, *before* Mafu supposedly incarnated in Torres.

My conclusion was that "Mafu" is probably, at best, a dissociated part of Torres's own consciousness, and at worst, her conscious creation. But *in any case,* through practicing the biblically forbidden art of mediumship, she has become a satanically energized and guided agent of deception. In other words, even if Mafu is unreal, Torres is probably possessed.

It would seem that the facts call for a refining of the usual Christian conception of voluntary possession. As many channels are willing to admit,[11] in most if not all cases it is not simply a matter of a spirit taking over his channel's body and directly expressing his own words. To varying degrees, the channel's subconscious and/or conscious mind is also involved.

Thus the typical "entity" in channeling is partly—but not entirely—an objective reality. He is the combined creation of the channel and a *hidden* entity, which is in fact *real.*[12]

Brooks Alexander and Robert Burrows of the Spiritual Counterfeits Project have made an important point relative to this discussion: "Real entities do not have to be channeled for real lies to be told and real damage to be done. . . . The runaway popularity of a flagrantly demonic message is cause enough for concern."[13] With this thought in mind, we now turn from the entities themselves to the common message they bring.

Channeled Teachings—A Description

In spite of its many obvious commonalities with other New Age traditions, the channeling movement has developed a distinctive message of its own. As I mentioned in Part One, the central "truth" of this channeled "gospel" is the twin doctrines "You are God/You create your own reality."

"You Are God/You Create Your Own Reality"

At the core of channeled teaching is what might be called an "antibelief belief." It is held that our worst enemies are our own misplaced beliefs. Jane Roberts's Seth said that our beliefs are like fences that set boundaries to our experience—the only limitations we know are those *we* create.

There was one belief that Seth *did* recommend, though, which he set forth under three headings: (1) "The self is not limited"; (2) "There are no boundaries or separations of the self"; (3) "You make your own reality."[14]

There is therefore an interdependence between this antibelief belief, the doctrine that each person creates his or her own reality, and the belief in unlimited human potential. And all of these are based on a *pantheistic* world view which presupposes that the human self is by nature unlimited; a personal god who shares a common essence with the ultimate, impersonal God ("All That Is").

Taking their cue from Seth, every channeled entity has made this message his dominant theme, tirelessly and monotonously driving it home. Ramtha exhorts his followers:

> You be unequivocally God! You say you are tired of hearing the word? Never tire of hearing the word; you cannot say it nearly enough. . . . Do not reckon yourself less for if you do you will become the lessness of your reckoning.[15]

Certainly, the doctrine is not unique to channeling. Human potential groups like The Forum (formerly est) and Lifespring have always been based on it. But the entities apply it with a new consistency and boldness, taking it to its logical conclusions. Channel Iris Belhayes ("Enid") is not unrepresentative when she writes:

> It is difficult for someone living in some kind of intolerable situation, experiencing the throes of terrible physical illness or financial ruin, to think of it all as a game, but that is what it is, nonetheless. Not only are they playing a game, but they are playing their own game. The game that they created for themselves to play.[16]

"You Are Your Own Savior"

Deploring the way the Christian church has exalted Jesus Christ, the entities unanimously stress that they, like him, have not come to the world to be saviors, but to tell us that we are our own saviors. In Lazaris's words:

We have chosen to communicate not in order to save the planet, and not to save humanity, because clearly that is the human condition: to be saving itself. Rather, we are here to help people understand, to help people grow. . . .[17]

During an audience with Ramtha, a follower of Indian guru Bhagwan Shree Rajneesh was admonished: "You never become, ever, you never know God, ever, and you never know who you are, ever, as long as you follow another entity—ever."[18]

It is maintained that to follow another is to give away one's inherent power as a god. To achieve one's potential one must instead *take back* his or her power, becoming totally autonomous and independent.

"Love"

A lack of "love" is also blamed for our individual and collective problems. The entities affirm that our failure to love others results from our failure to love ourselves, and so they all extol self-love far above all other loves. Some carry this to a point of clear-cut narcissism, showing disdain for any expression of altruism. In a dialogue with one of his "masters" (that is, followers), Ramtha gave some typical advice:

MASTER: My main concern is what my path of service is in my life.
RAMTHA: To you.
MASTER: To myself and my fellow man.
RAMTHA: Don't worry about your fellow man. If you become happy, however they look upon you doesn't make any difference. The fact that you are happy and in service to Self is quite enough.[19]

In addition to self-love, "unconditional love" is a favorite channeled topic. This means total acceptance: not taking into account anything that is wrong with the one loved.

The difference between this and the biblical teaching of unconditional love (for example, Matt. 5:43–48) is subtle, yet radical. Love is so defined in channeling as to be the antithesis of judgment—where one is, the other cannot be.

When applied to God, this view of love would eliminate ultimate justice from the universe. God is absolutely permissive and accepting—there is no accounting for past sins, no retribution for wrongdoing. Ramtha expresses it quite clearly:

> Contemplate the love of God; how great this Entity-Self is, that is all encompassing; that will allow you to be and do anything you wish and hold you judgeless. God has never judged you or anyone.[20]

There Is No Death

The entities are also united in their affirmation that death, as such, is an illusion. What we call death, they say, is merely a transition to a higher plane, from which we will probably reincarnate in time, either on earth or elsewhere.

"Jesus," supposedly speaking through Northern California channel Virginia Essene, affirms that

> death is an automatic and nearly immediate entrance into a greater sphere of learning, growth, and service to which you are well-accustomed already. You then simply live at that higher level of purpose, joy and understanding. . . .
>   . . . .As you join daily with the greater YOU of God's expression, you will stop thinking of death as a catastrophic event and can assist others to cope with their fear or even terror of death.[21]

The Higher Self and Life Purpose

Another common theme in channeled teaching is the "Higher Self." Jon Klimo provides a good definition:

> **Higher Self.** The most spiritual and knowing part of oneself, said to lie beyond the ego, the day-to-day personality or self, and beyond the personal unconscious, and which can be channeled for wisdom and guidance; variations include the *oversoul*, the *superconscious*, the *Atman, Christ* (or *Krishna* or *Buddha*) *Consciousness, the God within*, or *the God Self*.[22]

Connecting with and channeling the Higher Self is a major goal for followers of channeled teachings. It is believed that one's Higher Self has all the answers, not only to specific problems, but to one's larger purpose in life. "Li Sung," channeled by Alan Vaughan, explains:

> Higher Self has the reasons why you came into this life in the first place. It was at the choice of the Higher Self.
>
> When you come into physical incarnation, you forget this, for you have to discover it moment by moment in this life. But the Higher Self's plan is geared not only to equalize karma from past lifetimes, but more importantly to promote the lessons in life that are most necessary for the soul.[23]

This near abandonment of karma (in fact, some entities have totally repudiated it) is a significant departure from classical Eastern and occultic thought. Instead of one's life circumstances being inexorably determined by the impersonal law of karma according to past deeds, they are determined by the subjective will of the Higher Self for the purpose of learning lessons. Apparently, the doctrine of karma was found incompatible with the current desire to create one's own reality immediately, directly, and autonomously.

Iris Belhayes lets us in on how the Higher Self plans its various physical lives between incarnations:

> After a period of rest and renewed joy, one may decide upon a new game to play in this physical universe. The time spent in between could be years or even centuries of Earth time. New game plans will be devised and shared—new or old spirit guides will be "chosen" for the new body experience. New parents and situations will be chosen, and off we go again.[24]

Spirit Guides

The "spirit guides" chosen before incarnating are believed to play a supplementary role to the Higher Self, prompting and inspiring people toward their higher goals.

"Orin" and "DaBen," the guides of *Opening to Channel* authors Sanaya Roman and Duane Packer, tell us that spirit guides are the reality behind the Christian conception of guardian angels: ". . . they will work with you whether or not you stick to your highest path or are even aware of them."[25] But Packer, Roman, Belhayes, and others encourage their readers to open up to the presence of these "old friends from the spirit world," so that they can receive direct guidance, enjoy their companionship, and even allow them to channel through them.

Channeled Teachings—An Evaluation

In Part One I noted that a particularly significant aspect of channeling to the Christian is its function as "special revelation." It needs to be clarified that only a loose use of the word "revelation" (that is, "spiritual information from beyond") can be applied to channeling.

In strict theological terms, a "special revelation" is a miraculous event: a breaking into the world of space and time by a supernatural, personal, speaking and acting God, to bring otherwise inaccessible and necessary knowledge pertaining to himself.

In a pantheistic world view like that of the New Age, however, God and nature are conceived as one, meaning that the category of the supernatural is ruled out, and with it the concept of miracles. Furthermore, the pantheistic God is impersonal, neither speaking nor acting, and space and time are illusions ("maya"). Thus, in classical pantheistic Hinduism there is no concept of revelation, strictly or loosely defined. Rather, spiritual knowledge is held to be always available, but it takes clear minds capable of penetrating maya to perceive it, like the ancient sages who wrote the Hindu scriptures. Revelation is therefore a concept that historically and properly belongs to the Judeo-Christian tradition.

The Irony of It All

In light of all this, how is it that the current rage of the New Age movement is a practice which purports to bring a loosely defined special revelation? If, as New Agers have consistently maintained, all answers lie within and therefore we do not need special revelation (that is, the Bible), why do we need channeling?

Azena Ramanda's Saint Germaine is typical of the other entities in his effort to "transcend" this logical obstacle:

The air is heavy laden with your questions. Leave your incomplete answers in your conscious mind, for within you, you have it all.

You have all the answers already. I am merely here to assist you and remind you that it is so. That you are already complete.[26]

But this only makes the discrepancy more apparent. Here we have special revelation (Saint Germaine's proclamations) to bring to our attention the *necessary* truth that we *don't need* special revelation! If we are complete and perfect, what's *wrong* with us that we don't know it? Isn't this very deficiency of knowledge (which is blamed for all the world's woes) an imperfection? The New Agers' endless quest for external help and answers corroborates the biblical view of man.

Sadly, because they pay more attention to intuition than reason, New Agers are increasingly recognizing the value and importance of special revelation without even noticing the inherent conflict:

> There are many times when celestial counsel is the only kind that has the perspective and vision to suffice.[27]
> . . . channels . . . can offer each of you an *otherwise unattainable* view of your past, present, and future.[28] (emphasis added)

Referring to a channeled message given by respected teacher David Spangler, psychologist Barry McWaters asked some important questions, but also indicated that he and other New Agers are not intent enough on finding the answers:

> This is just one of many such revelations, and of course we will receive them with caution and wonder. From whence do they come? Are they ill or well-intentioned? How shall we judge their validity? In spite of our suspicions of subjective projections and astral injections [that is, deceptive messages from "lower astral entities"], we *are* beginning to pay attention. We are listening for messages of guidance from every possible source; tuning in our astro-radios, talking to dolphins, and listening more and more attentively to the words of those among us with psychic abilities. Is there help out there? Is there guidance in here? Will anyone respond?
> "Yes" is the response, loud and clear—surprisingly with a good bit of general consensus.[29]

At this point the irony becomes almost unbearable for the Christian. New Agers are so desperate for transcendent guidance that they are willing to trust these new revelations even though they know of no sure way of testing them. If they now approve of the idea of special revelation, why don't they consult the Bible, the first and most influential revelation, for insight on these new arrivals?

In most cases, the sad answer reads as follows: because the New Ager began his (or her) spiritual quest with a bias against special revelation, he never gave serious consideration to the Bible's claims to be such. By the time he does recognize his need for outside help, his objectivity has been profoundly affected by mystical experiences (*see* chapter 2), and he now has a pantheistic bias. Naturally, then, he is attracted to the pantheistic revelations of channeling. When he finally does consider the Bible, he does so selectively and subjectively, interpreting it according to pre-established spiritistic categories, rather than seeking to understand it on its own terms (as any seeker of truth should do with a text claiming to be *the* written revelation of God). The result is that if the Bible is respected at all, it is respected as one more spiritistic revelation, while its actual meaning never penetrates his mind.

In this regard the Christian needs to challenge the New Ager with his inconsistency. If he recognizes that we lack knowledge and thus need spiritual information from higher sources, then he should also recognize that there *could be* critically important facts he has not considered—facts which would radically alter his world view. He should therefore not assume *anything* about reality *a priori*, even pantheism (which is by no means a self-evident fact; *see*, for example, Appendix C).

Were the New Ager to make an honest inquiry into the Bible, the Christian can be reasonably assured of three things. First, he would encounter a wealth of compelling evidence that it *is* a special revelation, including scores of historically verifiable miracles (the Exodus of the Jews from Egypt, the Resurrection of Christ, and so forth), hundreds of unambiguously fulfilled prophecies, the sublimity of its teachings and their absolute consistency with the world and man as we find them, and (not least) the peerless person of Jesus Christ, who endorses the *entirety* of Scripture as God's Word, and is himself its fulfillment (Matt. 5:17–19).

Second, in objectively reading the biblical text he would discover that theism, not pantheism, is among the truths it clearly reveals. God is assumed throughout to have an essence and identity distinct from his creation, and such is explicitly affirmed to be the case in numerous passages (*see* Pss. 113:4–6; 102:25–27; Rom. 1:18, 25; Ezek. 28:2).

Third, based on the above-mentioned evidence for the Bible's claims, he would find a *reliable* criteria for judging all subsequent "revelations." It would then become painfully clear that the channeling movement is blithely following the very voices the authentic revelation explicitly and repeatedly warned *would* come, and should *not* be listened to (for example, Matt. 24:4–5, 11, 23–25; 2 Cor. 11:3–4; Gal. 1:6–8; Col. 2:8–10, 18–19; 1 Tim. 4:1–3; 2 Peter 2:1; 1 John 2:18–23; 4:1–6).

Having identified "from whence they come," the seeker could now understand *why* there is "a good bit of general consensus" among the entities. For this consensus does not pertain to matters of past, present, or future fact, about which they constantly contradict each other.[30] Rather, it pertains to their antichristian teachings, and here the unanimity is so thorough as to indeed suggest an otherworldly source.

Unmistakably, then, biblical revelation answers the question of whether channeled teachings are "ill or well intentioned." But, specifically, what might the diabolical intentions behind the various teachings be?

Detecting the Demonic in Channeling

The repeated teaching that we are perfect, autonomous, and totally self-sufficient gods conditions New Agers to vehemently reject the basic gospel message that we are sinners, accountable to God for our sin, and incapable of saving ourselves (Rom. 3:9–20). The related teaching that we are in need of no savior but ourselves obviously is intended to close them to receiving salvation through Jesus, which is the primary satanic objective for each individual soul (Luke 8:12; 2 Cor. 4:3–4).

Because it implies that there is no objective truth, the idea that "we create our own reality" can effectively "short-circuit" a sincere quest for such truth, which could have led to Jesus. Once the New Ager accepts this premise, an almost insurmountable barrier to Christian penetration is erected. No matter how strong a case the Christian makes, the New Ager will respond: "That's *your* truth," incapable of seeing any direct relevance for his or her own personal "reality." (Again, *see* Appendix C for my suggested response.)

The channeled teaching on self-love is an exact inversion of biblical truth. Scripture portrays self-love as being right at the root of man's problems (*see* John 12:25; Rev. 12:11; 2 Tim. 3:1–5), while the entities offer it as the solution. (It needs to be noted that the entities combine in their definition of self-love the selfishness that the Bible condemns with the concepts of self-esteem and self-acceptance, which are not necessarily unbiblical, if viewed as by-products of a right relationship with Christ.)

The equation of unconditional love with total nonjudgment has insidious ramifications, since it creates a false picture of the biblical God as unloving, when in truth he perfectly integrates the equally necessary qualities of mercy and justice (Ps. 85:10). It also leaves the New Ager with the idea that the Christian message is essentially negative and unloving, putting us down to keep us down as unworthy sinners. In fact, its purpose is simply to face us with the truth about ourselves, for only then can we avail ourselves of what Christ has done to forever raise us *above* that condition. By teaching their followers to revolt against the very suggestion of judgment, the entities ensure that they will be unprepared to face it when it inevitably comes.

It has been rightly noted by many Christian observers that the core New Age/channeling doctrines, "You can be as God," and "You shall not die," were first uttered by the serpent in the Garden of Eden (Gen. 3:4–5). Embraced then, this "gospel" produced all of the world's misery. Embraced now, it will make all that God has done in Christ to remedy the situation of no avail to the individual in question.

We see then how the entities' endless hammering away at the above themes is evidence that a diabolical conditioning process is currently in an advanced stage, discernibly calculated to harden people's hearts against biblical salvation. At the same time, the entities' advocacy of getting in touch with and channeling the Higher Self and spirit guides is intended to result in a breaking down of the natural, God-given barriers to spirit influence and intrusion. As this transpires in an ever-widening cultural circle, the implications for our society are sobering, to say the least.

Implications for Society

Having considered several demonic intentions behind channeling for the individual, we must now contemplate what might be in

store for society, or even the planet. New Ager John White enthusi-
astically proclaims that

> it will not be long, fifty years perhaps, before "channeling" will be
> considered the norm rather than the exception . . . One's "teachers"
> or "spirit guides" will be as common as one's professors at a univer-
> sity.[31]

William Kautz and Melanie Branon envision channeling's being
integrated into the work of science, business, education ("side by
side with conventional, rational instruction"), the decision-
making process of government ("a step beyond democracy"), and
virtually every branch of society.[32]

The reader should be advised that this vision is not mere fantasy.
While its fulfillment is not likely to happen overnight, significant
trends in this direction can be observed in all of the fields mentioned, with the partial exception of politics.

What are the implications? First, our already torn social fabric
would be virtually shredded by a broad acceptance of the amorality,
hedonism, social and familial irresponsibility, lack of compassion,
and devaluation of human life (at least in *this* "incarnation") that
can be found in much, and strongly characterizes some (for example, J. Z. Knight's[33]) channeled teachings. But second, a larger
pattern is becoming discernible. The New Age/channeling movement is signaling a return to a superstitious, animistic culture.

Progressively, facets of nonhuman nature are having intelligence
(equal, if not superior to, humans) ascribed to them. Dolphins, plants,
and heavenly bodies together with an ever-expanding pantheon
of spirits are supposedly concerned with and seeking to influence
human affairs—just as in ancient and modern primitive cultures.

The socially static nature of such primitive cultures is directly
related to the control that the spirit world (or their belief in it) has
over them. World religion authorities typically use the word *fear* to
characterize these socioreligious systems. While the world they
believed in may seem mythical to us, it seemed plausible enough
to their limited knowledge, and was probably reinforced by actual
spirit manifestations.

It could be that a similar kind of situation is being orchestrated
today by the same spirits, only pandering now to the *Space Age's*
conception of what the "beyond" must be like—a slightly more
sophisticated mythology.

Satan's intention for society would then be, at the minimum, to bring it under an abject subjugation to himself, not unlike the hold he has had over the darkest pagan cultures. Beyond this, I expect that there are apocalyptic designs behind this activity, especially since the channeled material seems to be preparing New Agers for events chillingly similar to those described in the Book of Revelation.[34]

A Critical Shortage of Discernment

With all this cosmic evil lurking just beneath the surface of channeling, it is staggering to observe how unreservedly and unquestioningly many New Agers throw themselves into the experience. "There is absolutely nothing to fear in delving into one's inner beingness. There is only truth and beauty to be found there," says Iris Belhayes.[35]

It is true that the more critically thinking participants (including Jach Pursel[36]) recognize that not all entities can be trusted, and stress the need to "test the spirits." But the criteria they suggest are always faulty, containing pantheistic presuppositions which themselves are not open to testing, and which result in a naivete where the entities are concerned. (After all, if everything is a part of God, how can any entity *really* be evil?)

For example, a typical New Age approach to discerning the spirits was arrived at by sociologist Earl Babbie and his wife Sheila after interviewing several entities through their channels:

> Assuming it's real, how do you tell a good from a bad entity? The way we've been approaching it is, ask the entities that. And we're starting to see some consensus emerging . . . it has to do with *empowerment:* If the entity is trying to get you to follow it or is trying to get you to give up your power to it, then you should really watch out . . . Many of the entities say they are intending to put themselves out of business. They want to just empower people to get in touch with their own intuition or higher Self or whatever . . . [so] that in the future everyone will be kind of channeling something.[37]

Clearly, the Babbies are not prepared to match wits with supernatural evil. It is folly to assume that the entities' motives can be discovered by merely asking them if they are good or bad: "Even

Satan disguises himself as an angel of light" (2 Cor. 11:14). Biblically it is clear that whether the entity wins someone as his follower, or teaches him or her how to be possessed by another entity,
Satan's purposes are well served.

All New Age approaches to discernment are critically flawed by
the assumption that *any* channeled entity could be good. Were
they to consult Scripture they would see, as we saw in Part One,
that God condemns *all* forms of spiritism, and thus any real entity
involved is evil. Channeling, therefore, will invariably be harmful
to all participants, active or passive.

Robert Shell was head in the 1970s of the Roanoke, Virginia,
Ordo Templi Orientis (OTO), a secret society based on the teachings of the notorious occultist Aleister Crowley. Shell believed he
was in contact with the "secret chiefs," a group of entities roughly
equivalent to the "masters" of Theosophy. After two years of objective research into spiritism, he made an observation which is particularly noteworthy, since it was not at all influenced by Scripture:

> It seems that at any given point in history these entities, whatever
> they are, couch themselves in the form most likely to be accepted
> by the mind they contact. Thus the occultist has his invocations of
> spirits, good and evil, and the Saucerian has his space people. How-
> ever, on one point only can we look to the literature and be certain:
> that such contacts are always detrimental to the physical and the
> mental well-being of the contactee. . . .[38]

Though not directly referring to spiritism, in John 10:10 Jesus
made an observation that is applicable to our discussion: "The
thief comes only to steal, and kill, and destroy; I came that they
might have life, and might have it abundantly." Historically,
though the entities are capable of appearing quite benevolent, they
have always proved themselves in the long run to be thieves, robbing and destroying, not giving and healing.

Such a warning will understandably be difficult for many New
Agers to hear, since the entities have seemingly filled a deep void in
their lives, bringing a sense of purpose and love, and the hope of a
happy life beyond the grave. But no one who takes heed to this
warning need remain empty. Those of us who have taken Jesus at
his word have not been disappointed, receiving, as he promised, an
abundant, purposeful life. We've also found that the "sting of
death" has been removed by the historic reality of his own triumph

over it, which he has promised to share with those who are his (John 10:25–26; 1 Cor. 15:51–57). All that the entities offer can only be a fleeting counterfeit of what Jesus permanently gives.

Had we the power to fully create our own realities (which we do not; *see* James 4:13–16), we could never dream of a future as glorious as that which he has offered to create for each of us (Rev. 21:5–6; 1 Cor. 2:9; Eph. 3:20). To experience it, we need only turn our futures over to him.

Appendix A
Eight Common Questions Answered

When I lecture on the New Age movement (NAM) I need to leave plenty of time at the end for questions and answers. It seems that everyone has a particular set of unanswered questions on this exceptionally broad and varied subject. And though this book itself has been exceptionally broad in its scope, there have inevitably been questions (pressing to some) that did not fall within the range of its main chapter topics. The purpose of this appendix, then, is to list and then provide answers to several of these questions, while at the same time providing a handy summary of the relevant facts on the NAM.

1. What exactly is the New Age movement?

Please note that definitively answering this seemingly direct and simple question is actually so complicated and involved that I have devoted all of chapter 1 to doing it. But to be as concise as possible: The New Age movement, properly defined, is an extremely large *metanetwork* ("network of networks") composed of people and groups who share common values and a common vision. These values are based in Eastern/occult mysticism and pantheistic monism (the world view that all is One, and this One is God), and the vision is of a coming era of peace and enlightenment, the "Age of Aquarius."

New Agers come from a wide variety of independent traditions and persuasions, and may differ on a number of more peripheral matters. But their agreement as to their basic values and vision is sufficient for them to "network" (cooperate) with one another to help influence society in the direction of their values and vision.

The fact that New Agers are actively seeking to shape our cultural future suggests a second, more loosely defined way in which people think of the NAM: It has become a *third major social force* vying with traditional Judeo-Christian religion and secular humanism for cultural dominance. But this would make the

183

NAM more than *just* a network or movement: it is also a *major cultural trend*. It represents a *historical movement* that can be traced over a period of more than two centuries in the West *from* orthodox Christianity *back to* paganism.

In this perspective secularism can be viewed as little more than a "bridge" that has made this cultural return to our pre-Christian roots intellectually and psychologically possible. And so, finally and most significantly, the New Age movement is a *resurgence of paganism*. It is the *occult going public* or *"coming out of the closet"* after centuries of hiding itself (in fact, "occult" *means* "that which is hidden") at the cultural periphery because of the dominance of Judeo-Christian beliefs and values. (*See* chapter 1 for a more detailed description of this).

2. Why is "New Age" so popular today?

It would be impossible to attempt here a comprehensive description of the many factors contributing to the rise of the NAM, but five in particular seem noteworthy: 1. The New Age appears to offer a spiritual basis to life (purpose to life, life after death, a means to directly experiencing transcendent realities, and so forth), thus filling the void created in our culture by secular humanism. 2. While orthodox Christianity also offers the above, it is often perceived as being at odds with science and therefore obsolete, while New Age teaching affirms the theory of evolution and claims to be right at the "leading edge" of all the newest theories in the physical, social, and behavioral sciences (*see* chapters 2 through 4). 3. In keeping with this emphasis on being contemporary, it claims to have answers to the personal and social complaints of modern life (for example, materialism, loneliness, powerlessness, pollution, the nuclear threat). 4. It often tolerates rather than challenges such unchristian behaviors as sex between unmarried partners, homosexuality, and (in some circles) recreational use of drugs, thus providing a spiritual alternative to the many in our time who are unwilling to abandon such lifestyles. 5. Perhaps most significantly, it appeals to man's primordial, sinful desire to be a god, independent of the creator God (Gen. 3:4–6).

3. In what ways and to what extent has the New Age movement penetrated our culture?

One way of gauging the growing popular interest in things "New Age" is the exploding demand for New Age books in the stores of major retailers like B. Dalton Booksellers and Waldenbooks. Both of these chains now have New Age sections, reflective of a 60 percent growth of interest evident in 1987 alone. As one representative of Waldenbooks put it: "Now the average mainstream customer is shopping in these sections, which they never would have done before." (*Publishers Weekly,* 25 Sept. 1987, 30). Add to this the fact that New Age or "metaphysical" bookstores have doubled over the past five years to 2,500. Major publishing houses like Bantam and Ballantine have developed entire New Age divisions.

One of the most influential cultural establishments, the arts and entertainment media, has been deeply infiltrated by the New Age movement. Shirley MacLaine is the most visible and best example of a celebrity using her popularity and influence to promote the New Age. But there are numerous others, including singer and actor John Denver, singer and actor Willie Nelson, singer Tina Turner, jazz musician Paul Horn, film producers George Lucas and Steven Spielberg, actor Dennis Weaver, actress Sharon Gless ("Cagney and Lacey"), and actor Levar Burton ("Roots" and "Star Trek: The Next Generation"). Films like Lucas's *Star Wars* and Spielberg's *Poltergeist* and television series like "Star Trek: The Next Generation" and the 1972–75 favorite "Kung Fu" (starring David Carradine) have propounded pantheism, mysticism, and occultism.

In addition, New Age views have been given frequent airing on all three of the major daytime "talk" shows: "Oprah Winfrey" (who is a self-professing New Ager), "Phil Donahue," and "Geraldo."

The Public Broadcasting System (PBS) has often served the New Age cause, not only by the frequent proevolution, anti-"fundamentalist" bias that colors much of its otherwise commendable programming, but more recently by bold ventures into New Age propagandizing. These include two 1988 efforts. "The Power of Myth," Bill Moyers's extensive interviews with the recently deceased mythologist Joseph Campbell, subjected the viewer to heavy and extended "doses" of New Age indoctrination (were evangelical beliefs so promoted on public television, it seems highly unlikely that it would have been tolerated). Extremely successful with viewer and critic alike, the series was rated the top television program of 1988 by *The Boston Globe*. The other, a nine-part series "How then Shall We Live?", is perhaps *the* classic example of the "Aquarian Conspiracy" utilizing television—intended to produce "psychological transformation, political empowerment, and spiritual awakening" in the viewer ("PBS Series Enters 'New Age,'" *Satellite TV Week*, Pacific Edition, Feb. 7–13, 1988).

Other social arenas into which the NAM has made substantial inroads include health care, education, and business. All of these are described in some detail in chapter 5. New Age inroads into science and politics, which are less pervasive but still significant, are described in chapters 2 and 6 respectively. A particularly disturbing area of New Age penetration is the church (*see* question 6).

The NAM's growing entrenchment in such cultural structures as those described above is a strong sign that it is not a passing fad. The NAM as cultural trend could continue long after the NAM as recognizable movement inevitably disperses into new cultural forms (as happened with the counterculture of the 1960s). Embedded in our cultural establishments, New Age beliefs and practices are now able to exert a much stronger influence on the popular mind than they did when they were clearly identified with an occult cultural fringe.

4. What are good criteria for identifying New Agers?

By definition a New Ager is someone of whom all of the following is true: he or she (1) *believes in pantheism and many or all of its attendant doctrines* (for example, salvation by "gnosis" or experiences of enlightenment, karma, and reincarnation, spiritual evolution, ascended masters); (2) *engages in mystical or occult practices and/or has had such experiences* (for example, astrology, psychic healing, magic, various methods of inducing trancelike states of consciousness, use of crystals or pyramids for psychic reasons, out-of-body experiences like "astral projection"); (3) *believes in the coming New Age* (that is, an age of peace and mystical enlightenment); and (4) *seeks to hasten this New Age by participating at some level in the New Age networking process.* If some but not all of these criteria are true of an individual, then it can be said that the person has *affinities* with the NAM, but not that he or she is a New Ager. (Of course a person who does not fully fit the criteria of a New Ager, like a secular humanist or a Hare Krishna, is not necessarily any closer to the Christian position for not being New Age.)

In addition to the certain criteria given above, there are numerous signs of *possible* New Age involvement. These include questionable *terminology* (for example, use of the term "New Age" itself, "new paradigm" or "paradigm shift," "transformation," "global vision"); questionable *political convictions* (such as, advocacy of a "new world order," a "planetary guidance system," "Green" politics—*see* chapter 6); and questionable *personal or organizational associations* (for example, has ties with or recommends the Association for Humanistic Psychology, the Association for Holistic Health, or some New Age writer like Norman Cousins or Elizabeth Kübler-Ross).

Please note that while such signs can indicate a need for further inquiry, they are *not reliable in themselves* for determining if someone is a New Ager (unless, of course, the *organization* the individual belongs to fulfills the criteria for "New Age" given above). There are no (or almost no) political convictions that automatically make one a New Ager (as unchristian as the views *may* be). And New Agers do not have "copyright" on such terms as "new age" or "transformation," which Christians were using long before occultists adopted them. Furthermore it is possible and permissible for Christians to appreciate and quote the insights of a Norman Cousins or an Elizabeth Kübler-Ross in particular respects, without agreeing with their basic spiritual message. Therefore, to avoid the harmful, all-too-common extreme of branding non-New Agers as New Agers, it is vital to evaluate the *context* of their language, convictions, and relationships. Do they exhibit the four defining features of a New Ager listed above?

5. What should one be alert to if he or she wishes to avoid New Age influences and activities?

No Christian is immune from exposure to New Age influences. This is because some New Agers consider themselves Christians, and thus move about in Christian as well as New Age circles. Furthermore, many Christians are unclear as to exactly what is unchristian about the New Age, and thus ignorantly absorb and then impart such influences to other Christians.

"Christian" New Age language can at times sound very close to that of biblical Christianity. However, there are certain distinctively New Age phrases that an orthodox Christian is highly unlikely to use. These include such names and terms as "Christ consciousness," "Jesus *the* Christ" (though not unbiblical *per se*, this phrase is used to accentuate the supposed difference between the man Jesus and the "Christ principle"), "the Master Jesus," "the I Am Presence," and the "God" or "Christ within."

The Christian may also cross paths with the New Age while simply conducting the mundane business of his or her life. This is particularly the case when it comes to health care. New Age healing techniques are often being employed, not just by the unorthodox healers that can be found in most any town, but by the family doctor or community hospital. To discern New Age therapies, a key word to be aware of is *energy*. Most New Age healing invokes some theory of energy to explain how it works, but upon inquiry one finds that it is not a *scientifically explainable* or *physical* energy. Instead there will be a vague reference to something like *"cosmic"* or *"universal"* or *"life"* energy, based on a pantheistic view of the universe. Most often the practice itself has been derived from occultism, or some pagan tradition. Thus if it *does* work, it could well be by an ungodly supernatural force, which would predictably have a destructive spiritual effect on the patient.

Another doorway to the New Age that is often ignorantly entered is various human potential "trainings." In general, Christians should avoid *any* approach to "getting your life together" that is not biblically based and Christ-centered. The claim of human potential programs like the Forum and Lifespring to be religiously neutral is false—they are based on humanistic and Eastern mystical presuppositions that directly contradict biblical faith. And any method for achieving more in life that portrays low self-esteem as the *root* of *all* our problems should likewise be avoided.

Additionally one should steer clear of all techniques for increasing relaxation, creativity, concentration, and so forth that involve repeating words or visualizing objects in order to suspend normal thought processes. Such altered states of consciousness are the breeding ground for mystical and occult activity of all kinds. This warning also applies to using the imagination (whether on one's own or in some form of guided imagery) to leave the body, contact "counselors" or "wise persons," or in any way *manipulate* the spiritual realm.

Finally New Age influences must also be watched for in the realm of social and political causes. Concerns which may be innocent and valid in themselves are often utilized by New Agers to promote ends in conflict with Christian values and interests. If an evangelical gets involved in a seemingly nonreligious or "neutral" cause, he (or she) should ask himself whether the approach being advocated to meet the particular need would contribute to the New Agers' "grand solution" of a one-world political arrangement based on New Age values. (For more on this, *see* chapter 6.)

6. Do you agree with Dave Hunt *(The Seduction of Christianity, Beyond Seduction)* that the New Age movement has profoundly infiltrated the church?

If the word *church* is used broadly to include all of the historically orthodox communions, including Roman Catholic and mainline Protestant, then my answer would be an unqualified *yes*.

A dramatically growing movement within Roman Catholicism goes by the name of "Creation Spirituality." Conceived and spearheaded by Dominican priest Matthew Fox, it espouses hard-core New Age philosophy with a Catholic Christian gloss. (Although Fox is under Vatican discipline at the time of this writing, this may only serve to add fuel to his movement.)

In both liberal Catholic and liberal Protestant circles, the widespread acceptance of meditation, yoga, *A Course in Miracles,* and various human potential trainings has long provided an open door to New Age inroads, so that now it is not uncommon to find a local parish or congregation saturated with such elements.

"Process theology," currently in vogue among liberal Protestant theologians, has many affinities with New Age thinking (*see* chapters 3 and 4). This theology is now making inroads into evangelical circles, especially among those who do not hold to the complete inerrancy of Scripture.

It is possible indeed to envision how such trends could increasingly lead to "the seduction of Christianity."

What made Hunt's *Seduction* one of the most controversial Christian books of the 1980s, however, was its emphasis on *evangelical* leaders and movements knowingly or unknowingly promoting New Age teachings and practices. It seemed as though no quarter of the evangelical church was safe from Hunt's "heresy hunt" or "inquisition," as some termed it. But many of the trends Hunt has been critical of are deserving of criticism.

For example, the distinctive teachings of the "positive confession" or "word-faith" movement—that believers are "little gods" who have a divine right to health and prosperity, and who can sovereignly "speak things into being" through the power of their own words and faith—do have more in common with New Age "metaphysical" teachings than with the biblical doctrines of regeneration and faith. But the larger context of these positive confession teachings is biblical theism (however imperfectly stated), not New Age pantheism. The people responsible for them would all appear to be biblically erring Christians, not maliciously conspiring New Agers.

The same probably applies to most of those evangelical movements which are deserving of Hunt's criticism. Therefore, while such teachers can rightly be charged with compromising some of the distinctives between biblical truth and New Age error (which could lead their "spiritual descendants" directly into the New Age), they should not be viewed as an incursion of the New Age movement itself into the church. This is not to deny, however, that there are some actual New Agers operating within the field of evangelical Christianity, even in leadership positions! And we can realistically expect this to be a worsening problem in the years ahead.

Beyond making some (at least partially) valid criticisms Hunt has made a contribution that many have failed to appreciate. He has provoked the church to address several issues that critically *need* to be examined, lest we risk contamination from the increasingly pagan culture that surrounds us: To what extent is psychology compatible with Christianity, and how dependent should the church be on it as a pastoral resource? Are the concepts of self-love and self-esteem valid for the Christian, and, if so, how important are they as compared to other Christian values? What is the place of the imagination in the Christian's devotional life and ministry? Is the practice of "inner healing" a valid biblical ministry?

Unfortunately the answers which Hunt provides to these questions tend to be simplistic, thus fueling unnecessary controversy and division within the church. For example, while I agree with him that there are many ungodly elements in the field of psychology, I find his blanket condemnations unconvincing and inflammatory. Even unchristian men like Sigmund Freud and Carl Jung were/are capable of discovering true principles of human behavior and personality dysfunction. There is no reason why a biblically grounded Christian could not discern what is true in these systems and then integrate such truth into a biblical framework. Thus, I disagree with Hunt when he claims that there can be no Christian psychology, and that all attempts at it are only a "Trojan horse" bringing humanistic and New Age influences into the church.

Hopefully, the long-term good derived from Hunt's having raised these issues will outweigh the immediate harm caused by his divisive approach.

7. What is a Christian to make of the New Age "crystal craze"?

New Agers place a lot of stock in "vibrations." Everything in the spiritual realm is supposed to operate according to exact scientific law, so spiritual energy or healing energy is thought to transmit at definite, very high vibration levels or frequencies. Aware that crystals serve as good energy transmitters in electronics (used in watches, radios, computer chips, lasers, and so forth), New Agers assume that they must also be good for transmitting and amplifying other kinds of frequencies as well. Consequently an incredible body of lore has quickly developed about the energizing powers of crystals (for example, crystals supposedly generated the power supply for the lost continent of Atlantis).

The energy receiving and sending capacities New Agers attribute to crystals (without scientific basis) seem endless: They can attract desirable and repel undesirable forces. They can store information that New Agers psychically program into them, and then radiate these "positive images" back to the New Agers to help them achieve goals like weight loss or confidence. They can absorb, stimulate, amplify, and focus every spiritual and healing force, and thus are used to aid a variety of New Age therapies, like psychic healing, acupuncture, "dream work," and aura and "chakra" cleansing and balancing. They are also used to enhance meditation, visualization, magic, "astral" or "soul travel", channeling, and various forms of divination. They are worn on the body to attract prosperity, the opposite sex, and general good luck, and are even placed on or near plants to help them grow, carburetors to keep them running, and refrigerators to bring electric bills down.

Is all of this pure superstition, or might there be some occult power in back of it? In all probability New Age credulity and the power of suggestion are sufficient to explain most testimonies of "crystal power." However, the sheer volume of such testimonies suggests the possibility that psychic forces are at times involved.

Obviously, this does not mean that crystals are inherently occultic or spiritually dangerous. They are a part of God's creation, and if a Christian has a nonoccultic interest in or attraction to crystals, he or she should be able to pursue this attraction (with due moderation) in good conscience.

Although Scripture does not allow for a New Age idea of psychic energy pervading the universe, it would support the view that demonic energy can be misidentified as such. And though there is no reasonable basis to hold that crystals are inherently good transmitters of demonic power, such power *can* work through people's belief in magical objects. Thus when people associate crystals with an occult understanding of the universe and look to them for healing or other desired ends, they are opening up a door with their free wills to demonic intrusion and deception.

When a dozen people met at a Corona del Mar, California, metaphysical center to "swoon over hundreds of quartz crystals recently unearthed in Arkansas," a woman came up to the New Ager who was selling the rocks and whispered: "I have a severe injury in my foot. I'm a skeptic, but I felt a real charge when I held the crystal. What would happen if I put it on my foot?" (Robin Pierson, "The Crystal Connection," *The Orange County Register*, 4 January 1988, 5.) Seeking relief from pain, and encouraged by the sensation she experienced, this woman would be a likely convert to the New Age if she experienced some dramatic relief after applying the crystal to her foot. No doubt Satan is willing to provide such phenomena if it will persuade someone of a false view of God and the universe.

8. How "New Age" is New Age Music?

There can be no disputing that the increasingly popular and profitable "New Age music" has roots in the New Age movement—the identical names are not a coincidence. The trend began with jazz luminaries like Paul Horn and John Fahey seeking to create music especially conducive to New Age spirituality. Then, as recounted by New Age seminar leader and entrepreneur Dick Sutphen, in the latter 1970s Steven Halpern created a "soothing music that was . . . great for visualization. Structured on a pentatonic scale, there was no tension, no resolve, and it inspired without distracting." ("The Emergence of New Age Music," *Self-Help Update*, issue 29, 14.) Halpern, who holds a master's degree in the psychology of music, was deliberately attempting to facilitate the development of "higher" levels of consciousness.

This has remained a central goal for many New Age musicians to this day. Even Swiss harpist Andreas Vollenweider, whose records have sold in the millions, explains that the purpose of the tranquil sound is to "build a bridge between the conscious and the subconscious. We have to somehow excite our spirituality." (Bill Barol with Mark D. Uehling and George Raine, "Muzak for a New Age," *Newsweek*, 13 May 1985, 68.)

For many involved in this burgeoning field, however, the primary incentives appear to be artistic expression and/or financial gain. The leading New Age label, Windham Hill, has in 10 years grown into a $21 million record company. Its artists include such popular names as George Winston and Shadowfax. While strongly expressing their commitment to creative over monetary values, they explicitly deny any commitment to the New Age movement. Correspondingly, they do not pursue the more "hard-core" New Age music (which Sutphen calls "Inner Harmony New Age Music") that is used as background for meditation and healing sessions. Instead, they have become associated with "New Age jazz," a progressive blend of jazz, rock, folk, and other influences.

It is this jazz-oriented form of New Age music, along with the electronic sound associated with names like Vangelis *(Chariots of Fire)* and Tangerine Dream, that is played on most "New Age" radio stations. Prominent among these is KTWV, Los Angeles ("The Wave"), which is syndicating its programming nationwide.

The common thread that unites these otherwise diverse forms of New Age music is supposed to be *feeling*—listening to them generates a peaceful and uplifting mood.

How dangerous is New Age music—if at all? The primary means for conveying spiritual influences through music is words. Since most New Age music is nonverbal, except for song titles, this opportunity rarely exists.

When it comes to melodies and rhythms, there is much greater possibility than with words for the original intention to become diffused in the medium. Thus, while the composer may intend to elicit a particular mystical mood, the noninitiate listener simply becomes more relaxed. I believe this would be the case even with most inner harmony New Age music. After all, even when New Agers are specifically attempting to induce altered states of consciousness through their music, much of their applied theory is based on New Age presuppositions that Christians would not be inclined to accept. These include belief in the correspondence of particular sound frequencies with more or less mystical levels of consciousness, and an equation of certain relaxed or emotional states with mystical states. In any case, by and large only the inner harmony school appears to be seriously attempting such an effect.

The strongest potential for a truly *New Age* musician to use his music for the New Age cause would lie in live performances. He could evangelize between tunes, or lead the audience in a meditation or visualization. For example, Hawaiian New Age musician Robert Aeolus Myers likes to share the spiritual basis behind his music with his audiences. "I just feel like there's a personal responsibility to allow people the opportunity for awakening," he explains. (Mike Gordon, "The New Age of Music," *Honolulu Star-Bulletin*, 5 Nov. 1987.)

Additionally, some New Age melodies are so obviously patterned after familiar mystical or meditative rhythms (such as, the mystical refrain *om*) that their pagan associations are all but inescapable. Listening to such music for entertainment or relaxation could easily result in someone being stumbled— either the listener or another believer (*see* 1 Cor. 8).

Although these are valid concerns, I must say that I have listened extensively to the Southern California New Age stations, and have found almost nothing objectionable (though this does not exonerate *all* New Age stations *everywhere*. Some are clearly New Age in every sense of the word). It would seem to me that if the discerning Christian remains alert to the possibility of undesirable influences occasionally coming through, he or she could listen to the progressive varieties of New Age music, in moderation, without ill effect.

Given the heavily mystical orientation of inner harmony New Age music, I would advise against the Christian going out of his or her way to listen to it. As a general practice, it is not wise to passively receive the influences of one who is seeking by those influences to produce an unchristian effect. But if such music happens to be playing within earshot (for example, a relative or fellow worker is listening to it), the likelihood of being adversely affected is slight. And even then it would probably have more to do with the believer's *perception* of the music (such as, associating it with his or her past as a New Ager) than any hypnotic or occultic power in the music itself.

Appendix B
Constance Cumbey's New Age Conspiracy Theory: A Summary Critique

Most evangelical readers will need little introduction to Constance Cumbey, Christian attorney turned ardent opponent of the New Age movement (NAM). During the years 1983–85 Mrs. Cumbey and her best-selling book *The Hidden Dangers of the Rainbow* (Huntington House, 1983) were perhaps the greatest cause of controversy within the evangelical church.

Since 1985 both the controversy and Cumbey's popularity have seemingly waned. In late 1988 she announced her retirement from full-time NAM opposition, and her return to legal practice. Why then should a critique of Cumbey's New Age conspiracy theory *still* be considered necessary? Might it not simply revive a bitter debate that is better off forgotten?

Although a large number of Cumbey's former supporters have indeed become disillusioned with her methodology, it is my observation that many of these same people continue to bear the marks of her influence. This is because, having received their first exposure to the NAM through her, they have unconsciously retained many of her most basic assumptions. Since a number of these assumptions are unfounded, a widespread distortion in the American church's perception of the NAM *continues* to exist. One of many possible examples of this is Texe Marrs's *best-selling* Crossway Book, *Dark Secrets of the New Age* (1987, followed in 1988 by his *Mystery Mark of the New Age*). Though less controversial, Marrs's rendition of the NAM is almost an exact reproduction of Cumbey's original thesis.

It is my hope that this review of Cumbey's *Hidden Dangers* and her 1985 sequel *A Planned Deception* (Pointe Publishers) will help to clear up this continuing distortion by casting a light on the unwarranted assumptions that are responsible for it. (Due to space limitations I must regretfully refrain from addressing Cumbey's claim that the NAM is a revival of Nazism, and her implications of several prominent Christians with a New Ager conspiracy.)

The Hidden Dangers of the Rainbow

The Hidden Dangers of the Rainbow met with considerable criticism from the Christian apologetics community. What made the book so controversial was not so much its bare assertion that there is an "Aquarian Conspiracy," nor even its suggestion that this conspiracy would somehow lead to the Antichrist. Facts and possibilities such as these had been addressed in Christian countercult literature for years. It was rather the peculiar nature and operation that Cumbey attributed to this conspiracy that drew objections.

As Cumbey represented it, the leadership of the *entire* NAM had been united for decades in following the instructions of esotericist and former Theosophist Alice Bailey (d. 1949):

> One familiar with the Movement and the Bailey teachings cannot help but note the close patterning of developments within the New Age Movement along the lines set forth by Mrs. Bailey. She is literally followed like a recipe (p. 90).
> The writings of Alice Bailey, which have been followed meticulously by the New Age Movement . . . (p. 115).

In addition to Bailey, Cumbey cited British author H. G. Wells (d. 1946) as the second major source for this New Age conspiracy:

> The esoteric thrusts of the Movement as well as the aims of its groups are largely derived from the Alice Bailey books. Its overall direction and tactical strategy may be found in *The Open Conspiracy: Blueprints for a World Revolution* by H. G. Wells (p. 55).

In Cumbey's view, at some point Wells's "Open Conspiracy" had merged with Bailey's New Age conspiracy, so that both were working toward identical ends, and those participating in one were also participating in the other:

> There is other evidence that Wells was an insider and that the present structure is no coincidence. The first clue that one investigating the Movement should look for in Wells' writings comes from *The Aquarian Conspiracy*.
> Wells is mentioned in that work as an author of importance in at least three places.
> A more important clue comes from the presses of Lucis Trust [founded by Bailey] with its subsidiary Lucis Publishing Company. In their official organ, *The Beacon*, on page 310 of the May-June edition of 1977, appears an article entitled "H. G. Wells, a Forerunner" (p. 124).
> The New Agers/Open Conspiracy people were more interested in a dictatorship of the "Hierarchy" headed by Maitreya the "Christ" (p. 123).

The blueprint that this conspiracy had long been executing was known as "the Plan." Intricately detailed, it involved major behind-the-scenes manipulation of seemingly unrelated and spontaneous world events and cultural developments. Thus, the growing influence of Eastern religions, the nuclear freeze movement, and virtually everything potentially leading in the direction of the New Age were carefully engineered events. The world was to be secretly prepared until 1975, and then the movement was to go entirely public. Its ultimate goal was to conquer the world for its true god, Lucifer. This would be accomplished by the enthronement of a "New Age Christ" named "Maitreya" (actually the Antichrist). The Plan's final stage, she warned, was nearing completion:

> Step by step they plotted the coming "New Age". . . . Plans for religious war, forced redistribution of the world's resources, Luciferic initiations, mass planetary initiations, theology for the New World Religion, disarmament campaign, and elimination or sealing away of obstinate religious orthodoxies . . . (p. 50).
>
> Other things were to be taught to prepare the world for the "New Age" and the "New Age Christ" as well. Mind control and meditation were to be taught. Color therapy was to be emphasized. Music therapy and holistic health were additional items to be added to this eclectic diet for a "New Age." New Age symbols such as the rainbow, Pegasus, the unicorn, the all-seeing-eye of freemasonry, and triple-sixes were to be increasingly displayed.
>
> The Movement was to keep a low profile until 1975. Then it had permission to make everything public—including the very fact and nature of "The Plan" itself. Everything hidden was to be revealed and there was to be a no-holds-barred propaganda drive after that time, spreading the previously esoteric teachings of the New Age along with the anticipation of a New Age Christ by every media vehicle available. However, even before 1975, the stage had been carefully set (p. 12).
>
> Her [Bailey's] disciples are now on the last stage of the New Age scheme to take the world for Lucifer (p. 50).
>
> An *imminent* coup by a New Age cabal is not outside the range of *probability* (p. 58) (emphases added).

Contributing to Cumbey's sense of imminency was a media campaign being conducted by esotericist Benjamin Creme. His Tara Center ran an advertisement that appeared in major newspapers on April 25, 1982, proclaiming that "THE CHRIST IS NOW HERE," and affirming that his appearance would be forthcoming. Creme followed this up with a press conference in which he predicted that "Maitreya" would appear before summer arrived. Since Cumbey was convinced that the entire NAM was working in concert, Creme's declarations were not to be taken lightly:

> *The Movement* is even bold enough to run full-page newspaper ads proclaiming "THE CHRIST IS NOW HERE" (p. 41) (emphasis added).
>
> Benjamin Creme's announcement of "Maitreya the Christ" is the culmination of over 100 years of meticulous planning and labor by those seeking this "Age of Aquarius" (p. 17).

The reader should note that the NAM cannot be as Cumbey portrayed it in *Hidden Dangers* and at the same time be the loosely structured, leaderless (that is, nonhierarchical) metanetwork (network of networks) that both New Agers like Marilyn Ferguson *(The Aquarian Conspiracy)* and Christian observers like myself have claimed. For the entire movement to be following one detailed Plan "like a recipe" it would *have* to be tightly organized and hierarchical. Such perfectly coordinated activity is unheard of (among occultists, Christians, or anyone else) where such controls do not exist.

More than that, for the NAM to be coldly orchestrating major developments on every level of society and capable of an imminent world takeover, it would have to be almost omnipotent and omnipresent! In short, we would no longer be talking about a *movement*, but a conspiracy in the most subversive and menacing senses of the word, similar to the all-pervasive, monolithic conspiracies attributed by some to the Illuminati, Jesuits, international bankers, and so forth.

In such a scenario, Marilyn Ferguson would be deliberately concealing information in her book about the *true* nature of the conspiracy (which Cumbey has in fact claimed), and someone like myself would likely be a "plant," deliberately spreading disinformation (which Cumbey has also suggested). In other words, any information which seems to counter the conspiracy theory can easily be viewed as deliberate cover-up work *by* the all-powerful conspiracy. But when a theory can no longer be *disproved*, neither can it ever be *proved*. It loses all possible value as a source of reliable, relevant knowledge.

If, on the other hand, a theory is to have potential value, it must be made *testable*—certain evidence must be determined that would be sufficient to disprove it. I contend that sufficient evidence against Cumbey's theory would be to show that *all* New Age leaders have not been following one detailed blueprint— that, in fact, the movement is *not* tightly organized and hierarchical. If that can be *proved*, Cumbey's entire conspiracy theory would necessarily be *disproved*.

A Planned Deception

Self-published and difficult to read for its obvious lack of professional editing, *A Planned Deception* is largely devoted to defending the thesis of *Hidden Dangers* against the criticisms of "Christian cult 'experts.'" Both by name and by allusion, Walter Martin in particular is berated on several occasions.[1]

Little new is added to Cumbey's original theory, although new documentation is brought forth to support old claims. There are a few slight but detectable changes in Cumbey's overall thrust. Maitreya, to whom she devoted an entire chapter in her first book, is *never* referred to as an actual, living man, and receives passing mention only twice. Benjamin Creme, who occupies a central place in *Hidden Dangers*, is only referred to a few times incidentally.

In *A Planned Deception* Cumbey is ready to qualify some points that were stated as absolutes in *Hidden Dangers*. For example:

> At any rate, it is clear that there has been much working out of "The Plan"— consciously or *unconsciously*. It appears that much more of it is conscious that [sic] Christian cult "experts" wish to concede (p. 46) (emphasis added).

As the tone of the above quote indicates, however, such qualifications are always made in a grudging manner, while in the same breath the basic thesis of the original conspiracy theory is upheld. Although some of its points are stated less forcefully, none are retracted; there is no admission of past error. Rather, the original thesis is assumed and defended throughout the book.

It needs to be recognized why it would be difficult for Cumbey to retract openly any of her original unqualified claims about the NAM. Her conspiracy theory was pieced together from a multitude of New Age sources under the assumption that whenever one New Age leader spoke, he/she did so for the entire movement. If it were to be allowed that this is not at all the case, that in fact the movement is not nearly so organized as she first thought, then Benjamin Creme's announcement of Maitreya's soon appearing would not necessarily mean that the NAM was ready to take over the world. David Spangler's references to a "Luciferic initiation" would not prove that all New Age leaders hold to a positive belief in Lucifer. Alice Bailey's antisemitic statements, her reference to the atomic bomb as the "saving force," even her belief in the "Masters" and a coming "New Age Christ," could no longer be indiscriminately attributed to the entire movement. Ultimately, Cumbey's distinctive conspiracy theory would entirely unravel.

Problems with Cumbey's Thesis

Particularly for those lacking much prior exposure to the NAM, Cumbey's presentation can be very persuasive. Since she is a trial lawyer, one naturally assumes that she must follow the rules of logic and know how to interpret evidence. And *evidence* she appears to have—thousands of New Age books out of which she can endlessly cite quotes and facts in seeming support of everything she says. Christians are usually unable to check out this overwhelming amount of bizarre material, but often reason that since it all seems to fulfill biblical prophecy, it *must* be true. But those who *are* familiar with the evidence do not need to be trained logicians to see that Cumbey's thesis is riddled with mishandled facts and logical fallacies. To prove this we will now apply the aforementioned "test" and see if all New Age leaders have unitedly been following one detailed blueprint.

Concerning Bailey and the Plan

It must first be acknowledged that Cumbey often displays excellent instincts as a researcher. She has tracked down just about all of the important players in the NAM. Alice Bailey is the best example of this. If we were to call H. P. Blavatsky (the founder of Theosophy) the "grandmother of the New Age movement," Alice Bailey would be its "mother." It was she more than any other adherent of Blavatsky's teachings who took these ideas and shaped them into the ideological/mythological system we now call "New Age."

It must also be recognized that in the Alice Bailey writings a "Plan" for preparing the world for the New Age and a New Age Christ *is* described in much detail. And, over the past seventy years there *have been* self-conscious disciples of the "Master D.K." (the supposedly advanced being who Bailey claimed telepathically wrote most of the books through her) working to further the Plan.

The following questions remain to be answered: (1) Is the Plan essentially like Cumbey described it? (2) Did the present New Age movement arise out of a step-by-step following of the Plan? (3) Are all (or even most) New Age leaders self-conscious followers of Bailey and the Plan?

Regarding the nature of the Plan, Cumbey fails to make clear that the Plan is never described as a complete blueprint held in human hands. Rather it is in the possession of the "hierarchy," a group of superhuman "Masters," and most of its details have not been revealed to human beings. It is largely carried out by the Masters themselves, without the assistance of self-conscious disciples.[2]

There are, however, specific instructions in the Bailey books on how the disciples can help with the Plan's outworking. A major focus was the forming of an international "network of light and service" by organizing "triangles": groups of three who would use and promote the Great Invocation (a "world prayer" which invokes the return of the "Christ" and the establishing of the Plan on earth).[3] They were also to teach the principles of goodwill or "right human relations" and spread the hope of the "coming one" to the general public.

On the whole, the instructions for working out the Plan are not nearly as many as Cumbey implies. It is true that "D.K." describes the future work of the disciples in a manner that at times strikingly parallels what has actually been done by various movements over the past couple decades (for example, in education, religion, health, politics). However, the very book from which Cumbey draws most heavily in support of her thesis can also be used to destroy it.

In *The Externalization of the Hierarchy* (p. 530), the same book in which the year 1975 is given significance in the Hierarchy's Plan, we are also told that "in 2025 the date in all probability will be set for the *first stage* of the externalization [bodily appearances] of the Hierarchy" (emphasis added). Later, on page 559, we are told that *after* these first Masters appear, "if these steps prove successful, other and more important reappearances will be possible, *beginning with the return of the Christ*" (emphasis added). Obviously, if Bailey's disciples are following her "like a recipe," and this is why 1975 is important, then the "Christ" *cannot* appear until some time after 2025. In context, 1975 only represents a stepping up of preparatory activity over a 50-year period, and yet Cumbey has used it sensationally to argue for an *imminent* appearance of Maitreya.

Also, even according to Bailey or "D.K.," most of the disciples who would really be working out the Plan in the world would *not* be doing so consciously. They would be "disciples" purely on the basis of *reincarnation* (which means they could only be *true* disciples if Bailey's belief system were true!):

> The disciples sent out from the various ashrams [that is, reincarnated] do not arrive on earth conscious of a high mission or knowing well the nature of the task to which they have been subjectively assigned. . . . They will find their way into politics, into the educational movements and into science; they will work as humanitarians, as social workers in the field of finance, but they will follow these lines of activity through natural inclination and not because they are being "obedient" to instruction from some Master. . . .
>
> . . . . They will work . . . in response to impression from the Ashram, but of this, in their physical brains, they know nothing and care less.[4]

On the other hand, those disciples who were aware of the hierarchy and the Plan (that is, the only true disciples from a nonreincarnationist perspective) were *not asked to do that kind of work*.

> Disciples who are intensely interested in personal responsiveness to the soul, who work diligently at the problem of soul contact, who are busy with the art of serving consciously and who make service a goal, who are keenly alive to the fact of the Ashram and to the Master, *will not be asked to do this work of preparing for the externalization of the Hierarchy*. Advanced disciples [that is, those unconscious of the Plan] . . . can be trusted to work along right lines in the world and do the work of preparation. They cannot be sidetracked or deflected from one-pointed attention to the task in hand by any soul call to urge: hence they are free to do the intended work (emphasis added).[5]

So what have those who we would all agree are Bailey's disciples been doing for these past several decades? Mainly occult work (using the Great Invocation, chanting various mantras, and so forth).[6] According to their world view, that's the most effective preparatory work they can do, but it lends little support to Cumbey's thesis.

No doubt, Bailey's followers would be happy to take credit for the rise of the NAM. They would point to their occult activity and say that they unleashed the energy that engendered the NAM. They might also point to the second major thrust of their work, the widespread promotion of the Great Invocation, Bailey's books, and related teachings, as a way in which they have helped bring it about.

This latter claim would be legitimate. Many New Age leaders have been directly influenced by Bailey's teachings (for instance, Donald Keys, Robert Muller, David Spangler [although Spangler has been much more strongly influenced by estotericist Rudolf Steiner, who predated Bailey]), and many more indirectly. But even Bailey's followers would readily admit that most who have been influenced by her are not following her "meticulously." New Agers are typically eclectic, drawing on many sources and combining them in their own personal mix. Furthermore, there are many New Age leaders who show little or no Bailey influence at all (for instance, Marilyn Ferguson, Fritjof Capra, Mark Satin).

The evidence indicates that true disciples of Bailey, those who *would* follow her every word, are small in number and *not* that united (several splinter groups formed off the original organization, Lucis Trust, after Bailey died.)[7] One thing is certain: her followers by no means encompass the entire New Age leadership, as Cumbey's theory *requires*.

Concerning H. G. Wells and the Open Conspiracy

In singling out H. G. Wells, Cumbey again put her finger on someone of undeniable importance. If Bailey might be called "the mother of the New Age movement," Wells is certainly "the father of the world-state movement" (two distinct though overlapping movements). At the turn of the century Wells began to preach his gospel of world government with missionary zeal, and through his great popularity (which lasted until the mid-1920s) as an author and social "prophet" the minds of an entire generation were taught to think in global terms. Even today his indirect influence is still quite evident.

Again, it is Cumbey's *interpretation* of her research findings with which issue must be taken. First, Wells was no New Ager, nor an "occult initiate," as she describes him in *A Planned Deception* (p. 98). W. Warren Wagar, an authority on Wells, observes:

> Wells made quite clear . . . that the passivity and mysticism and other-worldliness embedded in most Eastern faiths would have no place in the Great State of the future. In an age when Western intellectuals are re-examining with a deepening distrust the "mood of the Western peoples" and opening their minds more than ever before to Eastern religious insights, Wells' rejection of the characteristically Eastern varieties of religious experience identified him all the more with the boldly self-reliant rationalism of the nineteenth century.[8]

After extensive research I could find no evidence that Wells even knew of Bailey. But he was extremely critical of those "New Agers" of his time that he did know, such as Aldous Huxley, P. D. Ouspensky, and Gerald Heard.[9]

Certainly, much of Wells's ideology could be considered "New Age" by today's standards, and he even entertained the notion of an evolving racial Being or Mind. It was this he termed "God" in *God the Invisible King* and *Mr. Britling Sees It Through*. But, however inconsistently, he never appealed to pantheism as a metaphysical basis for this doctrine. He remained a philosophical materialist.

Second, and more importantly, Cumbey is seriously mistaken about Wells's "Open Conspiracy." It is not that he did not outline several practical steps toward a world revolution—he did, much more so than Bailey. Nor is Cumbey wrong in saying that much of what Wells envisioned has come to pass. Where Cumbey makes a critical error (as she does also with Bailey) is in concluding that these correspondences between Wells's blueprint and subsequent history are so strong that the case is closed—no further evidence is needed to prove that Wells has been followed by the NAM.

In fact the evidence Cumbey cites is purely circumstantial, and crumbles under the weightier evidence of the historical record, and the context of Wells's own words.

Published after Wells's popularity began to decline, *The Open Conspiracy* did not sell particularly well—maybe a little over 30,000 in its three editions. Reviews from critics were mostly unenthusiastic.

In the Depression-struck 1930s, interest in revolutionary programs of all kinds was great, and thus a couple of efforts *were* made to organize the Open Conspiracy. However, the right kind of people (industrialists and scientists) did not become involved, and so these amateurish attempts floundered, and completely disappeared amid the chaos of the late 1930s.

The Open Conspiracy failed partly because Wells failed to give it strong leadership:

> A disillusioned Wellsian, Odette Keun, complained in 1934, it was tragically disconcerting "to expect from a social thinker a system to which you can rally and which you can put into execution, and receive instead a swamping cataract of rush-

ing broken notions." Wells shifted and changed, she said, "almost from one moon to another, his ground, his angle, and his solutions," shattering the confidence of "the men and women who aspired to be his disciples."[10]

As Wells approached the end of his life he viewed his mission as a complete failure. This despair is evident in his final book, *Mind at the End of Its Tether*.

W. Warren Wagar's book *H. G. Wells and the World State* is the authoritative work on the Open Conspiracy. Wagar, himself a disciple of Wells and a member of the Institute for World Order, was writing to people of sympathetic mind when he made the following observations. It would be a case of "invincible ignorance" to assume he was *not* telling the truth.

> Wells' warnings and proposals and Utopias were *not accepted as a single system by a self-consciously Wellsian intellectual movement*[11] (emphasis added).
> The Open Conspiracy will probably go down in history as *a curiously interesting failure, a creed that never caught hold*, although it was by no means the most wild-eyed of twentieth-century creeds[12] (emphases added).
> All of his attempts to proselyte the intellectual avant-garde of the generations which came to maturity in the years after 1914 had failed. The Open Conspiracy had not materialized, either directly in answer to his books or as a great spontane-ous wave of enlightened militant action . . . *since his death in 1946, his already declining prestige has dwindled to almost nothing*[13] (emphasis added).

This evaluation is confirmed by virtually every other authority on Wells.[14]

Wagar's book was written in 1961. Over the past two decades there has been a great resurgence of interest in global government. H. G. Wells has been rediscovered by some in this movement, and therefore Cumbey can cite references to him in *The Aquarian Conspiracy*, and a Lucis Trust article calling him a "forerunner" (which indeed he was). That is to be expected. But surely it offers no proof that the entire NAM is closely following his blueprint. There is much that indicates otherwise.

Cumbey and I would both agree that the Club of Rome's Aurelio Peccei is a guiding force in the current move toward "planetization." Peccei granted an interview with cultural historian and leading New Ager William Irwin Thompson. Thompson reports that "Peccei had said that he was *not familiar with the work of H. G. Wells;* nevertheless Peccei and the Club were the very men Wells had been waiting for [that is, industrialists and scientists]"[15] (em-phasis added).

In truth, the world state called for by Wells and the "planetary guidance sys-tem" envisioned by New Agers are worlds apart, both in structure and in under-lying values. Consequently, Wells's appeal even today is quite naturally limited.

How then can we explain the remarkable similarities between Wells's blue-print and what has actually happened? H. G. Wells was, perhaps, the greatest social prognosticator in history (the word "prognosticator" not applying to the biblical prophets). His mind had a phenomenal capacity to foresee the natural lines along which history would likely move. Around 1900, he predicted avia-tion and its strategic use in warfare. In 1933 he foretold the outbreak of World War II, just missing the date by a few months. In 1913 he described the invention and use in war of the atomic bomb! He also perceived the increasingly global character of our age, and foresaw the natural emergence of an "open conspiracy" similar in several respects to what we now have with the NAM.

In reading *The Open Conspiracy* Cumbey failed to pay sufficient heed to Wells's own clarifications:

> In such terms we may sketch the practicable and possible opening phase of the open conspiracy. We do not present it as a movement initiated by any individual or radiating from any particular center. It arises naturally and necessarily from the present increase of knowledge and the broadening outlook of many minds throughout the world. It is reasonable therefore to anticipate its appearance all over the world in sporadic mutually independent groups.[16]

Wagar accurately comments:

> The movement Wells envisioned could not have thrived as a "society" in any case, however vigorous or articulate. It had to be a movement in the historical sense, a tidal wave, an irresistible and spontaneous outbreak of understanding. When Wells groped for words to describe his Open Conspiracy, he was in effect trying to say that unless the idea occurred independently and simultaneously to tens of thousands of able men in responsible positions all over the world, there was no hope for it. *Wells had too much fatalism in his blood to expect history to obey H. G. Wells* (emphasis added).[17]

Having looked carefully at the two primary sources for Cumbey's conspiracy theory, the following comments can be made. While some New Agers have certainly acted on the suggestions of Alice Bailey and H. G. Wells at times (Donald Keys of Planetary Citizens being a likely example), the NAM is best understood as a dynamic, spontaneous movement, not the deliberate execution of an elaborate plan. Though there are elements of conspiracy (as described in chapters 5 and 6), the word can conjure up misleading images. New Agers themselves believe the very force of evolution is the *prime* mover, carrying them along. They see (all too correctly) a spontaneous social transformation occurring, and they do what they can to help further it. No doubt *Satan* has a well-defined "plan," but it is almost sure folly to think it can be learned by studying Alice Bailey, H. G. Wells, or any other ungodly source. The Bible is the only reliable source for learning the truth about the "father of lies" (John 8:44).

Concerning Benjamin Creme and "Maitreya"

Particularly in her first book, Cumbey attached too much significance to Benjamin Creme and "Maitreya." This was probably partly due to the fact that when she first started researching the NAM in 1981, Creme was big news. It must have seemed as though he was important in the NAM. But for those of us who had been watching New Age trends for years, it was simply "par for the course" that Creme had been making media appearances, had drawn a following, and was attracting widespread interest from the New Age community at large. Whenever someone comes along prophesying the arrival of the New Age or some apocalyptic event within a limited period of time (such as the more recent

New Age excitement about a "harmonic convergence" occurring August 16 and 17, 1987), he/she receives an enthusiastic hearing. But this does not signify (as Cumbey wrongly surmised) that the entire movement is sponsoring or following that person. Therefore, after "Maitreya" predictably failed to show by the end of spring 1982, we were not surprised to see Creme quickly slip back into relative obscurity.

Cumbey, however, refused to drop the matter. Rather than drawing the natural conclusion that Creme was at the most demonically deluded when he thought Maitreya was telepathically communicating with him, Cumbey interpreted the nonevent as further evidence that Maitreya is the real Antichrist!

> Although the full-page newspaper ads said Maitreya would soon appear, he has not done so yet. This worries me. For it could cause many Christians to develop a false sense of confidence over the fact that he has not yet appeared.
> The average false Christ—and there have been many—is not bashful. He comes out, collects his followers, his accolades, and especially the money. Then, he lives like a king.
> The real antichrist cannot appear until the Lord permits it. And I believe the Lord will not let it happen until his people are fully warned (*Hidden Dangers*, p. 23).

This reasoning illustrates a key problem with Cumbey's entire approach: an *eschatological bias*. Rather than first getting a good understanding of the facts on their own terms and *then* applying a biblical world view to them, Cumbey has too often run the facts immediately through the grid of her own end-time expectations, rejecting all which do not agree. Thus, because Creme's message seemed to fit biblical prophecy so well, no amount of evidence could convince her that the entire NAM was not behind him.

At an April 21, 1983, lecture at Costa Mesa, California's Orange Coast College, Marilyn Ferguson was asked about Creme's message:

> I remember thinking at the time that is crazy. Benjamin Creme is a really sweet guy, [but] this is a crazy idea. And somebody asked me about that at this Detroit lecture where Constance [Cumbey] was, and I *said* that my opinion was that their intentions were good but I couldn't arouse any interest in it. And she *still* refers to him as "your good friend Benjamin Creme." . . . I mean, I *told* about the conspiracy that exists in [my] book. [The conspiracy's] open and I'll tell people anything they want to know about it, about what I know. . . .

Later, during a conversation with *Media Spotlight's* Steve Wurglund, Ferguson said:

> The thing is that the sense of a lot of people. . . . is that the spirit that is abroad now is a *collective* messianic spirit. We're not looking for some new person to show up, like this guy in the outskirts of London [that is, Maitreya]. It just doesn't seem possible.

It is not that Christians should completely ignore the Benjamin Cremes when they come along saying, "The Christ will soon appear." Though improbable, it is possible that one day the Antichrist *will* appear in such a manner. But based on the occult world's track record, such claims should be met with a healthy amount of skepticism.

The "Creme event" provides no proof whatsoever that the Antichrist is in the world today, or that he will be identified as "Maitreya" when he does appear (though, again, both are *possible*). And yet one *still* encounters Christians who, having been influenced by Cumbey, assume that Maitreya is the central fact of the entire NAM. This is a prime example of how Cumbey's message has left the church with a distorted view of the NAM.

Concerning New Age Organization

I have already described the nature and extent of New Age organization in chapters 1, 5, and 6. I will only reemphasize here that the NAM is a *network*, and that means, by the common usage of the term, that it is *not* centralized and tightly organized. As New Agers Jessica Lipnack and Jeffrey Stamps explain it:

> Bureaucracies tend to bring parts together through *centralized* control and to *maximize* the dependency of parts on the whole. Networks tend to bring parts together under *decentralized* cooperation and to *minimize* their dependency on the whole. Network parts are dispersed and flexibly connected, whereas bureaucratic parts are concentrated and rigidly connected.[18]

Cumbey seems to be profoundly confused on this point. On the one hand she will make completely accurate statements like this: "It should also be kept in mind that the Movement is not a hierarchical structure, per se, but is composed of thousands of networking organizations" (*Hidden Dangers*, p. 193). And then on the same page she will affirm:

> It may safely be said that Lucis Trust is truly the brains—at least from an occult planning basis—of the New Age Movement. One only has to study the course of the Movement to see that her [Alice Bailey's] instructions to New Age "disciples" have been followed like recipes (*Hidden Dangers*, pp. 193–94).

But if Lucis Trust is the "brains" of the movement, and the NAM has followed Bailey's instructions "like recipes," then it *must* be a hierarchical structure with tremendous control.

That New Agers have not always been organized as a conspiracy, but are *becoming* organized as a network, is evident in the following quotes from Donald Keys and Fritjof Capra:

> Thousands of organizations of concerned people throughout the world have been conscious of the global crisis and have been responding with activities to increase awareness and to propose positive alternative suggestions for a human world. However, *these significant efforts have usually been unrelated*. Their convergence can greatly strengthen their impact (emphasis added).[19]
>
> The philosophical, spiritual, and political movements generated in the '60s and '70s all emphasize different aspects of the new paradigm and all seem to be going in the same direction—though, so far, most of these movements still operate separately and have not yet recognized how their purposes interrelate.[20]

Cumbey has read these statements and many more like them. Why doesn't she believe them? Undoubtedly it is because she is convinced she has more reliable evidence to the contrary. And yet all of her evidence for a monolithic conspiracy (for example, "organizational charts, matrixes, statements of purpose, and directories"—*Hidden Dangers*, p. 6) could just as easily be interpreted by the network model, especially when one realizes that such evidence invariably refers to organizations and networks *within* the movement, and not the movement as a whole.

Why is this important? The main reason Cumbey's vision of the NAM is distorted is because she has failed to grasp this point. She saw the degree of organization that *does* exist and jumped to the conclusion that when one teacher or group says or does something, all must be involved. For examples:

The New Age Movement . . . seeks to replace the cross with . . . the swastika (*Hidden Dangers*, p. 118).
They openly propose to give every world resident a number and require the usage of this number in all financial transactions of any sort (Ibid., p. 256).

It is bad enough that these incredible claims are not documented, but even if they were, since the NAM is a loose network and not a centralized organization, what one member says or does is not necessarily representative of the whole. The last quote cited illustrates a seemingly simple but nonetheless serious flaw in Cumbey's entire representation of the NAM—her frequent use of the word *they*.

This approach can be evangelistically self-defeating because it alienates most New Agers. They feel they are being maliciously misrepresented by a "reactionary type" that is not interested in truth and does not care enough to take the time to understand them.

Space permits only one example. I once conversed with the minister of a New Age "church" who explained to me that he had been regularly watching a local Christian talk show, and was being drawn away from his New Age beliefs to the gospel. Then Constance Cumbey was a guest on the program and managed to alarm the hosts about the NAM. Afterward they began to preach regularly about the threat of the New Agers—how they worship Lucifer and want to take over politically so they can exterminate Jews and Christians. When this man heard the hosts making charges his own experience told him were false, he recoiled against them and everything they stood for. His offense was so great that I am not sure that any of my words succeeded at reconciling him.

I do not mean to deny that *Satan's* goal in all of this New Age activity is the establishment of the Antichrist. And if he appeared there is no doubt that all (unrepentant) New Agers would follow him: *everyone* will except those whose names have been written in the Lamb's book of life (Rev. 13:8). Nor do I wish to deny that persecution is in store for Christians if the "New Age" becomes a reality. But it is simply erroneous to say that all New Agers *now* are looking for a "New Age Christ," or that violent repression of Christians is part of a widely accepted "Plan."

My point here is that Christians should strive for truth and accuracy. I must stress that when I criticize Cumbey's depiction of the movement's size and dangers, I am not advocating the *opposite* position—it *is* big and it *is* dangerous.

Some Christians have replied, "If you agree that the movement is a serious threat, then why criticize brave Christians like Constance who are taking an unpopular stand and sounding the warning? You should be supporting them." My reply is that, for a Christian, means (in this case, *how* a message is presented) are as important as ends. I am critical for the same reason that Christians will criticize other believers who speak about the dangers of communism, Satanism, or Satan himself in such a simplistic and sensational manner that the skeptics are only made *more* skeptical about the dangers of these things. Although not referring to Cumbey, Dave Hunt put the matter well:

> Exaggerated reports like the above play into the hands of the internationalists by causing reasonable persons to doubt the whole idea of a conspiracy to set up a world government. That could be dangerous.[21]

It is very real concerns such as these, and not "jealousy" (as Cumbey has suggested), that prompt these criticisms. I freely acknowledge that, in spite of the problems noted above, Constance Cumbey has made several valuable contributions to the Christian church. Her enterprising research has brought to light many important organizations and personalities within New Age politics, and I myself am indebted to her for this. By her own report, many New Agers have become Christians through her efforts. Certainly, she has alerted many Christians to the subtle dangers of programs like the Forum, Silva Mind Control, *A Course in Miracles*, and so forth. And while her treatment of Christians that she believes have New Age connections (sometimes rightly, more often wrongly) has been anything but conciliatory, at least she has taken a stand for biblical doctrine in an age of growing apostasy. Her warnings against such men as Matthew Fox, Rodney Romney, Thomas Merton, and Robert Schuller have no doubt saved many believers from deception.

For all these contributions and more, Constance Cumbey deserves credit and appreciation. But although she has succeeded more than anyone else at waking the church up to the New Age movement, the "New Age movement" that the church awoke to is decidedly different from the New Age movement that is really out there, as our "test" of Cumbey's theory has shown. It is time for the church to wake up *fully*, shaking off its dreamy fantasy of a monolithic New Age conspiracy. Only then can it truly rise up to the very real and formidable challenges of the New Age movement.

Appendix C
Breaking Through the "Relativity Barrier" (How to Make Points Effectively with New Agers)

Ever wonder what trying to communicate with someone from a different planet would be like? Christians who try to share their faith with New Agers may have some idea. This communication gap runs deeper than mere terminology: it involves outlooks on the world that are themselves *worlds* apart.

One major reason for this is what I have termed the "relativity barrier." Underlying much New Age thinking is a relativistic assumption that *anything* can be true for the individual, but *nothing* can be true for everyone.

To many New Agers, truth is intensely personal and entirely subjective. In their view, it is the height of presumption to think that one knows *the* key truth for all people. On the other hand, it is the apex of love to "allow" others to have their own "truth." "Thou shalt not interfere with another's reality" might be called the First Commandment of New Age revelation. Thus, the New Ager views him or herself as open-minded, tolerant, and progressive, while viewing the Christian evangelist as narrow-minded, intolerant, and repressive.

The "relativity barrier" is therefore a great obstacle to Christian evangelism. No matter how carefully the Christian directs his or her testimony, it is deflected with the reply, "That's *your* truth." Ironically, the New Ager remains rigidly closed-minded to the possibility that one person's "truth" might be critically relevant to all.

If New Age thinking continues its rapid permeation of our culture (as most long-time observers expect), Christians will face this evangelistic challenge everywhere they turn. How might they respond?

It is important first of all to explode the myth of New Age tolerance. The difference between Christians and New Agers is not fundamentally a question of greater or lesser open-mindedness. A conversation between the channeled spirit

207

"Ramtha" and one of his "masters" (disciples) will help the reader see what I mean:

> **RAMTHA:** Now, if one believes in the devil and another doesn't, who is right, who is true?
> **MASTER:** Both of them are.
> **RAMTHA:** Why?
> **MASTER:** Because each one of them has their own truth.
> **RAMTHA:** Correct, correct.

Up to this point we are witnessing classic New Age relativism. But in the comments which immediately follow Ramtha gives away the larger metaphysical context behind this seemingly impeccable tolerance:

> **RAMTHA:** Now, the devil was a masterful ploy by a conquering institution to put the fear of God, most literally, unto [sic] the hearts of little ones—that God had created a monster that would get them lest [sic] they be good to him. The devil was used to control the world most effectively and even today it is still feared and believed. Someone conjured it up—a God—and thus it became, but only to those who believed. *That is how it is.* (emphasis added) ("Ramtha" with Douglas James Mahr, *Voyage to the New World,* Friday Harbor, WA: Masterworks, 1985, 246.)

Ramtha's explanation illustrates what is generally the case in New Age thinking: it really isn't a matter of each person's "truth" being *equally* true. At a deeper level, we are all gods creating our own realities. Some, like fundamentalist Christians, are blind to this truth, and thus have created some rather unfortunate "realities." When they become "enlightened," they will drop these creations and see things as New Agers do.

By bringing this larger picture to the New Ager's attention we can demonstrate to him or her that the New Age world view is based on an absolute "truth" after all—pantheism (that is, the belief that God and the world are one). This just allows them to acknowledge multitudinous private "truths" (like the Christian's belief system) at lower levels.

It turns out that the very nature of existence won't permit us to make *everything* relative. Some ultimate view of reality must be assumed, and whichever we choose will necessarily exclude all other views. This holds true for New Age pantheism no less than Christian theism (that is, the view that God is an infinite-personal being separate from his creation). Therefore, the real question New Agers and Christians should be addressing is not whether there *is* a universal truth, but rather, *which* "universal truth" is true, pantheism or theism?

The Christian can point out to the New Ager that since this is a *metaphysical* question, and science only answers *physical* questions, we must look for other means than science to test the truthfulness of these world views. One good approach is to ask ourselves if either one is compatible with life and the world as we find them. Can they be consistently lived out?

After securing the New Ager's approval of this approach, the Christian can proceed to demonstrate that New Age beliefs fail the test, while Christian faith passes it. For example, the New Ager can be shown that (1) we all *inescapably* live by a belief that certain things are right and wrong; and (2) the ethical relativism of New Age pantheism cannot supply a sufficient basis for this belief, while the moral absolutes of Christian theism can.

Since New Agers often avoid critical thinking in favor of an intuitive approach to truth, the Christian should not expect cold logic to suffice. To make a point, it is important to impact their emotions as well as their minds. This explains the rather shocking and disturbing approach of the following demonstration.

Christian: Do you mean that there are no moral principles that are absolutely true and right for everyone?

New Ager: We each create our own reality and have our own truth.

> *Note:* A less-consistent relativist might invoke a universal law of love or karma. To this the Christian could reply: "First of all, if there are such universal laws which are absolutely true for everyone, why should you take offense when I say the gospel is not just my truth but *the* truth? But second of all, if everything is God, then karma is as much an illusion to be transcended as the world, and there is ultimately no one for my Self (which is God) to love. So why should I take such illusory "absolutes" seriously?"

Christian: What if in my reality it is wrong for people to own things, and so when you're not looking, I elect to play "Robin Hood" by relieving you of your new two-thousand-dollar-crystal and giving it to someone else?

New Ager: Well, uh, I guess I'd have to conclude that my Higher Self wanted me to learn a lesson about material things.

Christian: Okay, if stealing is not a sin, let's take it further. Now let's pretend I'm a "pedophile"—it's part of my reality to "love" children in every way possible. So, while you're at work I'm going to invite your children into my home to play a "game" that I've made up. Is that all right with you?

New Ager: It most certainly is not! It would be part of my reality to report you to the police.

Christian: Why? After all, it's the reality I've sovereignly chosen to create for myself. What gives you the right to interfere in the reality of another god?

New Ager: Simple. Your reality is infringing on my children's reality.

Christian: But according to your belief system, before they incarnated *they* chose *you* as their parent and they also chose *whatever* happens to them, including my act, and you've no right to interfere.

New Ager: I do too, in *this* case.

Christian: Can you see my point now? You are naturally and rightly outraged at the very suggestion of such an act. Something within you *knows* that it is wrong *in and of itself.*

New Ager: You're right.

Christian: But that can *only* be so if there are absolute rights and wrongs *independent* of our personal realities. Yet, try as you may, you will not find a ground for such moral absolutes in your world view. Your God is impersonal and amoral, "beyond good and evil," so you can't appeal to it. And, since in your view we are all *equally* gods, my truth about any subject is as good as your truth. So you see, New Age beliefs fail the test of human experience—they can't be consistently lived out. But Jesus said in John 14:6 "I am *the* truth." As the unique, infinite, and holy God incarnate he provides a sufficient basis for saying that certain acts such as child molestation are *absolutely* wrong.

New Ager: Hmm. I see your point.

Christian: Now let me share with you more about what the Bible says concerning Jesus. . . .

When the Christian compellingly depicts to the New Ager the natural implications of his or her beliefs, the "relativity barrier" can be sufficiently cracked to allow the glorious light of biblical truth to shine through.

Appendix D
From New Age "Christ" to Born-Again Christian: The Author's Story

Was I a New Ager? In the most technical sense, the answer is *no*. I became a Christian in 1970, and, as I explained in chapter 1, the "New Age movement" did not take its present form until the mid-1970s when the networking process began in earnest and several distinct movements converged. On the other hand, as I also pointed out in that chapter, one of those forerunning movements was the counterculture of the 1960s and early 1970s, and I was intensely (though briefly) involved with the New Age aspect of *that*. So I do believe that I understand today's New Age movement from the inside out, and feel that in many ways my own experience typifies that of a generation. Perhaps you will agree after I share my story with you.

"Bless Me, Father, for I Have Sinned"

Until the age of seven I attended Sunday school in my Baptist grandparents' church, and I remember having a warm feeling toward Jesus when I said my nightly prayers. Then my Catholic mother repented of her backslidden ways, insisted that the entire family attend mass on Sundays, and enrolled me in Catholic school.

I believed what I was taught there, but amid the pre-Vatican II Latin liturgy, the perpetual standing and kneeling, and the stern glances of somber nuns, my heart turned cold.

"Bless me, Father, for I have sinned. It has been one week since my last confession. Since that time I have had impure thoughts six times." As I reached the age of puberty such reports to the parish priests (the Catholic sacrament of

211

"Penance") became increasingly provocative, and therefore difficult to make. At last I lost all hope of piety, and resigned myself to eternal damnation.

The week before I started eighth grade I convinced my parents to let me return to public school, and in my science class that year I was first exposed to the theory of evolution. Like a "domino effect," the following conclusions fell upon my mind in their turn: No Adam and Eve. No infallible Bible. No God. No hell. Freedom!

In the years that followed pleasure became my god, and I lost all sense of guilt about it. I realized that I could not prove or disprove anything positively, but there was positively no God in the universe as I experienced it.

Because I had been profoundly influenced by the anti-establishment lyrics of mid-60s "protest songs," when the "hippies" first received national publicity in early 1967, I found myself identifying with them. My handful of friends and I, who had not fit in with any of the preexisting social groupings in our Long Beach, California, high school, derived a new and exciting sense of belonging by joining a group of hippies that emerged during our junior year (1967–68).

I followed the crowd in smoking marijuana, "hanging out" on the streets of Hollywood and nearby Huntington Beach, and even participating in a high school branch of the radical Students for a Democratic Society (SDS). But toward the end of the spring semester the thrill was gone. I could see that we hippies were no less "plastic" (phony) and conformist than the "straights" we disdained. I withdrew, seeking to establish my own independent identity and life direction.

Cosmic Torture

During my senior year I would sit alone during lunch hour reflecting on every aspect of life. Little questions led to big questions until I found myself wrestling with the ultimate issues.

As I thought about death I realized that my youth was only an illusory barrier against its reach. Just as surely as my once-distant eighteenth birthday was now arriving, so one day would death. This realization incited a new urgency within me to find some meaning in life.

In my first year of college I looked to the philosophers for answers only to find that each successive school of philosophy was refuted by the one which followed it. If truth was that difficult to discern, how could one ever know if he or she was right? Could there even *be* any real purpose in a randomly evolving universe?

As these thoughts weighed heavily upon me, I would lay awake at night tortured by the insanity of being a purpose-seeking creature in a universe which either lacked purpose, or whose purpose was beyond finding out.

Out of this torment a deep hunger for truth and meaning grew within me, taking precedence over the hedonism that had governed me before. My search for an independent identity was evolving into a quest for the truth, but first I needed encouragement that truth could be found. Surprisingly this would come through drugs.

Doors of Perception?

After I broke away from my hippie peer group, I adopted the view that drug use was stupid and dangerous. I was therefore disappointed when a friend who had shared this view began to experiment with "psychedelic" (mind-manifesting) drugs like mescaline and LSD. For nine months I refused Steve's persistent beckonings to jump into this river of unfamiliar experience. However, in the fall of 1969 he enticed me to read Tom Wolfe's *The Electric Koolaid Acid Test*, which told the story of the original San Francisco hippies. Wolfe's intriguing description of their surrealistic drug experiences and a quote from Aldous Huxley gave me hope that psychedelics might open "doors of perception" that would enable me to penetrate the mysteries of life.

In his family's mountain cabin, Steve guided me through my first mescaline "trip." After some initial pleasantries, like a "mind blowing" walk underneath a blanket of stars, my "good trip" became a "bummer" as my awareness turned to myself. I was faced with what might best be called my own wretchedness (insecurities, hypocrisy, insignificance) in ways I'd never allowed myself to be before, and I couldn't turn the picture off. Weeping and unable to speak, I wrote on a piece of paper: "I will never do this again."

Two weeks later I was doing it again. Having seen these disturbing truths about myself, I couldn't just "sweep them under the rug." I decided the best way to change myself was to confront these areas of my psyche head-on. As I began to work on myself subsequent mescaline experiences were more positive, leaving me with a taste for more. Before I knew it I was smoking marijuana (which is mildly psychedelic) on a daily basis and taking mescaline about every two weeks (I never approved of the nonpsychedelic drugs like cocaine).

In altered states of consciousness my continuing philosophical inquiry took some radical turns. Habitual patterns of thought were interrupted, enabling me to see things in new ways. Like a tyrannical king whose claim to the throne is suddenly found to be spurious, some of my most fundamental and unwanted perceptions and beliefs lost their power as truisms in my mind. In a radical application of cultural relativism, I began to challenge everything about conventional reality I once took for granted, especially the "sacred cows" of the Establishment. The resulting sense of freedom made me feel like I had just begun to live, and was discovering the universe afresh.

While sitting "stoned" alongside a river in California's beautiful Big Sur, the evidence for some kind of intelligence behind creation suddenly came crashing through my evolutionary biases. Without entirely rejecting evolution, I was now once again a believer in God.

This revelation led me on to pantheism ("God is everything") instead of back to Christianity, though, partly because of a strong naturalistic bias—I could not conceive of anything beyond the universe and so if there was a God he must *be* the universe.

Also, the drugs themselves led me to pantheism because on them I experienced a loss of ego or self-image boundaries. I began to feel intrinsically connected to the universe as my larger and more real self—an infinite consciousness into which my finite consciousness was merging. Thus, if I was the universe and the universe was God, I was God! With very little outside help I'd seemingly gone through all the classic mystical experiences and come to all the standard pantheistic conclusions.

I began to receive "revelations" from an Inner Voice, which on one occasion I committed to writing. One such revelation was that love was the fundamental principle of the universe. In response to this truth I developed my own unconventional brand of religiosity. For the first time being a good person was an important goal in my life.

It may sound as though out of desperation for answers I threw all judgment to the wind, and was now ready to believe anything. But I must stress that throughout these experiences I reserved a portion of my mind to function as a "critical observer." It's just that as a skeptic of the supernatural I had been ill-prepared for two things I encountered in altered states. The first was a very real sensation of *expanding* awareness which made my old skepticisms seem like blind prejudices. The second "proof" was the occurrence of external corroboration in my newfound psychic abilities—telepathy (knowing what people were thinking) and precognition (knowing events before they occurred).

These experiences gradually persuaded even my "critical observer" that *something* paranormal was going on. Though I was being increasingly attracted to pantheism as the explanation, I remained open to all interpretations that could account for the phenomena. My desire for truth remained strong, and I was optimistic that I would find it. I reasoned that whatever Ultimate Reality was, it was probably loving (since love was the highest expression of being), and would "meet me halfway" if I sought it with my whole being.

Tune in, Turn on, Drop out

By this time I was fully involved in what could be called my "genuine hippie phase." I was not now, as before, *imitating* the lifestyle of the hippies. I had rather gone through the same inner changes that produced that lifestyle in the first place. I could no longer relate to the prospects of school, career, and compliant participation in the "System." Without consciously following the adage of hippie guru Timothy Leary, I had "tuned in" and "turned on" and was now ready to "drop out."

In August of 1970 I hitchhiked up to Portland to attend a "Woodstock"-like festival called "Vortex I." While there I decided to join a group of people who were forming a commune.

After only a few days of commune experience, a lost contact lens forced me to return temporarily to Southern California. Back at home I maintained contact with the commune by telephone and learned that they had settled outside of Grants Pass in Southern Oregon.

I shared my experiences "up north" and plans to move there with my close circle of friends, and with my friend Joe and his wife I also shared the relatively pure LSD I had brought down with me from Oregon.

All of my friends respected me for acting on the values that we all espoused.

But under the influence of LSD Joe's respect turned to a holy dread. As I was reading to him from my private "revelations" he had a "vision" (hallucination): "My God, Elliot, you've turned into Christ!"

For several minutes Joe kept insisting that I was the Second Coming of Christ. Laughing I assured him that I was *not* Christ, though I allowed that I might be a prophet, since I was receiving these revelations.

After a two-week-wait my new contact lens was finally ready. This meant I could drive again. To celebrate, I decided to drive to some natural setting and "drop" (ingest) a capsule of organic mescaline that I'd also brought down with me.

As I stood alone in my family's kitchen formulating this plan, I suddenly received a powerful premonition that in the midst of this drug experience a new truth would be revealed to me. By this time I'd learned from experience that when such "intuitive knowings" came on so strongly, I should pay serious attention to them.

My immediate response was excitement, since my life was now entirely devoted to seeking truth. But then the premonition was expanded—there was a sense of challenge attached to it. What if this new truth could not be followed without my giving up certain things that I held dear? I saw clearly that I could not be consistent with my truth-seeking profession without being willing to make *whatever* changes truth might require. And so I resolved within myself to "flow with" and not resist whatever truth might be revealed to me that day, or ever.

A State of Suspended Identity

Driving south on Pacific Coast Highway I ended up on a somewhat isolated beach in Laguna Beach, a "hippie haven" in conservative Orange County. By sunset I was all alone, experiencing an exceptionally pleasant "trip." Feeling as though I was in perfect harmony with the universe, I waited patiently for my new revelation.

After some time my privacy was broken. About fifty feet in front of me a couple of my own age were making their way along the rocky shore. I strongly sensed that their appearance was not an accident. They didn't seem to notice me sitting there in the dark, and so I greeted them. The girl came over and sat in front of me, silently smiling. "Wow, I'm really stoned," I said—hoping for an understanding response. "Jesus really loves you, brother," she replied.

My mind reeled. Was *this* the "new truth" that would challenge my commitment to follow truth? For years I had been *thoroughly* convinced that no one who really understood modern knowledge could believe in a supernatural Jesus. Furthermore, the Christian lifestyle seemed as unattractive as any I could think of. I was therefore both confounded and shaken by this revelation. How far was I to take it?

Joining us, the girl's boyfriend expounded the same old evangelistic "pitch" I'd heard many times before from the mouths of "Jesus Freaks"—young converts mostly from the drug culture. In the past I'd been impossible for them to reach.

But this time, when he asked me to pray with him and receive Jesus into my heart, I remembered my commitment to flow with and not resist whatever happened that day. So I joined him in prayer, and whereas I'd been "peaking" on the drug a few minutes earlier, its effects were now almost imperceptible.

I was still so shaken that when they started to leave me, I asked them not to. We talked further as they took me for a drive. They suggested I visit Calvary Chapel, a church in Costa Mesa which was an "epicenter" for the up-and-coming Jesus Movement among the young. Trying to get a grasp on how "straight" I was going to have to become, I asked, "Does anyone at Calvary smoke marijuana?" For whatever reason, the young man responded by asking his friend, "Doesn't [so-and-so] smoke marijuana?" From this I wrongly gathered that although smoking marijuana was not the most popular practice, it was still tolerated.

After they dropped me off I returned to the beach. Whereas earlier I'd serenely sat there in the yogic "full lotus" position, I was now on my knees, beseeching God to reveal to me the significance of the evening's events.

In the days that followed my thinking was a confused mixture of Christian and New Age notions. This reflected a state of suspended identity: was I now a Jesus Freak or some kind of "cosmic Christian"? The answer, of which I was painfully unsure, all depended on whether the revelation on the beach was compatible with the spirituality I had previously developed in altered states.

I tried reading our gigantic family Bible, but didn't make it past the genealogies in Genesis chapter 5. I couldn't remember where the couple said Calvary Chapel was. Because I had not been flatly told to abstain from drugs, I continued using them, but I now had an uneasy conscience about it.

While visiting Kurt, an outwardly straight "pothead" who enjoyed getting stoned with me, I recounted what happened in Laguna, expressing my uncertainty as to its significance. He straightfacedly replied that its significance was very clear: just as Jesus had gone out into the desert and there was shown that he was the Son of God, so I had gone down to the beach and there was shown that *I* was the Son of God—the Second Coming of Christ! I laughed, informing him that Joe had suggested the same preposterous thing. "Out of billions of people you're telling me *I'm* going to play that role? Come *on!*"

Afterward I drove to another friend's home and waited for him to return in my car. While sitting there, Kurt's words came back into my mind. This time I sensed a great power in this suggestion, sucking me into itself. "You *are* the Son of God. You *are* the Son of God," a voice repeated ever louder in my mind. I felt some kind of spiritual presence pressing in heavily upon me. Fearing that I might go "off the deep end" I grabbed hold of myself and fought this delusion off.

In early October two other friends dropped me off at a freeway entrance for my return trip to Oregon. Already hitchhiking at that spot were a couple of "Jesus Freaks" who lived in a commune in Berkeley associated with the Christian World Liberation Front. They invited me to spend a night there when I passed through, and it turned out I was able to take them up on their offer.

Because of my experience on the beach, I identified myself as a Christian, and so I was accepted as such and not evangelized by the commune members. Things went smoothly enough until the next morning when a Christian sister brought my inner conflict to the surface by making an unfavorable reference to drugs. I argued in reply that drugs could make one more conscious of God, and pressed her to tell me exactly what was wrong with them. "We don't need drugs," she responded. "Jesus makes us high."

This pat reply was intellectually unsatisfying, and so I refused to give up drugs on the basis of it. Nonetheless, her disapproval intensified the "illogical" (as I told myself then) pangs of conscience I was already experiencing.

After several days and adventures on the road, I finally tracked down the commune only to find that it had deteriorated into two small groups of no more than six people each. What was worse, all of the remaining people were individuals I had previously discerned to be mystically "unaware." (Most hippies were not nearly as spiritually inclined as I now was.)

Before the full weight of my disappointing discovery could sink in, some hippies from another commune in Cave Junction (about a half-hour away) drove up in a truck, "turned us on" to some mescaline, and took me with them to spend the night at their place.

"There Is No Conflict"

When we arrived I thought I had finally made it to paradise—it was everything I'd hoped to find in Oregon. There were over forty people residing on a large acreage in the woods. Not your stereotypically lazy hippies, they were industriously striving to forge an alternative culture to that of the straight society.

Evening fell. I sat on the floor in a large cabin coming on heavily to the mescaline. Several men were sitting around a table discussing spiritual things. I could tell that for the first time I'd found a *group* of people who were actively pursuing the same kind of spirituality I had been. They were literally talking my language—using terms (like "ego death") to describe spiritual concepts and experiences I had previously either thought of on my own or received from my Inner Voice. This proved to me that what I'd been going through was not my own private creation, but a universal spiritual experience, presumably grounded in an Ultimate Reality. The force of this realization was electrifying.

In spite of this seeming confirmation for my drug experiences, the unanswered questions raised in Laguna refused to leave me alone. Finally I got up and joined them at the table. "I can really relate to what you guys are talking about," I began, "but I'm going through a conflict." After I recounted what had happened to me, Earl, the communal family's unofficial spiritual leader, replied: "There's no conflict if you want to pray to Jesus, and he [another at the table] wants to meditate on Buddha, and I want to smoke a joint. We're all experiencing the same God."

After Earl finished speaking, his words continued to reverberate in my mind: "It's all the same God. It's all the same God." Somehow this common conception hit me like a new revelation. Could it really be that beneath the outward quibbling the Jesus Freaks and the hippies were all experiencing the *same* God?

Immediately, as though in confirmation of what Earl said, I had a visionary experience more powerful than any I'd had before. I lost all consciousness of the room and the people in it. I felt as though I'd transcended all finite boundaries. I could hear very distinct, audible voices speaking to me in the most intimate and reassuring manner. Intuitively I "knew" who they belonged to—people from distant points in space and time. The explanation for such "long-distance communication" seemed to be that we were all "plugged into" the same Universal Mind.

I also had a vision of a blue or positive energy, which I sensed represented God, and a red or negative energy, signifying the devil (which, like God, was impersonal). The blue energy was drawing me to enlightenment and peace—the transcendence of this unnecessary conflict I'd been going through. The red energy was seeking to keep me locked into ignorance and self-destructive ego patterns, and was using this conflict to do so.

Once my consciousness returned to my body, I felt moved to go outside. Emotionally overwhelmed, I looked up at the stars and thanked God for answering my prayer. My inner conflict was now entirely gone.

That first night in Cave Junction had a transforming effect on me. I now had a seemingly unshakable confidence in my mystical experiences and the validity of using drugs to achieve them. Nevertheless drugs were no longer so necessary to have such experiences. To some extent I was always in a state of "cosmic consciousness" now. Also, my psychic abilities now seemed five times stronger. Telepathy and precognition (often verified) were almost becoming daily parts of my experience. And I was becoming increasingly aware of "spiritual presences" hovering around me, especially as I'd lie in bed at night.

I was led to believe by a few members of the commune that I was welcome to stay on and join the family. A month later I would find out that this was not the majority verdict. There were too many people to fit comfortably in a large two-story dome that had recently been completed. Those who had not contributed to its construction were to move on for the winter. But during the month I was there I had what could have under different circumstances been several years' worth of spiritual experiences.

One of Many Christs

Truly, the belief that "there is no conflict" was foundational to the commune's spirituality. Eastern mystical scriptures, occult books, tarot cards and other occult paraphernalia, drugs, and unself-conscious nudity were combined with an abundance of well-read Bibles, Christian art and symbols, and frequent, reverential references to Jesus.

The commune's seemingly Christian orientation made it easy for me to reason that I was being true to the revelation given me at the beach. Jesus *could* be integrated with my drug-based spirituality, I'd concluded, and God had brought me here so I could learn how to do it.

The significance of my beach revelation was particularly "explained" to me by one of the books on hand at the commune, "Levi's" *The Aquarian Gospel of Jesus the Christ* (a turn-of-the century work). Its account of Jesus' life and mission (based on the ethereal "Akashic Records" which only special psychics like Levi can read) was similar enough to seem consistent with the familiar gospel story, and yet the Jesus depicted there was a mystical master who spoke of the very kinds of "realities" I had encountered during my drug experiences.

The Aquarian Gospel's Introduction explains that we are now in a transition phase from the Piscean to the Aquarian Age. In the New Age the level of consciousness manifested by Jesus ("Christ consciousness") will become widespread, making it an era of enlightenment and peace.

This scenario seemed to explain the rash of people like myself in the inchoate New Age movement who were suddenly experiencing cosmic consciousness. We were the forerunners of a new age and a new phase in evolution. Whereas I had not been able to accept the suggestion that I was *the* Second Coming of Christ, I did find acceptable the idea that I was becoming *one* of *many* Christs, sort of a collective Second Coming. It now seemed that the experience in Laguna was God's way of moving me in this direction, and so attaining Christ consciousness became a major objective of my spiritual life.

During that month I read from several other books as well, including Eastern and Western scriptures. Each seemed to confirm my spiritual experiences, including the Bible. For instance, I understood John 3:3 ("You must be born again") to be speaking of the mystical "ego death" I was going through.

"Ego death" was a critical aspect of my experience. Even when not on drugs my consciousness was to some degree in what mystics term "the Now"—very aware of my immediate surroundings and of an interpenetrating spiritual dimension, but very out of touch with my past and a normal sense of self. Increasingly I identified myself with the God within rather than the Elliot Miller without.

In spite of such feelings of high attainment, during my stay in Cave Junction it seemed I could not quite achieve Christ consciousness as I understood it. My ego refused to remain completely dead. Instead, I found myself going through moments or even hours in which the most painful pieces of my past would rematerialize and torment me. I was struggling to find a way to completely extinguish Elliot Miller so that Christ could fully "incarnate" in me (as I imagined Jesus successfully did at the time of his baptism).

When I was asked to leave the commune, I went through a brief emotional upheaval. Although I understood and respected their decision, it still hurt. I had felt like I was already a part of the family, but obviously the majority did not share that sentiment. And had not God brought me here? I'd assumed this was my ultimate destination—my own ideally suited environment.

Pacing back and forth in a nearby grove, I got hold of myself. "Surely, God is in control of this turn of events as much as the previous ones. He must have lessons for me to learn that I can't learn here." My faith once again grew strong, and I committed myself to God to take me wherever he wanted me between Cave Junction and Long Beach.

Surrendering Control to "God"

Completely triumphant over this uprising of "ego," the next day I packed up my things and was driven in a huge van to Interstate 5 in Grants Pass. As I quietly sat thinking about my spiritual struggles, my Inner Voice distinctly sounded within my mind: "The reason you keep having battles with your ego is because you're afraid to let go of it. If you want to become a Christ, you must die in your mind and let me take over."

This guidance seemed reasonable enough; like the next logical step on my spiritual path. And so, without reservation I began at once to surrender control of my entire being to "God." I found that it was a gradual process that would take perhaps hours to complete. But within minutes there were already dramatic results.

By the time I was let out of the van, I felt like I was surging with power. It was raining, and so I decided to put my new power to a test. Based on the belief that all reality is one Mind, and that a Christ is so connected to that Mind that he can control external reality (as Jesus did with his miracles), I looked up at the completely overcast sky and confidently commanded the rain to stop and the sun to shine. *Immediately,* the clouds parted and the afternoon became sunny and dry.

My "power surge" continued to accelerate. In spite of uncertain circumstances, I had no fear in the world; nor had I any doubts about what I was experiencing. This was the consummation of my spiritual quest—God had ordered everything I had gone through before to bring me to this moment.

I sensed that if and when I returned home, I would as a Christ have the spiritual authority and power needed to kill the egos of my friends, and bring them to this same spiritual "place." A role of leadership in the emerging New Age movement seemed to be unfolding before me.

The spot where I was dropped off turned out to be a miserable place to catch a ride; there was absolutely no traffic. So I decided to use my new power again. I simply *willed* for someone to come by and pick me up. Again, "nature's" response was immediate. I was picked up and driven south to Ashland, twenty miles north of the California border, where I was dropped off at the crossing of Highway 5 and a road going west into Ashland.

I stood there hitchhiking south for a couple of hours. The process of possession continued, and I felt as high as if I'd taken LSD, though I was now under the influence of no drug.

Suddenly, my euphoria turned to alarm. I strongly sensed that my soul was in great danger, as though something evil was trying to consume me. I began to resist the entity taking possession of me, but then the thought crossed my mind: "This is just your ego putting up its last fight for survival. God is good! He wouldn't do anything to hurt you." Satisfied with this explanation, I yielded again. The negative sensation was now gone, and it began to feel as though I was fading out and something else was moving into my place.

As I stood there hitchhiking, I watched a steady succession of cars heading west toward Ashland. For no earthly reason, one of those cars off in the distance caught my attention. Intuitively I knew that they were going to stop and ask me to get in, even though I was hitchhiking in a different direction! I further sensed that this car would take me to the place God wanted me.

Not surprisingly (by now), as they approached, the driver slowed down, rolled down his window, and asked me if I'd like to have dinner. "Sure," I replied, telling myself as I headed toward the car: "When I get in they'll be talking about God, because these are God's people." I opened the door and the driver greeted me with the words: "Praise God!" "Praise God!" I replied, "God told me you were going to pick me up."

A Moment of Truth

We pulled up in a residential area to a two-story home called the "Shiloh House," a commune as large as the one I'd just left, only its long-haired members were clearly Jesus Freaks. Now convinced that there was no conflict, I no longer felt uncomfortable in this kind of atmosphere—Jesus Freaks, too, knew God.

As I sat down in the living room my mind was throbbing with so much energy that it felt like it was pressing against the walls. After identifying myself as a Christian, I proceeded to extol the insights of Kahlil Gibran's *The Prophet*. The more informed and discerning in the room no doubt recognized that they had a less-than-orthodox "Christian" on their hands.

One particularly discerning observer, named Tom, came over and engaged me in a one-on-one discussion. As I expressed my peculiar views about God, Christ, and drugs, Tom would calmly but firmly correct me with the biblical view (for example, "God is no more the universe than the maker of that chair is the chair.").

The more we talked, the more I "lost my cool," annoyed that I would have to "butt heads" with another narrow-minded Jesus Freak right during my moment of spiritual triumph. *When will these Christians stop being so bigoted?* I asked myself. *Why can't they accept the validity of other people's spiritual experiences?*

In the midst of my arguing, a realization came over me like a tidal wave. God had clearly brought me to this house. But if his goal was to possess me, and everything I'd gone through was intended to bring me to this point of surrender, then why during his moment of success would he bring me *here?* Why at such a critical time would God bring me to a place where I'd be told, in effect, that what I thought was God was a demon, unless the entity that was possessing me *was* a demon, and *that's* what God wanted me to hear?

Within a couple of minutes my entire perspective had "done a 180." Instead of seeing my life as a continual progression toward Christhood, I now saw it as a spiritual battleground, particularly since I'd been searching for the truth. Because I was not yet fully aligned with either side of the battle, I'd remained wide open to the influences of both. Through messengers and direct messages (for example, giving me advance notice of crucial events) God had indeed "met me halfway"—pointing me to Jesus as the only way to him. But Satan also was using messengers and direct messages—pointing me to myself and reinterpreting God's unique revelation in Jesus as a revelation of my own Christ potential.

Since I'd been completely happy on my mystical path and had no desire to be a Jesus Freak, I was now facing a real moment of crisis. It was also a moment of truth. The first thoughts that came into my mind were: "Go back on that freeway and start hitchhiking. Put all of this out of your mind. After all the power and triumph that have come within your grasp today, do you want to start all over again on a new spiritual path? And what of your friends in Southern California? If you become a Jesus Freak, they'll think you flipped out!"

But I knew it could never be the same again. How could I continue my quest for truth if I ignored what happened here? I'd be living a lie. Now was the time to "put my money where my mouth is," or else know forever that I wasn't *really* interested in finding truth and God. And besides, who would want to go back on that freeway knowing it was the devil he'd be returning to?

At Tom's suggestion I agreed to stay on a few days and study the Bible. That was the only pronounced "decision" I made—a nonthreatening way of saying, "I surrender." But *surrender* I had, and simultaneously the spiritual presence that I *had* been surrendering to fully retreated.

The spiritual battle over my soul did not entirely end that night, however. For example, during my second day at Shiloh I ran into a fellow alone upstairs (a visitor, but I had thought he was an established member) who engaged me in a metaphysical discussion. After he made reference to "om," the primordial "hum" of the universe (a Hindu concept), I was at once intrigued and ill-at-ease. "Most people here don't seem to believe in such things," I observed. He replied that different people were at different stages of advancement. *Hmmm, maybe there's a place for mysticism after all,* I thought.

At that instant Tom came rushing up the stairs, rebuking the visitor and proclaiming: "The Holy Spirit told me you were stumbling this brother." The visitor cowered before Tom's spiritual authority like a bad, little boy who had been caught by his mother inciting his friend to steal some cookies.

False Peace and False Light

It seemed at every turn I received further confirmation that my decision to follow Jesus and abandon my New Age path had been a moral choice between good and evil. I finally yielded once and for all to this heavenly verdict, but I still had difficulty understanding exactly what had been wrong with my former "sacramental" use of drugs. After all, hadn't it made me a better, more spiritually minded person?

After a couple weeks of painful confusion over this, I finally turned to prayer: "God, you know I've given up drugs for you and I'm willing to never use them again. But it would really help if I understood why. Please show me what is wrong with them."

Rising up from prayer I headed downstairs and sat on a couch next to Tom's fiancee Liz, just in time to overhear her refer to "drugs" in conversation with Tom. "What was that you were saying?" I asked, wondering if my prayer would be instantaneously answered.

"I was just talking to Tom about my sister. She'd accepted the Lord with us before, but has now gone back to smoking marijuana. So I'm writing a letter to warn her not to use drugs, because they open your mind to a spiritual realm, but that realm is not of God. It gives you a false kind of a peace and a false kind of a light, like the peace and light the Antichrist will give to the world. And so you can have a false sense of security that you're on the road to God when you're actually on the road to hell."

Liz's answer once and for all delivered me from my conflict. I could finally understand why drug use, or for that matter, Eastern meditation or any method of inducing altered states of consciousness, was not the way to reach God. It was possible to have a spiritual experience—even to feel blissfully enlightened and serene—without *really* experiencing God. Spiritual evil can and does masquerade as spiritual good (2 Cor. 11:14), and trancelike states of consciousness tend to open one up to such influences.

As I submitted to the spiritual regimen of the house, including daily personal and group Bible study and prayer, I gradually began to understand experientially what *authentic* spirituality is—entirely different from what I'd known before. I remember its dawning upon me after three months in Ashland that I now really knew what it was to be "born again"; what everyone meant when they spoke of having a *personal* relationship with the Lord. I no longer just knew *about* him—I *knew* him. I found this intimate fellowship with Christ to be the sweetest thing I'd ever known in life. It surpassed the "bliss" of cosmic consciousness—which I had previously thought to be the ultimate experience—just as one would expect the genuine to surpass the counterfeit.

In my more than eighteen years of experience I have found orthodox Christian faith to be entirely satisfying, both experientially and intellectually. It has profoundly answered the questions and met the needs that first propelled me on my search for truth. It is my sincere hope that New Agers will not take this testimony lightly, for I believe I had the same intellectual and experiential reasons for rejecting orthodox Christianity in favor of a more esoteric path as they. If I can find abundant satisfaction in evangelical faith, it seems to me they could too.

Actually, I have no reason to doubt that I would have gone on to become an active participant in the contemporary New Age movement were it not for one thing only: through all my spiritual experiences I remained *open* to the possibility of another world view being true than the one to which I was currently attracted. For this reason it is ironic when New Agers now accuse me of closed-mindedness *because of* my Christian beliefs.

My biggest concern about today's New Agers is that they seem to be closed to everything but pantheism. Today's seekers do not appear as interested in finding objective truth as those of fifteen to twenty years ago. Spirituality without such commitment falls right into the hands of the Evil One. Jesus said, "Seek and you shall find" (Matt. 7:7). He also said "I am . . . the truth . . ." (John 14:6). My experience, and that of numerous others I know of, testifies to the piercing accuracy of both these claims.

Notes

Chapter 1: What Is the New Age Movement?

1. Jessica Lipnack and Jeffrey Stamps, *Networking* (Garden City, N.Y.: Doubleday & Company, 1982), 7.

2. Ibid., 6.

3. Ibid., 8.

4. Ibid., 226–27.

5. Lillie Wilson, "The Planetary Initiative: A Plot to Save the World," *New Age*, Jan. 1982, 43.

6. It is true that mystical experience can *precede* and *stimulate* belief—a fact that gives New Agers a tactical evangelistic advantage over Christians. (We will see how they exploit this in chapter 5.)

7. Mark Satin, *New Age Politics* (New York: Dell Publishing Co., 1978), 328.

8. David Spangler, "Old Voyage, New Voyagers: The Maturing of Planetary Culture" (Foreword), in *The New Times Network*, comp. Robert Adams (London: Routledge & Kegan Paul, 1982), x.

9. Reported in "New Age People: We Are a Political Force," *The New Age Harmonist*, Vol. 1, No. 1, 2.

10. In areas where it is strongest, like the West Coast, the Northeast, and Colorado, it has made its political presence felt, however. For example, former California governor Jerry Brown is a true New Age politician, and former Colorado Senator Gary Hart has strong affinities with the NAM.

11. Several other Eastern religions have contributed to the New Age Move-

ment, such as Zen, Tantric (Tibetan) Buddhism, and Taoism. But they all share the same monistic world view, and all but Taoism are indebted to Hinduism for it.

12. Satin, *New Age Politics*, 98.

13. Ibid.

14. As helpful as this basis for ethics may seem to New Agers, it is doubtful that it could survive the test of time. There is a much stronger inclination in human nature toward evil than even the most realistic New Ager is willing to recognize, and ethical frameworks that *we* build, *we* can take apart. Furthermore, New Agers must realize in the back of their minds that, in spite of whatever good may be said for it, the world perceived in the "religious" state is still relative, while the world perceived in the "spiritual" state remains absolute, ultimate reality. Therefore, what's to stop a New Ager from reverting back to the "beyond good and evil" mindset of classical Hinduism and occultism? He can always resort to the position New Age writer Paul Williams (not the songwriter) does here:

> Who is God trying to kid?
> God is All. There is nothing that is not God.
> Lucifer is God. There is no distance.
> Dear God, the jig is up.
> Stop chasing your tail. Embrace your Self.
> Lucifer returns to Heaven!
> Let there be dancing in the streets.
> (*Das Energi* [New York: Warner Books, 1973], 1–2).

15. Quoted in Robert Tucker, "Back to Basics: The New Age Conspiracy," *New Age Source*, Feb. 1983, 10. The article originally appeared in *PSA* magazine.

16. Bill Barol with Mark D. Uehling and George Raine, "Muzak for a New Age," *Newsweek*, 13 May 1985, 68.

17. Sabine Kurjo, "Growth and Human Potential—Introduction," *The New Times Network*, 33.

18. Barry McWaters, *Conscious Evolution* (Los Angeles: New Age Press, 1981), xiv.

19. Spangler, *New Times Network*, x.

20. Levi, *The Aquarian Gospel of Jesus the Christ* (Santa Monica, Calif.: DeVorss & Co., 1907), 10–11.

21. Rick Ingrasci, M.D., "Up from Eden: A New Age Interview with Ken Wilber," *New Age*, April 1982, 38.

22. *See*, for example, Archibald Thomas Robertson's *Word Pictures in the New Testament*, Vol. VI (Nashville: Broadman Press, 1933), 217, and Merrill C. Tenney, *New Testament Survey* (Grand Rapids: Wm. B. Eerdmans Publishing Co., 1961), 376, 77.

23. Satin, *New Age Politics*, 114.

24. Ibid., 292, 93.

25. Ibid., 112.

26. While occultism is not always New Age (as, for example, with Satanism or the Cuban-based cult Santeria), New Age spirituality is always occultic. The

defining features of occultism (mentioned previously in this chapter as characteristic features of paganism) appear in all quarters of the movement.

Chapter 2: A New Age of Science

1. Brad Steiger, *Revelation—The Divine Fire* (Englewood Cliffs, N.J.: Prentice Hall, 1973), 186.
2. Robert Kirsch, "New Frontiers Explored in Parapsychology, Physics," *Los Angeles Times*. (Undated clip on file.)
3. Richard Maurice Bucke, *Cosmic Consciousness* (Secaucus, N.J.: The Citadel Press, 1961), 14.
4. Quoted in William James, *The Varieties of Religious Experience* (New York: New American Library, 1958), 295n.
5. Quoted in Mark Satin, *New Age Politics* (New York: Dell Publishing Co., 1978), 284.
6. Marilyn Ferguson, *The Brain Revolution* (New York: Bantam Books, 1973), xiii.
7. *The American Heritage Dictionary of the English Language* defines *scientific* as, "Broadly, having or appearing to have an exact, objective, factual, systematic or methodological basis."
8. James Gorman, "Righteous Stuff," *Omni*, May 1984, 48.
9. Ibid.
10. Ibid., 98.
11. Quoted in a 1985 Institute of Noetic Sciences appeal letter by Edgar Mitchell.
12. Efforts have been made to explain "psi" (psychic ability or phenomena) in terms of purely physical (nonspiritual) energy, but they have proved less than convincing: "The biggest barrier to acceptance of psi by conventional science, however, involves neither disputes over methodology nor the suspicion of fraud. It is centered instead on the very real failure of parapsychology to develop a plausible theory to account for phenomena that appear to transcend our concept of time and space. For science requires not only facts but also a way of explaining them. Thus far, there has been no want of speculation; to explain psi various theorists have invoked virtually every possibility, from electromagnetic fields generated by the brain to the seemingly chaotic dance of subatomic particles. Yet no researcher has come up with a coherent theoretical framework in which to fit all the fragments of psi research." (Will Bradbury [ed.], *Into the Unknown* [Pleasantville, N.Y.: The Readers' Digest Association, 1981], 219.)
13. "Bhagwan Shree Rajneesh Speaks Again," *The Rajneesh Times*, 2 Nov. 1984, 4–5.
14. Quoted in Satin, *New Age Politics*, 336.
15. Ibid., 115.
16. Ibid.
17. Quoted in Dan Wakefield, "The Hallucinogens: A Reporter's Objective View," *LSD: The Consciousness-Expanding Drug*, ed. David Solomon (New York: Berkley Medallion Books, 1966), 61.

18. Ibid., 60–61.

19. Kenneth L. Woodward with Gerald C. Lubenow, "Physics and Mysticism," *Newsweek*, 23 July 1979, 85.

20. Fritjof Capra, *The Turning Point* (Toronto: Bantam Books, 1982), 78.

21. Beverly Rubik, Ph.D., "Healing the Rift Between Science and Spirituality," Festival of Lights Program Guide, Nov. 1985, B-11. While it is certainly true that *absolute objectivity* is beyond human reach, this does not license subjectivism in science and life, as some New Agers seem to think. We are still capable of *relative* (either more or less) *objectivity*, and should strive to be as objective as possible.

22. Capra, *The Turning Point*, 95.

23. Marilyn Ferguson, *The Aquarian Conspiracy* (Los Angeles: J. P. Tarcher, 1980), 172.

24. Pat Means, *The Mystical Maze* (San Bernadino, Calif. Here's Life Publishers, 1976), 43.

25. Quoted in John Warwick Montgomery, *The Shape of the Past* (Minneapolis: Bethany Fellowship, 1975), 295.

26. This theme is developed at great length in J. N. D. Anderson's excellent book, *Christianity & Comparative Religion* (Downers Grove, Ill.: InterVarsity Press, 1971).

27. *See* Gleason, L. Archer, Jr., *A Survey of Old Testament Introduction* (Chicago: Moody Press, 1973).

28. *See* John Warwick Montgomery, *History and Christianity* (Downers Grove, Ill.: InterVarsity Press, 1971).

29. This is a presentation of the "cosmological argument." For an elaboration of its see Norman L. Geisler's *Philosophy of Religion* (Grand Rapids: Zondervan, 1974).

30. For a helpful discussion of deism, naturalism, and pantheism in contrast with biblical theism, *see* James W. Sire, *The Universe Next Door* (Downers Grove, Ill.: InterVarsity Press, 1976).

31. New Agers claim that Kirlian photography has detected this energy: "Kirlian photographs verify what psychics often point out, that we are actually interpenetrated with an energy body whose luminescence is the aura." (Geri Afshari, "Kirlian Photos Show Life Colors," *Holistic Living News*, Dec. 1982/ Jan. 1983, 28.) This is highly debatable, however. Many Kirlian researchers dismiss such claims out-of-hand. Richard Petrini of California's Lawrence Livermore Laboratory wrote in *Science*: "Kirlian photography, if properly controlled, is an excellent way to measure the moisture content of objects, period." (Quoted in Edward Edelson, "Aura Phenomenon Puzzles Experts," *Smithsonian*, April 1977, 112.)

32. Quoted in John Weldon and Clifford Wilson, *Occult Shock and Psychic Forces* (San Diego: Master Books, 1980), 158.

Chapter 2: Addendum

1. Marilyn Ferguson, *The Brain Revolution* (New York: Bantam Books, 1973), xiii–xiv.

2. For a popular description of this kind of experimentation, *see* Adam Smith, *The Powers of Mind* (New York: Random House, 1975).

3. Robert J. Mandell, "Some Insights into Psychic Abilities," *Los Angeles Times*, 5 June 1981, Part 5.

4. Lee Koromvokis, "Faith Healers in the Lab," *Science Digest*, May 1982, 95.

Chapter 3: The "New Myth": An Outline

1. Quoted in Marilyn Ferguson, *The Aquarian Conspiracy* (Los Angeles: J. P. Tarcher, 1980), 39.

2. Kristin Murphy, "United Nations' Robert Muller . . . A Vision of Global Spirituality," *The Movement Newspaper*, Sept. 1983, 10.

3. Robert Lilienfeld, *The Rise of Systems Theory—An Ideological Analysis* (New York: John Wiley & Sons, 1978), 264.

4. The systems movement encompasses a number of disciplines and schools of thought, including Ludwig von Bertalanffy's General Systems Theory (GST), cybernetics, information theory, game theory, operations research, and computerized simulation techniques. These disciplines are being linked by a growing common acceptance of von Bertalanffy's GST (which is briefly explained in this chapter). *This does not mean*, however, that everyone involved in the above disciplines embraces the new ideology.

5. The movement toward "planetization" is examined in depth in chapter 6.

6. Fritjof Capra, *The Turning Point* (Toronto: Bantam Books, 1982), 22.

7. Ibid., 25.

8. Ferguson, *The Aquarian Conspiracy*, 28.

9. Ibid., 26–28.

10. New Agers usually fail to recognize that they contradict this belief by their unyielding allegiance to monism and pantheism as absolute truths.

11. Roger Walsh, M.D., *Staying Alive* (Boulder, Colo.: New Science Library, 1984), 69.

12. Capra, *Turning Point*, 31.

13. Ibid., 59.

14. Walsh, *Staying Alive*, 36.

15. Capra, *Turning Point*, 77, 78.

16. Ibid., 266, 67.

17. Von Bertalanffy contended that this new-found mathematical precision would lend the behavioral and social sciences a new exactitude and scientific respectability.

18. Capra, "The Turning Point—A New Vision of Reality," *New Age*, Feb. 1982, 30.

19. Ludwig von Bertalanffy, *Perspectives on General Systems Theory* (New York: George Braziller, 1975), 136.

20. Mark Davidson, *Uncommon Sense* (Los Angeles: J. P. Tarcher, 1983), 84.

21. Ibid.

22. Quoted in Ferguson, *The Aquarian Conspiracy*, 383.

23. Capra, *The Turning Point*, 302.

24. Ibid., 297, 98.

25. The theme of Smuts's book is that "the fundamental activity underlying and coordinating all others" in the universe is "holism," a movement toward synthesis, or the creation of ever-deepening wholes (*Holism and Evolution* [New York: The MacMillan Company, 1926], 317). A "whole" in this context is the equivalent of a "system." Von Bertalanffy dismissed Smuts as a "vitalist," but his "organizing force" seems ultimately no less vitalistic than Smuts's "holism."

26. Process philosophy inspired process theology, associated with such names as John B. Cobb, Jr., Norman Pittenger, Shubert Ogden, and Nelson Pike. In the words of Norman Geisler, it is "perhaps the major movement, in contemporary theology." *See* Geisler's evaluation of process theology in *Tensions in Contemporary Theology*, ed. Stanley N. Gundry and Alan F. Johnson (Grand Rapids: Baker Book House, 1983).

27. Rick Ingrasci, M.D., "Up From Eden—A New Age Interview with Ken Wilber," *New Age*, April 1982, 77.

28. Donald Keys, *Earth at Omega: Passage to Planetization* (Boston: The Branden Press, 1982), iv.

29. Peter Russell, *The Global Brain*, quoted in *Brain/Mind Bulletin*, 14 Feb. 1983, 1.

30. John White, "Channeling, A Short History of a Long Tradition," *Holistic Life Magazine*, Summer 1985, 20.

31. Keys, *Earth at Omega*, iv.

32. Robert Burrows, "New Age Movement: Self-Deification in a Secular Culture," *SCP Newsletter*, Winter 1984–85, 4.

33. Jerry Adler with John Carey, "Is Man a Subtle Accident?", *Newsweek*, 3 Nov. 1980, 95.

34. Ferguson, *The Aquarian Conspiracy*, 158, 59.

35. Ibid., 159.

36. Ronald S. Miller, "The Evolutionary Journey—An Interview with Barbara Marx Hubbard," *Science of Mind*, Jan. 1983, 8.

37. Barry McWaters, *Conscious Evolution* (Los Angeles: New Age Press, 1981), xii, from the foreword by David Spangler.

38. Quoted in Walsh, *Staying Alive*, 81.

39. McWaters, *Conscious Evolution*, 27, 28.

40. Walsh, *Staying Alive*, 82.

41. Keys, *Earth at Omega*, iii.

42. Jessica Lipnack and Jeffrey Stamps, *Networking* (Garden City, N.Y.: Doubleday & Company, 1982), 193.

43. Ferguson, *The Aquarian Conspiracy*, 55.

44. Ibid., 50.

45. Pierre Teilhard de Chardin, *The Phenomenon of Man* (New York: Harper & Row, 1961), 300.

46. Ibid., 258.

47. Ibid., 181.

48. Ibid., 182.

49. Ibid., 259.
50. Ibid., 251.
51. Pierre Teilhard de Chardin, *The Future of Man*, quoted in Keys, 69.
52. Teilhard de Chardin, *The Phenomenon of Man*, 250, 51.
53. Keys, *Earth at Omega*, 70.
54. Capra, *The Turning Point*, 292.
55. Keys, *Earth at Omega*, 71.
56. McWaters, *Conscious Evolution*, 10.

Chapter 4: The "New Myth": A Critique

1. *See* Dave Hunt and T. A. McMahon, *The Seduction of Christianity* (Eugene, Oreg.: Harvest House Publishers, 1985), 191.
2. Duchrow's paper, accompanied by responses from several Christian scholars, appeared in *Gospel in Context* 1 (Oct. 1978): 4–23. All quotes from Duchrow are taken from pp. 5–6.
3. Mark Davidson, *Uncommon Sense* (Los Angeles: J. P. Tarcher, 1983), 188.
4. *See* Robert Lilienfeld, *The Rise of Systems Theory—An Ideological Analysis* (New York: John Wiley & Sons, 1978).
5. *Gospel in Context*, 15–16.
6. Davidson, *Uncommon Sense*, 159.
7. Fritjof Capra, *The Turning Point* (Toronto: Bantam Books, 1982), 38.
8. *See*, for example, Jack Kornfield, "Sex Lives of the Gurus," and Dia Urmilla Neff, "Tumbling from the Pedestal: What Makes Spiritual Teachers Go Retrograde?", both of which appeared in *Yoga Journal*, July/August, 1985.
9. It should be observed that in seeking such a basis New Agers are unconsciously attempting to embrace two mutually exclusive Gods and inhabit two mutually exclusive worlds. In other words, while retaining their basic pantheism (all is God) they are also adopting aspects of process philosophy's panentheism (all is *in* God). The latter world view allows for the world to be real as it appears, and for history to have purpose. If New Agers should recognize the logical impossibility of their present position and fully move over to panentheism, they will then inherit *new* logical impossibilities. The interested reader will find these detailed in Norman Geisler and William Watkins's *Worlds Apart* (Grand Rapids: Baker Book House, 1989).
10. Ian G. Barbour, *Issues in Science and Religion* (New York: Harper Torchbooks, 1971), 289–90.
11. For an incisive treatment of the claim that the biblical God *is* process, *see* Norman Geisler's chapter on process theology in *Tensions in Contemporary Theology*, ed. Stanley N. Gundry and Alan F. Johnson, 2d ed. (Grand Rapids: Baker Book House, 1976, 1983).
12. Barbour, *Issues*, 297.
13. From a letter to this writer dated April 11, 1986. The reader interested in more information on punctuated equilibrium is referred to Dr. Morris's Institute for Creation Research (P.O. Box 2667, El Cajon, Calif. 92021).
14. Jerry Adler with John Carey, "Is Man a Subtle Accident?," *Newsweek*, 3

Nov. 1980, 96. It should be noted that *Newsweek* goes on to report the punctuationalist response of Harvard biologist Pedro Alberch. Alberch argues that a new species may only require a mutation in a single gene if the gene controls a crucial developmental pathway. "He points to a race of salamanders which have a cluster of six unique characteristics, including webbed feet and fused tarsal bones. The identical mutation has appeared at least six different times in the evolution of salamanders, suggesting that only a single small genetic change is involved." *(Ibid.)* In reply it may be observed that even if only a single gene was involved in the salamander mutations it would lend little support to punctuated equilibrium. Punctuated equilibrium by definition involves *macroevolution* (the change of one species into another), and is supposed to operate according to a *different* mechanism than *microevolution* (changes *within* the genetic limits of a species). The webbed-feet salamanders are *still salamanders*. Since punctuated equilibrium postulates more *radical* structural changes the objection that it would "set awry" an organism's "delicate systems" was not satisfactorily answered by Alberch.

15. See, for example, Josh McDowell, *More Evidence that Demands a Verdict* (San Bernadino, Calif.: Here's Life Publishers, 1975).

Chapter 5: Tracking the "Aquarian Conspiracy" (Part One)

1. For example, Willis Harman, Ph.D., "Peace Is Possible," Festival of Lights Program Guide, Nov. 1985, B-8.

2. This deceptive proselytizing methodology was first exposed by the Spiritual Counterfeits Project in tracts like "TM: Penetrating the Veil of Deception."

3. Marilyn Ferguson, *The Aquarian Conspiracy* (Los Angeles: J. P. Tarcher, 1980), 35–36.

4. Ibid., 258.

5. Ibid., 242.

6. Jerry Driessen, Ph.D., "Health Sharing: Comments on the Characteristics of Holistic Health" (fact sheet), Holistic Health Education—Association for Holistic Health, May 1978.

7. Dana Ullman, M.P.H., "Holistic Health: Friend and Foe of Progressive Health Care," *International Journal of Holistic Health and Medicine* 2 (Winter 1984): 22.

8. Cited in Meme Black, "M.D.'s and Magic," *Science Digest*, May 1982, 92.

9. Lee Koromvokis, "Faith Healers in the Lab," *Science Digest*, May 1982, 95.

10. "Therapeutic Touch," New York Open Center catalog, Jan.–Mar. 1984, 9.

11. Ibid.

12. William Falk, "Meditation Merges with the Mainstream," *Esquire*, Mar. 1983, 249.

13. Quoted in Adam Smith, *Powers of Mind* (New York: Random House, 1975), 153.

14. Brooks Alexander, "The Rise of Cosmic Humanism: What Is Religion?" *SCP Journal* 5 (Winter 1981–82): 4.

15. Jack Canfield and Paula Klimek, "Education in the New Age," *New Age,* Feb. 1978, 28.

16. Ibid.

17. Ferguson, *The Aquarian Conspiracy,* 295.

18. There is nothing necessarily New Age about the practice of guided imagery *per se.* However, as the forthcoming quote from Beverly Galeyan indicates, it can easily be used for New Age purposes.

19. Ferguson, *The Aquarian Conspiracy,* 288.

20. Ibid., 281.

21. Canfield and Klimek, *New Age,* 36.

22. Ibid., 27.

23. Beverly Galeyan, "Meditating with Children: Some Things We Learned," *AHP Newsletter,* Aug.–Sept. 1980, 16. (This quote, but not the following, was taken from the AHP's introduction to the article.)

24. Ibid., 18.

25. Richard A. Baer, Jr., "Parents, Schools and Values Clarification," *The Wall Street Journal,* 12 April 1982.

26. Lynn Smith, "Americans Take a Long Look Inward," *Los Angeles Times,* 20 July 1982, part 1.

27. For example, after observing several disturbed Lifespring graduates, Dr. George Fulop, chief psychiatric resident at Mt. Sinai Medical Center in New York, commented that Lifespring's combination of "an overwhelming group experience with forced exposure to confrontational, emotional exercises can be very dangerous." ("Lifespring's Growth Called 'Phenomenal,'" *The Cult Observer,* Jan./Feb. 1988, 11.) Similar observations have frequently been made regarding the Forum/est.

28. Cited in Robert Tucker, "Back to Basics: The New Age Conspiracy," *New Age Source,* Feb. 1983. The article originally appeared in *PSA Magazine.*

29. Robert Lindsey, "Spiritual Concepts Drawing a Different Breed of Adherent," *New York Times,* 28 Sept. 1986, sec. 1.

30. Norman Boucher, "Transforming Corporation," *New Age Journal,* Feb. 1985, 38.

31. Ibid., 39–40.

32. Jessica Lipnack and Jeffrey Stamps, *Networking* (Garden City, N.Y.: Doubleday and Company, 1982), 108.

33. In addition to the information that is offered in this chapter, those seeking help in resisting New Age advances should consult Douglas Groothuis, *Confronting the New Age* (Downers Grove, Ill.: InterVarsity Press, 1988), Mel and Norma Gabler, *What Are They Teaching Our Children?* (Victor), and Elliot Miller, "Saying No to the New Age," *Moody Monthly,* Feb. 1985.

34. *See* William F. Willoughby, "Man Shall Not Live by Raw Carrots Alone," *Liberty,* 8 July 1982, 9.

35. The excerpt from this interview quoted here was first published in "Saying No to the New Age," *Moody Monthly,* 25.

36. Quoted in "Training Shall Not Clash with Religion," *Insight,* 16 May 1988, 26.

37. Quoted in "EEOC Guidelines on Religious Discrimination and Trainings," *The Cult Observer,* May/June 1988, 6.

38. Ibid.

39. Ibid.

Chapter 6: Tracking the "Aquarian Conspiracy" (Part Two)

1. "New Age People: We Are a Political Force," *New Age Harmonist,* 1, 1:2.

2. The nature and characteristics of networks were described in detail in chapter 1.

3. *See,* for example, Jessica Lipnack and Jeffrey Stamps, *Networking* Garden City, N.Y.: Doubleday & Company, 1982), 228.

4. That Ferguson overstated the case is acknowledged even among those who embrace the new ideology. *See* Donald N. Michael, "Aquarians Riding the Third Wave," *Journal of Humanistic Psychology* 25 (Winter 1985): 81.

5. John Vasconcellos, *Politics for Beginners* (tape) (San Anselmo, Calif.: Conference Coordinating Company, 1986).

6. Willis Harman and Donald Keys, *Sharing Personal and Planetary Security* (tape) (San Anselmo, Calif.: Conference Coordinating Company, 1986).

7. For an in-depth treatment of the history and ideology of the international Green movement *see* Fritjof Capra and Charlene Spretnak, *Green Politics: The Global Promise* (New York: E. P. Dutton, 1984).

8. "What Is Green Politics?" (statement), Cascadia Green Alliance, n.d.

9. Jeffrey Perlman, "Beyond Pocketbook Politics," *Los Angeles Times,* 14 Mar. 1982, part 9.

10. Those interested in reading more on this new development in liberal politics are referred to Walter Truett Anderson, ed., *Rethinking Liberalism* (New York: Avon, 1983).

11. Mark Satin, *New Age Politics* (New York: Dell Publishing Co., 1978), 236, 240, 246–51.

12. It must be recognized here that there is no well-defined "Christian political outlook" *per se,* since Christians can be found endorsing a wide spectrum of political views, each of which appeals to biblical values for support. But what I am arguing for is that, owing to a common world view and values, there are certain distinct perimeters to consistently Christian politics. To wit: a Christian might hold to a utopian political theory, but in so doing he or she is not being consistent with the Christian doctrine of human sin and its pervasiveness in the individual and society.

13. John Vasconcellos, *The New Human Politics* (tape) (San Anselmo, Calif.: Conference Coordinating Company, 1986).

14. "Interview: Norman Cousins," *New Realities,* Jan./Feb. 1985, 9.

15. Ibid.

16. Donald Keys, "All About Planetary Citizens: A Seminar in Four Parts" (transcript), n.d., Seminar 2, 1.

17. The author has written a paper entitled "H. G. Wells—Father of the World State Movement," which traces the move toward global unification throughout the century. The interested reader can write him at Christian Research Institute for a copy (P.O. Box 500, San Juan Capistrano, Calif. 92693).

18. *See*, for example, *The Humanist*, Mar./Apr. 1986, which features several articles on globalism.

19. *See*, for example, Benjamin Creme, *The Reappearance of the Christ and the Masters of Wisdom* (London: The Tara Press, 1980), 30.

20. *See*, for example, Satin, *New Age Politics*, 149–52.

21. Mark Sommer, "Constructing Peace as a Whole System," *Whole Earth Review*, Summer 1986, 18.

22. Arnold Toynbee, *Surviving the Future* (New York: Oxford University Press, 1971), 113–14.

23. Robert E. Cummings, "Global Community Networks: Living Locally/ Thinking Globally," *Transnational Perspectives* 8, 2:15.

24. *See*, for example, Terry Cole-Whitaker, *How to Have More in a Have-Not World* (New York: Fawcett Crest, 1983).

25. E. F. Schumacher, *Small Is Beautiful* (New York: Harper Colophon Books, 1973), 63.

26. A more detailed description of the people, groups, and activities referred to in this paragraph can be found in my previously mentioned research paper (*see* note 17).

27. Peter Stoller, "A Conversation with Jonas Salk," *Psychology Today*, Mar. 1983, 56.

28. Willis Harman and Donald Keys, *Personal and Planetary Peace: An Impossible Dream?* (tape) (San Anselmo, Calif.: Conference Coordinating Company, 1986).

29. Keys, "All About Planetary Citizens," Seminar 3, 1–2.

30. Donald Keys, "Security Alternatives," *AHP Perspective*, Dec. 1985, 18.

31. Harman and Keys, *Personal and Planetary Peace* (tape).

32. This is also given more detailed attention in my research paper.

33. Quoted in Satin, *New Age Politics*, 331.

34. Donald Keys, *Earth at Omega* (Boston: Brandon Press, 1982), 101.

35. Marilyn Ferguson, *The Aquarian Conspiracy* (Los Angeles: J. P. Tarcher, 1980), 221.

36. Keys, *Earth at Omega*, 88.

37. *See*, as the prime case in point, Constance Cumbey, *The Hidden Dangers of the Rainbow* (Shreveport, La.: Huntington House, 1983).

Chapter 7: Is the End upon Us?

1. Constance Cumbey is the classic example here, especially since many of the later writers and speakers (including Texe Marrs) repeat her errors. *See* my review of her books in Appendix B.

2. The reader interested in studying the various eschatological views may write Christian Research Institute (P.O. Box 500, San Juan Capistrano, CA 92693) for our eschatology bibliography.

3. I realize that Matthew 24:34 ("This generation will not pass away until all these things take place") is interpreted by many to mean that the end *must* come in a matter of decades or even years. But this passage has interpretive difficulties that should discourage dogmatism (for example, *genea* can be translated "race" or "nation" as well as "generation." Who did Jesus mean by "this" generation? How long is a generation?).

4. Quoted in Mark Satin, *New Age Politics* (New York: Dell Publishing Co., 1978), 148.

5. Donald Keys, *Earth at Omega* (Boston: Branden Press, 1982), 3.

6. "U.N.'s Robert Muller to Speak at Universal Peace Conference," *The Movement Newspaper*, Feb. 1983, 21.

7. This potential is best explained and illustrated in Tal Brooke's *Riders of the Cosmic Circuit* (Tring, England: Lion Publishing Company, 1986).

8. Just a few examples: in various places esotericists call for a world government, economy, and religion (Vera Stanley Alder, *When Humanity Comes of Age* [New York: Samuel Weiser, 1974], 193), affirm that the coming world Christ will *not* be Jesus (Alice A. Bailey, *The Externalization of the Hierarchy* [New York: Lucis Publishing Company, 1957], 612), assert that he will not come primarily as a religious leader but as one advocating changes in our political, social, and economic life (Benjamin Creme, *The Reappearance of the Christ and the Masters of Wisdom* [London: The Tara Press, 1980], 66), and predict the gradual dissolution of orthodox Judaism and Christianity (Bailey, 544–45).

9. There are degrees of certitude that one may pass through before reaching *absolute* certainty. I acknowledge that throughout the twentieth century there have been mounting indications that the end is drawing near. But until *all* of the signs of the end are evident (including the revelation of the Antichrist), it is premature to conclude that Christ will come within a limited number of years (*see* Matt. 24:33).

10. Dave Hunt, *Peace, Prosperity, and the Coming Holocaust* (Eugene, Oreg.: Harvest House Publishers, 1983), 57, 58.

11. Arnold Toynbee, *The World and the West* (New York: Oxford University Press, 1953), 19.

Chapter 8: Channeling: Spiritistic Revelations (Part One: Background)

1. Jon Klimo, *Channeling* (Los Angeles: Jeremy P. Tarcher, 1987), 1.

2. Ibid., 185.

3. Carol Ostrom, "Pastor Resigns, Sticks with Disputed Belief," *The Seattle Times*, 28 July 1986, section B. Claiming to have lived in Jesus' time, Jonah says Jesus did not die on the cross but had a three-day out-of-body experience, married a Druid princess, and had children.

4. Ibid.

5. For a comprehensive historical overview of spiritism, *see* Klimo, *Channeling*, chapter 2.

6. Quoted in Klimo, *Channeling*, 5–6, from an interview with the author.

7. Ibid., 106.

8. *A Course in Miracles*, Vol. 1, *Text* (N.p., Foundation for Inner Peace, 1975), ix.

9. The Spiritual Counterfeits Project has published a careful analysis of *A Course in Miracles*, written by Dean Halverson. See *SCP Journal*, 7:1, 1987 (P.O. Box 4308, Berkeley, CA 94704). Halverson has also written a critique of *The Urantia Book* which appeared in the *SCP Newsletter*, August 1981.

10. Jane Roberts, *Seth Speaks* (Englewood Cliffs, N.J.: Prentice Hall, 1972), ix–x.

11. Ibid., x.

12. Hal Zina Bennett, Ph.D., "The Inner Guides," *Magical Blend*, no. 16, 40.

13. Craig Lee, "Messages from Channel Infinity," *LA Weekly*, Nov. 7–13, 1986, 20.

14. Carol M. Ostrom, "Tuning in on the Master's Channel," *Seattle Times*, 5 June 1983, section D.

15. "Ramtha—An Exclusive Interview with His Channel J. Z. Knight," *Holistic Life Magazine*, Summer 1985, 30.

16. Ibid.

17. "Ramtha," quoted in Ostrom, "Tuning in."

18. Lee, "Channel Infinity," 20.

19. In publicity flyer, "Lazaris, the Consummate Friend," quoted in Klimo, *Channeling*, 47.

20. "Lazaris," *Awakening the Love* (video tape) (Fairfax, Calif.: Concept: Synergy, 1985).

21. Mark Vaz, "Psychic! The Many Faces of Kevin Ryerson" (interview), *Yoga Journal*, July/Aug. 1986, 28.

22. Ibid., 29.

23. Klimo, *Channeling*, 65.

24. Darryl Anka, quoted in Caryline Waldron, "Bashar: An Extraterrestrial Among Us," *Life Times*, 1:3, 107.

25. Ibid.

26. Kathleen A. Hughes, "For Personal Insights, Some Try Channels Out of This World," *Wall Street Journal*, 1 April 1987, 1.

27. Ibid., 22.

28. Klimo, *Channeling*, 176.

29. Ibid., 56.

30. Hughes, "Some Try Channels," 22.

31. Advertisement, *The Whole Person*, July 1987, 71.

32. C. P. Jeffries, Editorial, *Cycles*, July 1987, 36–37.

33. "She's Having the Time of Her Lives," *People*, Dec. 1986.

34. *See* Nina Easton, "Shirley MacLaine's Mysticism for the Masses," *Los Angeles Times Magazine*, 6 Sept. 1987, 33.

35. William H. Kautz and Melanie Branon, *Channeling: the Intuitive Connection* (San Francisco: Harper & Row, 1987), 15–16.

36. Easton, "Shirley MacLaine's Mysticism," 8.

37. Ibid., 34.

38. Lynn Smith, "The New, Chic Metaphysical Fad of Channeling," *Los Angeles Times*, 5 Dec. 1986, Part V.

39. *The Whole Person*, 89.

40. Lee, "Channel of Infinity," 76.

41. *The Whole Person*, 1.

42. Easton, "Shirley MacLaine's Mysticism," 34.

43. For example, a follower of Ramtha boasts: "Whereas most other teachers speak in terms of suffering and hardship, deprivation, long years, Ramtha says you can begin to live in a moment. . . . Enlightenment is only a moment away." ("Ramtha," with Douglas James Mahr, *Voyage to the New World* [Friday Harbor, Wash.: Masterworks, 1985], 81.)

44. "Channels—Historic Cycle Begins Again," *Mobius Reports*, Spring/Summer 1987, 4.

Chapter 9: Channeling: Spiritistic Revelations
(Part Two: Analysis)

1. Mark Vaz, "Psychic! The Many Faces of Kevin Ryerson," *Yoga Journal*, July/Aug. 1986, 27.

2. Lynn Smith, "The New, Chic Metaphysical Fad of Channeling," *Los Angeles Times*, 5 Dec. 1986, Part V.

3. Sanaya Roman and Duane Packer, *Opening to Channel* (Tiburon, Calif.: H. J. Kramer, 1987), 55.

4. Jon Klimo, *Channeling* (Los Angeles: Jeremy P. Tarcher, 1987), 192.

5. William H. Kautz and Melanie Branon, *Channeling: The Intuitive Connection* (San Francisco: Harper & Row, 1987), 25.

6. Quoted in Klimo, *Channeling*, 42, from an interview with the author.

7. Alice A. Bailey, *Telepathy* (New York: Lucis Pub., 1950), 75–77, quoted in Klimo, 321.

8. Joey Crinita, *The Medium Touch: A New Approach to Mediumship* (Norfolk, Va.: Unilaw Library/Donning Company, 1982), 45, quoted in Klimo, 321.

9. George Hackett with Pamela Abramson, "Ramtha, a Voice from Beyond," *Newsweek*, 15 Dec. 1986, 42.

10. Klimo, *Channeling*, 243.

11. *See*, for example, Alan Vaughan's comments in "Channels—Historic Cycle Begins Again," *Mobius Reports*, Spring/Summer, 1987, 11.

12. It was both a surprise and a confirmation for me to find the same theory independently suggested by Brooks Alexander in his *Christianity Today* article, "Are the Entities for Real?" (18 Sept. 1987, 24).

13. Ibid., citing an observation made by Robert Burrows.

14. Jane Roberts, *The Nature of Personal Reality* (New York: Bantam Books, 1978), 21.

15. "Ramtha" with Douglas James Mahr, *Voyage to the New World* (Friday Harbor, Wash.: Masterworks, 1985), 24.

16. Iris Belhayes, *Spirit Guides* (San Diego: ACS Publications, 1985), 11.

17. "Lazaris," "Do Not Ignore Your Responsibility to Be Free, to Be Limitless, to Found a New World," *Psychic Guide*, Sept./Oct. 1987, 52–53.

18. "Ramtha" with Mahr, *Voyage to the New World*, 135.

19. Ibid., 228.

20. Ibid., 61.

21. "Jesus" (through Virginia Essene), "Secret Truths—What Is Life?," *Life Times*, 1:3, 105.

22. Klimo, *Channeling*, 347.

23. "Plugging into Your Higher Self," *Psychic Guide*, Sept./Oct. 1987, 20.

24. Belhayes, *Spirit Guides*, 19.

25. Roman and Packer, *Opening to Channel*, 44.

26. "Talking with Saint Germaine," *Life Times*, 1:3, 86.

27. John White, "Channeling, A Short History of a Long Tradition," *Holistic Life Magazine*, Summer 1985, 22.

28. Kautz and Branon, *Channeling*, 37.

29. Barry McWaters, *Conscious Evolution* (Los Angeles: New Age Press, 1981), 111–12.

30. Space permits but one example: in the same issue of *Life Times* (1:3), Mafu said there will be no cataclysmic "earth changes" such as earthquakes and polar shifts before the New Age (p. 97), while his fellow inhabitant of the "seventh dimension," Saint Germaine, affirms that these very things will occur (p. 69).

31. White, "Channeling, A Short History," 22.

32. Kautz and Branon, *Channeling*, 136–37.

33. For example, Ramtha counsels one follower: "Of guilt . . . you see the folly of it. The only damage you ever did, Entity, was to yourself by allowing you to feel that way—kept you from having a jolly good time. You understand?" ("Ramtha" with Mahr, *Voyage*, 218.) He advises another: "You know, God is everything—He is every thing. So any thing you do, you have an inner action in divinity. Remember that, and do what you want to do, and portray yourself how you want to portray yourself, and let the world alone." (Ibid., 36.)

34. *See*, for example, Klimo, *Channeling*, 61, where an end-time scenario is laid out which fits the Book of Revelation perfectly, only from the reverse perspective.

35. Belhayes, *Spirit Guides*, 5.

36. *See* Craig Lee, "Messages from Channel Infinity," *LA Weekly*, Nov. 7–13, 1986, 18.

37. Quoted in Klimo, *Channeling*, 184, from an interview with the author.

38. Quoted in Brad Steiger, *Revelation: The Divine Fire*, (Englewood Cliffs, N.J.: Prentice Hall, 1973), 244–45.

Appendix B: Constance Cumbey's Conspiracy Theory

1. The interested reader may write Christian Research Institute for our statement, "A Reply to Constance Cumbey's Charges Against Walter Martin and CRI" (P.O. Box 500, San Juan Capistrano, CA 92693–0500).

2. *See,* for example, Alice Bailey, *The Externalization of the Hierarchy* (New York: Lucis Publishing Company, 1957), 664, and Benjamin Creme, *The Reappearance of the Christ and the Masters of Wisdom* (London: The Tara Press, 1980), 249.

3. Bailey, *Externalization,* 312.

4. Ibid., 582–85.

5. Ibid., 586.

6. Ibid., 104.

7. Accounts of this can be found in the following authorities: J. Gordon Melton, *The Encyclopedia of American Religions,* 2d ed. (Detroit: Gale Research Company, 1987), 126–27, 607–610; J. Stillson Judah, *The History and Philosophy of the Metaphysical Movements in America* (Philadelphia: The Westminster Press, 1967), 119–33.

8. W. Warren Wagar, *H. G. Wells and the World State* (New Haven: Yale University Press, 1961), 258.

9. Ibid., 255–56.

10. Ibid., 265–66.

11. Ibid., 269.

12. Ibid., 174.

13. Ibid., 246.

14. *See,* for example, Lovat Dickson, *H. G. Wells: His Turbulent Life and Times* (New York: Atheneum, 1969) and Mark R. Hillegas, *The Future as Nightmare: H. G. Wells and the Anti-Utopians* (New York: Oxford University Press, 1967), 79–80.

15. William Irwin Thompson, *Passages About Earth* (New York: Perennial Library, 1973), 79.

16. H. G. Wells, *The Open Conspiracy* (Garden City, N.Y.: Doubleday, 1928), 144–45.

17. Wagar, *H. G. Wells,* 202–03.

18. Jessica Lipnack and Jeffrey Stamps, *Networking* (Garden City, N.Y.: Doubleday & Company, 1982), 225.

19. Donald Keys, *Earth at Omega: Passage to Planetization* (Boston: The Branden Press, 1982), 106.

20. Fritjof Capra, "The Turning Point—A New Vision of Reality," *New Age,* Feb. 1982, 30.

21. Dave Hunt, *Peace, Prosperity, and the Coming Holocaust* (Eugene, Oreg.: Harvest House Publishers, 1983), 48.

Bibliography

The following books are *recommended reading* in that they provide the reader with educational material on the New Age movement and related themes. They are not all *recommended* as to their spiritual or theological content, since many convey unchristian beliefs. To help the reader distinguish between books written from Christian, New Age, and secular perspectives, the letters *C*, *N*, and *S* are included at the close of each entry. It should be clarified that some books designated *N* actually predate the New Age movement *per se;* but they *do* affirm the basic New Age world view. And some books designated *S* may have New Age leanings; nonetheless, they attempt to provide purely scientific or scholarly rather than sectarian treatments of their subjects (although others in the same category may indeed be considered "sectarian" in that they communicate a *secular* bias). An asterisk follows the designation *N* if the work has strong *affinities* with New Age thinking, but is not *necessarily* or *strictly* New Age. This applies even where the author has written elsewhere in an explicitly New Age vein. There are numerous other important books that could have been listed (the subject is so vast that the candidates for inclusion seem endless!). The following books—which I have found particularly significant in my own research—have been selected to provide a broad cross section for further study. To keep the bibliography from being unwieldy, only books are listed. The reader will find extensive references to relevant periodicals and articles in the notes.

1. The New Age Movement—Comprehensive Critiques

Groothuis, Douglas R. *Unmasking the New Age.* Downers Grove, IL: Inter-Varsity Press, 1986. (C)

———. *Confronting the New Age*. Downers Grove, IL: InterVarsity Press, 1988. (C)

Hoyt, Karen, and the Spiritual Counterfeits Project. *The New Age Rage*. Old Tappan, NJ: Fleming H. Revell, 1987. (C)

2. The New Age Movement as a Movement

Ferguson, Marilyn. *The Aquarian Conspiracy: Personal and Social Transformation in the 1980s*. Los Angeles: J. P. Tarcher, 1980. (N)

Lipnack, Jessica, and Jeffrey Stamps. *Networking*. Garden City, NY: Doubleday and Company, 1982. (N)

Popenoe, Cris, and Oliver Popenoe. *Seeds of Tomorrow: New Age Communities that Work*. San Francisco: Harper and Row, 1984. (N)

3. Major Sources for the New Age Movement

Bailey, Alice A. *Initiation, Human and Solar*. New York: Lucis Publishing Company, 1922. (N)

———. *The Reappearance of the Christ*. New York: Lucis Publishing Company, 1948. (N)

———. *The Externalization of the Hierarchy*. New York: Lucis Publishing Company, 1957. (N)

Besant, Annie. *Esoteric Christianity; or, The Lesser Mysteries*. 1901. Reprint. Wheaton, IL: The Theosophical Publishing House, 1970. (N)

Blavatsky, H. P. *Isis Unveiled: A Master-Key to the Mysteries of Ancient and Modern Science and Theology*. 2 vols. 1877. Reprint (2 vols. in 1). Los Angeles: The Theosophy Company, 1968. (N)

———. *The Secret Doctrine: The Synthesis of Science, Religion, and Philosophy*. 2 vols. 1888. Reprint. Pasadena, CA: Theosophical University Press, 1970. (N)

Bucke, Richard Maurice. *Cosmic Consciousness*. Secaucus, NJ: The Citadel Press, 1961. (N)

Huxley, Aldous. *The Perennial Philosophy*. New York: Harper and Row, 1970. (N)

Jung, Carl G. *Modern Man in Search of a Soul*. New York: Harcourt Brace, 1936. (N*)

———. *Psychology and Religion*. New Haven: Yale University, 1971. (N*)

Kuhn, Thomas. *The Structure of Scientific Revolutions*. Chicago: The University of Chicago Press, 1962. (S)

Levi. *The Aquarian Gospel of Jesus the Christ*. Santa Monica, CA: DeVorss and Co., 1907. (N)

Leadbeater, C. W. *An Outline of Theosophy*. Chicago: Theosophical Book Concern, 1903. (N)

Maharishi Mahesh Yogi. *The Science of Being and Art of Living*. 1963. Reprint. New York: New American Library, 1968. (N)

Ouspensky, P. D. *Tertium Organum: A Key to the Enigmas of the World*. 1920. Reprint. New York: Random House, 1970. (N)

———. *In Search of the Miraculous: Fragments of an Unknown Teaching*. 1949. Reprint. New York: Harcourt Brace Jovanovich, 1977. (N)

———. *The Fourth Way*. 1957. Reprint. New York: Random House, 1971. (N)

Paramahansa Yogananda. *Autobiography of a Yogi*. 1946. Reprint. Los Angeles: Self Realization Fellowship Publishers, 1972. (N)

Stern, Jess. *Edgar Cayce: The Sleeping Prophet*. Garden City, NY: Doubleday, 1967. (N)

Steiner, Rudolf. *Knowledge of the Higher Worlds and Its Attainment*. 3d ed. Spring Valley, NY: Anthroposophic Press, 1947. (N)

———. *An Outline of Occult Science*. 3d ed. Spring Valley, NY: Anthroposophic Press, 1972. (N)

———. *The Reappearance of Christ in the Etheric*. Spring Valley, NY: Anthroposophic Press, 1983. (N)

Sugrue, Thomas. *There Is a River: The Story of Edgar Cayce*. 1942. Reprint. New York: Dell, 1967. (N)

Teilhard de Chardin, Pierre. *The Phenomenon of Man*. New York: Harper and Row, 1961. (N*)

4. New Age World View and Belief System

Albrecht, Mark C. *Reincarnation: A Christian Critique of a New Age Doctrine*. Downers Grove, IL: InterVarsity Press, 1982. (C)

Campbell, Joseph, with Bill Moyers. *The Power of Myth*. New York: Doubleday, 1988. (N)

Geisler, Norman L., and J. Yutaka Amano. *The Reincarnation Sensation*. Wheaton, IL: Tyndale House, 1986. (C)

Head, Joseph, and S. L. Cranston, eds. and comps. *Reincarnation: The Phoenix Fire Mystery*. New York: Julian Press, 1977. (N)

MacGregor, Geddes. *Reincarnation in Christianity: A New Vision of the Role of Rebirth in Christian Thought*. Wheaton, IL: The Theosophical Publishing House, 1978. (N)

Mark, Alexandra. *Astrology for the Aquarian Age: An Informative Guide to Casting and Interpreting Horoscopes*. New York: Essandess Special Editions, 1970. (N)

Sire, James W. *The Universe Next Door*. Downers Grove, IL: InterVarsity Press, 1976. (C)

Spangler, David. *Revelation: The Birth of a New Age*. Middletown, WI: Lorian Press, 1976. (N)

―――. *Towards a Planetary Vision*. 2d ed. Forres, Scotland: Findhorn Publications, 1977. (N)

―――. *Reflections on the Christ*. 3d ed. Moray, Scotland: Findhorn Publications, 1981. (N)

Strohmer, Charles. *What Your Horoscope Doesn't Tell You*. Wheaton, IL: Tyndale House Publishers, 1988. (C)

Trevelyan, George. *A Vision of the Aquarian Age*. Walpole, NH: Stillpoint Publishing, 1984. (N)

Watts, Alan W. *The Supreme Identity: An Essay on Oriental Metaphysic and The Christian Religion*. 1950. Reprint. New York: Random House, 1972. (N)

―――. *The Two Hands of God: The Myths of Polarity*. New York: The Macmillan Company, 1963. (N)

―――. *The Book: On the Taboo Against Knowing Who You Are*. New York: The Macmillan Company, 1966. (N)

Wilber, Ken. *Up from Eden*. Boulder, CO: Shambhala, 1983. (N)

5. New Age Physics

Barbour, Ian G. *Issues in Science and Religion*. New York: Harper and Row, 1971. (S)

Bohm, David. *Wholeness and the Implicate Order*. London: Routledge and Kegan Paul, 1980. (N*)

Capra, Fritjof. *The Tao of Physics: An Exploration of the Parallels Between Modern Physics and Eastern Mysticism*. Boulder: Shambhala, 1975. (N)

Gardner, Martin. *Science: Good, Bad, and Bogus*. New York: Avon, 1981. (S)

Zukav, Gary. *The Dancing Wu Li Masters*. New York: Morrow, 1979. (N)

6. Mysticism, Altered States of Consciousness, and Psychic Phenomena

Anderson, J. N. D. *Christianity and Comparative Religion*. Downers Grove, IL: InterVarsity Press, 1970. (C)

Castaneda, Carlos. *The Teachings of Don Juan: A Yaqui Way of Knowledge*. New York: Ballantine Books, 1968. (N)

―――. *A Separate Reality: Further Conversations with Don Juan*. New York: Simon and Schuster, 1971. (N)

————. *Journey to Ixtlan: The Lessons of Don Juan.* New York: Simon and Schuster, 1972. (N)

Ferguson, Marilyn. *The Brain Revolution.* New York: Bantam Books, 1973. (N)

Gopi, Krishna. *The Awakening of Kundalini.* New York: E. P. Dutton, 1975. (N)

James, William. *The Varieties of Religious Experience.* New York: New American Library, 1958. (S)

Koch, Kurt. *Christian Counseling and Occultism.* Grand Rapids: Kregel, 1972. (C)

Koestler, Arthur. *The Roots of Coincidence: An Excursion into Parapsychology.* New York: Random House, 1972. (N)

Lilly, John C. *The Center of the Cyclone: An Autobiography of Inner Space.* New York: Julian Press, 1972. (N)

Masters, Robert, and Jean Houston. *The Varieties of Psychedelic Experience.* New York: Dell, 1967. (N)

Mitchell, Edgar. *Psychic Exploration: A Challenge for Science.* New York: Capricorn Books, 1976. (N)

Moss, Thelma. *The Probability of the Impossible.* New York: New American Library, 1974. (N)

Pearce, Joseph Chilton. *The Crack in the Cosmic Egg.* New York: Simon and Schuster, 1971. (N)

Smith, Adam. *Powers of Mind.* New York: Random House, 1975. (S)

Tart, Charles T., ed. *Altered States of Consciousness.* 1969. Reprint. Garden City, NY: Doubleday and Company, 1972. (N)

Weldon, John, and Clifford Wilson. *Psychic Forces and Occult Shock.* Chattanooga, TN: Global Publishers, 1987. (C)

White, John, ed. *The Highest State of Consciousness.* Garden City, NY: Doubleday and Company, 1972. (N)

Wilber, Ken. *The Spectrum of Consciousness.* Wheaton, IL: The Theosophical Publishing House, 1977. (N)

7. New Age Ideology and Mythology

Capra, Fritjof. *The Turning Point: Science, Society, and the Rising Culture.* Toronto: Bantam Books, 1982. (N)

Davidson, Mark. *Uncommon Sense.* Los Angeles: J. P. Tarcher, 1983. (N*)

Geisler, Norman L. "Process Theology." In *Tensions in Contemporary Theology,* edited by Stanley N. Gundry and Alan F. Johnson. 2d ed. Grand Rapids: Baker Book House, 1983. (C)

Hubbard, Barbara Marx. *The Evolutionary Journey.* San Francisco: Evolutionary Press, 1982. (N)

Laszlo, Ervin. *The Systems View of the World*. New York: George Braziller, 1972. (N*)

Lilienfeld, Robert. *The Rise of Systems Theory: An Ideological Analysis*. New York: John Wiley and Sons, 1978. (S)

McWaters, Barry. *Conscious Evolution*. Los Angeles: New Age Press, 1981. (N)

Mumford, Lewis. *The Transformations of Man*. New York: Harper and Row, 1972. (N*)

Russell, Peter. *The Global Brain*. Los Angeles: J. P. Tarcher, 1983. (N)

Von Bertalanffy, Ludwig. *General Systems Theory*. New York: George Braziller, 1968. (N*)

8. Holistic Health

Benson, Herbert, M.D., with Miriam Z. Klipper. *The Relaxation Response*. New York: Avon Books, 1975. (N*)

Dossey, Larry. *Space, Time, and Medicine*. Boulder, CO: Shambhala, 1982. (N)

Krieger, Dolores. *The Therapeutic Touch: How to Use Your Hands to Help or to Heal*. New York: Prentice-Hall, 1979. (N)

Reisser, Paul C., Teri K. Reisser, and John Weldon. *New Age Medicine*. Chattanooga, TN: Global Publishers, 1988. (C)

Seigel, Bernie S., M.D. *Love, Medicine and Miracles*. New York: Harper and Row, 1986. (N)

Weldon, John, and Zola Levitt. *Psychic Healing*. Chicago: Moody Press, 1982. (C)

9. Humanistic Psychology

Goble, Frank G. *The Third Force: The Psychology of Abraham Maslow*. 1970. Reprint. New York: Simon and Schuster, 1971. (N*)

Kilpatrick, William Kirk. *Psychological Seduction*. Nashville, TN: Thomas Nelson Publishers, 1983. (C)

Maslow, Abraham H. *Toward a Psychology of Being*. New York: Van Nostrand Reinhold Company, 1968. (N*)

―――. *Religions, Values and Peak-Experiences*. New York: Viking Compass Books, 1970. (N*)

―――. *The Farther Reaches of Human Nature*. New York: Viking Compass Books, 1971. (N*)

Myers, David. *The Inflated Self*. New York: Seabury Press, 1980. (C)

Rogers, Carl. *On Becoming a Person: A Therapist's View of Psychotherapy*. Boston: Houghton Mifflin, 1961. (N*)

Ruitenbeek, Hendrik M. *The New Group Therapies.* New York: Avon Books, 1970. (S)

Vitz, Paul. *Psychology as Religion.* Grand Rapids: William B. Eerdmans Publishing Company, 1977. (C)

10. Humanistic/Transpersonal Education

Gabler, Mel and Norma. *What Are They Teaching Our Children?* Wheaton IL: Victor, 1985. (C)

Simon, Sidney B., Leland W. Howe, and Howard Kirschenbaum. *Values Clarification: A Handbook of Practical Strategies for Teachers and Students.* 1972. Reprint. New York: Dodd, Mead, and Company, 1978. (N*)

11. New Age Politics and Economics

Anderson, Walter Truett, ed. *Rethinking Liberalism.* New York: Dell, 1978. (N*)

Capra, Fritjof, and Charlene Spretnak. *Green Politics: The Global Promise.* New York: E. P. Dutton, 1984. (N)

Harman, Willis. *An Incomplete Guide to the Future.* San Francisco: San Francisco Book Company, 1976. (N)

Henderson, Hazel. *Politics of the Solar Age: The Alternative to Economics.* Garden City, NY: Doubleday, 1981. (N*)

Keys, Donald. *Earth at Omega: Passage to Planetization.* Boston: The Branden Press, 1982. (N)

Laszlo, Ervin. *A Strategy for the Future: The Systems Approach to World Order.* New York: George Braziller, 1974. (N*)

Mische, Gerald, and Patricia Mische. *Toward a Human World Order: Beyond the National Security Straight Jacket.* New York: Paulist Press, 1977. (N*)

Satin, Mark. *New Age Politics: Healing Self and Society.* New York: Dell, 1978. (N)

Schumacher, E. F. *Small Is Beautiful.* New York: Harper and Row, 1973. (N*)

Tindergen, Jan, coord. *Reshaping the International Order: A Report to the Club of Rome.* New York: E. P. Dutton, 1976. (N*)

12. Channeling

Kautz, William H., and Melanie Branon. *Channeling: The Intuitive Connection.* San Francisco: Harper and Row, 1987. (N)

Klimo, Jon. *Channeling: Investigations on Receiving Information from Paranormal Sources.* Los Angeles: Jeremy P. Tarcher, 1987. (S/N)

Ramtha, with Douglas James Mahr. *Voyage to the New World*. Friday Harbor, WA: Masterworks, 1985. (N)

Roberts, Jane. *The Seth Material*. Englewood Cliffs, NJ: Prentice-Hall, 1970. (N)

———. *Seth Speaks: The Eternal Validity of the Soul*. Englewood Cliffs, NJ: Prentice-Hall, 1972. (N)

Steiger, Brad. *Revelation: The Divine Fire*. Englewood Cliffs, NJ: Prentice-Hall, 1973. (N)

Weston, Robin. *Channels: A New Age Directory*. New York: Perigee Books, 1988. (N)

13. Christian Witness to New Agers

Brooke, Tal. *Riders of the Cosmic Circuit*. Tring, England: Lion Publishing, 1986.

Maharaj, Rabi. *Escape into the Light* (also published under the title *Death of a Guru*). Eugene, OR: Harvest House, 1984.

Means, Pat. *The Mystical Maze*. San Bernadino, CA: Here's Life Publishers, 1976.

Subject Index

Index of Persons

255

Scripture Index

HEAVENLY

BANQUET

A DAILY DEVOTIONAL FOR A SUSTAINED INTIMACY WITH GOD

VOLUME 5

JANUARY–DECEMBER 2015

PASTOR MICHAEL O. NWAMOH

HEAVENLY BANQUET: A DAILY DEVOTIONAL FOR A SUSTAINED INTIMACY WITH GOD

All copyright enquiries to:

The Agape Christian Church (Miracle Center),

100 East Timonium Road,

Timonium, MD 21214, USA.

Published by
GOFACH PUBLISHERS
P. O. BOX 5941,
BALTIMORE, MARYLAND 21282
Printed in the United States of America.

For electronic version of this book, please logon to: **Gofachbooks.com**

ACKNOWLEDGEMENT
My appreciation goes to the following individuals for their hard-work and tireless effort in proof-reading the manuscript of this book: Mrs. Julie Ibidapo, Ms. Ngozi Jonathan, Mr. Wole Abijo and Rev. Dachi Maduako. May God richly bless them for their contribution in making the publication of this Devotional possible.

Cover Design:
Enobong Bassey © The Agape Christian Church (Miracle Center).

FOREWORD

Glory be to God for the fifth edition of **Heavenly Banquet Devotional**—a tool that enables you to enjoy a sustained intimacy with God. The Word of God is so powerful that it is capable of turning difficult situations around. Therefore, you need a daily dose of it. With the Word of God, you can never walk in darkness, nor go astray.

This year is the year of abundant blessing As you journey through it, make a conscious effort to align yourself with God and make His Word your spiritual compass. The Word of God is the only navigational compass that is never out modeled; it's been tested through the centuries and still remains fresh and effective for each day's challenges. The Heavenly Banquet is rich in spiritual diet that will enrich your spiritual life. A daily banqueting with it will open the doors of heaven to enable you experience God's abundant blessings. This fifth edition focuses on wide arrays of topic—faith, love, forgiveness, righteousness, marriage, backsliding, victory, spiritual growth, spiritual discipline, fruitfulness, holy living, etc.

My humble prayer is that you will experience God's abundant harvest as you banquet with heaven through this devotional. Read the Bible passages in conjunction with the Heavenly Banquet Devotional; pray and meditate on what you have read. Make the most of the materials contained in this Heavenly Banquet Devotional and it will be well with your soul.

I wish you a happy and blessed New Year.

Pastor Michael O Nwamoh
December 2014

In each edition, we try to publish some excerpts of testimonies shared by our readers. Here are some of them:

"I recommend the **Heavenly Banquet** devotional to every born-again Christian. I call it a mini-Bible, fully loaded with thought provoking topics, well chosen, well articulated with Bible quotations to back them up. There is no doubt that the author is a very good and seasoned teacher of the word of God. It is a devotional for the modern day Christian for spiritual growth." *Mr. Michael Nwaogu, Lagos, Nigeria.*

"**Heavenly Banquet** has been a source of inspiration and blessing for me. As a daily devotional, it helps me to focus on pearls of wisdom in each lesson which provide guidance and help to search the Scriptures. It also motivates me to apply these life lessons to my daily walk with Jesus Christ. I look forward to the 2015 edition. May God bless the author." *Mrs. June Ryan Bell, Baltimore, USA.*

"Pastor Michael Nwamoh outlines fundamental aspects of understanding the Word of God and nothing can compare to the inner peace we can have as Christians when we walk in fellowship with God by studying the **Heavenly Banquet** devotional. This book is an indispensable companion to pastors, Bible school teachers, new converts and indeed, every child of God. It has blessed me abundantly to the glory of God" *Mrs. Tina Ndubunma Amanahu, Abuja, Nigeria.*

"I would like to express my profound gratitude to Pastor M. O. Nwamoh for allowing God to use him for the past five years in writing the **Heavenly Banquet** devotional, which I nickname **Heavenly Nuggets**. Heavenly Banquet is full of spiritual nuggets, which young and seasoned Christians need for growth. As a Pastor, I always make references to the Heavenly Banquet while planning or delivering my messages. I highly recommend this wonderful book for the spiritual growth of every spiritually minded Christian." *Pastor C. Azuoru, Christ The King Christian Center, Baton Rouge, USA.*

"The **Heavenly Banquet** devotional is a great gift from God, because it teaches the rarely heard truth with deep astounding revelations that only the Spirit of God can inspiringly pass on to man. It is a jewel of inestimable value, and we are blessed to have it." *Elder Chizu Okorocha, Enugu, Nigeria.*

"The **Heavenly Banquet** is a daily devotional, which teaches undiluted Word of God. The practical approach adopted by the writer in teaching the Christian ethics, will help any reader who genuinely desires to grow in the Christian faith and make heaven to accomplish God's eternal purpose." *Ms. Ngozi Jonathan, Baltimore, USA.*